COOKING
WITH
F·R·U·I·T

COOKING

The Complete Guide to Using Fruit Throughout

WITH

the Meal, the Day, the Year

F·R·U·I·T

Rolce Redard Payne

and

Dorrit Speyer Senior

Crown Publishers, Inc.
New York

To Ed and Boris

Published by Crown Publishers, Inc., 201 East 50th Street,
New York, New York 10022. Member of the Crown
Publishing Group.

CROWN is a trademark of Crown Publishers, Inc.

Manufactured in the United States of America
Design by Lauren Dong
Illustrations by Jennifer Harper

Library of Congress Cataloging-in-Publication Data
Payne, Rolce Redard.
   Cooking with fruit / Rolce Redard Payne, Dorrit Speyer
Senior. —1st ed.
      p.   cm.
   1. Cookery (Fruit)   I. Senior, Dorrit Speyer.
   II. Title.
TX811.P375   1992
641.6′4—dc20   91-4322
                                                        CIP

ISBN 0-517-58406-9

10   9   8   7   6   5   4   3   2   1

First Edition

❧ ACKNOWLEDGMENTS ❧

Our first thanks go to our children. To Edmund for his ever-patient persistence in prodding us into the computer age and word processing, without which this book could never have been produced. To Cymie for a discriminating choice of recipe suggestions and her availability for computer emergency consultations. Special thanks to Jeffrey, Deena, and Skipjack's for ideas, advice, and assistance. We are especially appreciative of Paul's research of Asian fruits and recipes for us. We also thank Alan, who so willingly sought out source material, and Liss, Stephen, and Gael for their interest and support.

We wish to thank Chuck Sandner for giving so generously of his time and expertise to assist us with recipe development, and June Speyer for cooking assistance and sharing her knowledge of tropical fruits.

To our editor Erica Marcus, our gratitude for her discerning eye, decisive pen, and great sense of humor throughout this project. And our thanks to everyone at Crown who worked on the book: Etya Pinker, Lindsey Crittenden, Lauren Dong, Jennifer Harper, and Nancy Maynes.

We appreciate the wealth of information, recipes, and suggestions supplied by the fruit growers' groups, the fruit distributors, and the various fruit advisory boards. We extend special thanks for their extraordinary help and continuing support to Bryan Silberman and Diana Lopez of Produce Marketing Association. Calavo Growers of California, Castle and Cooke Foods, Evans Food Group, Frieda's Finest/Produce Specialties, Inc., J. R. Brooke and Son, Inc., and Maine Wild Blueberry Company deserve special mention for their warm response to our queries and willingness to provide us with information. We also thank the Apricot Producers of California, California Apricot Advisory Board, California Avocado Commission, California Fig Advisory Board, California Granny Smith Association, California Prune Board, California Raisin Advisory Board, California Strawberry Advisory Board, Del Monte Tropical Fruit Company, Florida Department of Agriculture, Florida Department of Citrus, International Apple Institute, International Banana Association, Michigan Apple Committee, Michigan Blueberry Growers Association, Michigan Plum Advisory Board, National Cherry Foundation, New York Cherry Growers Association, North American Blueberry Council, Northwest Cherry Growers Foundation, Ocean Spray Cranberries, Inc., Oregon Washington California Pear Bureau, Produce Marketing Association, South Carolina Department of Agriculture, Sunkist Growers, Inc., TexaSweet Citrus Advertising, Inc., United Fresh Fruit and Vegetable Association, Virginia State Apple Board, Washington Apple Commission, Washington Red Raspberry Commission, Washington Rhubarb Growers Association, Washington State Fruit Commission, and Western New York Apple Growers Association.

CONTENTS

Introduction
1

COOKING WITH FRUIT

INTRODUCTION

Fruit is not only ideally suited to the concept of lighter and healthier eating but its sensory appeal provides so much added pleasure to meals. Few foods are as sensual as fruit, from the fragrance of a peach to the clear smell of lemons. Best of all is the variety of tastes: sweet, sharp, smooth, tangy, or subtle—and always unique.

We love fruit and had long collected fruit recipes, so we searched for—but could not find—a book devoted to fruit for all courses, from appetizer through entree to dessert. We concluded that if we really wanted such a book we would have to write it ourselves.

We have updated, streamlined, and sometimes slimmed down traditional recipes but have not abandoned old favorites. From the thousands of recipes we tested, some of which we created, others that we modified, we selected those that we felt were good enough in flavor, ease of preparation, and appearance to make more than once. Our recipes have clear directions for even the novice or infrequent cook, but also offer something new for everyone who enjoys cooking. At times it can be relaxing and satisfying to create more challenging dishes, so we have included some of our favorites that we think are worth the extra effort.

Although our emphasis is on the contribution of fresh fruit in preparing a meal, we also include recipes using frozen, dried, or preserved fruits and sometimes use combinations of all four. When fresh fruits are out of season the cost can be prohibitive and frozen or canned fruits are an acceptable substitute.

While in no way a diet book we do pay attention to contemporary concerns for less sugar, eggs, and cream but without sacrificing either taste or appearance. Fruit contains no cholesterol or saturated fat and very little salt while providing vitamins, minerals, and fiber. Besides the recipes we have also provided nutritional information, peak seasons, shopping, preparation and storage instructions, and cultivation tips.

Above all we have tested repeatedly to perfect these recipes that now make up our long-sought volume of fruit cuisine. May its use provide you with as much pleasure as it has us.

A·P·P·L·E·S

Curry Dip with Delicious Apple Slices

Danish Herring Salad with Apples

Curried Butternut Squash and Apple Soup

Apple and Celeriac Salad

Scandinavian Beet Salad

Acorn Squash Stuffed with Apples and Prunes

Apple and Sauerkraut Casserole

Apple, Onion, and Potato Casserole

Himmel und Erde (Heaven and Earth)

Apples with Beets

Mixed Fruit and Vegetable Casserole

Bluefish with Apples

Braised Red Cabbage with Apples and Pork

Cornish Game Hens with Apples

Breasts of Duck à la Normande

Sauté of Apples with Chicken Breasts

Applesauce

Oven Baked Apples

Microwave Stuffed Apples

American Apple Pie

Tarte Tatin

Viennese Apple Tart

Apple Crisp

Apple Cake

Apple Cobbler

The apple can easily lay claim to being the most familiar and generally liked of all the temperate-zone fruits. For hundreds of years it has been the subject of art and legend, yet its exact place of origin is not known. Because of the horticultural needs of apples, central Asia is thought to be a possible location, and carbonized apples dated from 6500 B.C. have been found in Turkey. They were planted along the Nile in the thirteenth century B.C. by Ramses II, were being cultivated in Greece in the seventh century B.C., and the Romans had several varieties under cultivation in the time of Cato the Elder (234–249 B.C.). The apple traveled to England with the conquering Romans in the first century B.C., where it soon became a major fruit crop.

Apples were not native to North America, but were brought here by the first colonists early in the seventeenth century. Once established, they became the most widespread and useful fruit in colonial America. Today they are grown in all states with enough frost to induce a dormant or resting period for the trees. Thirty-five states grow apples on a commercial level, with Washington taking first place and New York second in supplying national markets.

In colonial times the most important products of the apple were derived from its juice. Hard cider (wine) and applejack (brandy) were used as beverages, and cider vinegar was important for preserving food. While in the United States apples are used for a wide variety of purposes including juice and sweet cider, cooking, baking, and eating out of hand, in Europe and England much of the apple crop is still used for the production of cider—a popular alcoholic beverage.

In addition to multiple uses, the apple's great popularity probably owes much to the convenience of handling and the enormous variety available. More than 10,000 varieties of apples have been named, and of that number over 100 are grown commercially in the United States (fifteen of these account for 90 percent of production). These varieties may have a red, yellow, or green color, taste sweet or mildly tart, and vary in texture from hard to soft.

Apples have long been available year round because of their superb keeping qualities; however, in recent years, with modern temperature-controlled storage, we have been able to enjoy even better texture and flavor in this stored fruit. Increased importation of apples from countries of the Southern Hemisphere gives us the added luxury of buying the more perishable types when they are out of season here.

⊹ HOME CULTIVATION ⊹

You can grow your own apples successfully from as far south as Georgia and New Mexico north to Maine and Wisconsin. An apple tree is an attractive landscape addition, and as they age they take on a picturesque quality, with the gnarled branches set against winter snow, and breaking out into fragrant, pale pink blossoms in the spring. Semidwarf and dwarf varieties are a good choice because they take less room, are easier to harvest, and tend to bear fruit earlier than standard trees. For a small property you might even try a grafted tree to produce several varieties from a single trunk. Given the time and effort involved in growing fruit trees, it is well worth the cost to purchase a known variety adapted to your climate from a reputable nursery rather than take your chances with planting seeds, since of the ten or so seeds in an apple, each can produce an apple different from the parent. You should check with your local nursery about cross-pollination; some varieties are self-pollinating while others require another tree for fertilization.

⊹ NUTRITION ⊹

A medium apple (2½-inch diameter) contains 87 calories with 21 grams of carbohydrate for quick energy. It is a good source of fiber, is high in vitamin C and potassium and low in sodium, and is virtually fat-free.

⊹ SELECTION ⊹

In selecting apples look for smooth skins without bruises. These brownish soft spots will cause early spoilage. The flesh should feel firm under slight pressure. In a ripe red apple the background color should be a pale green; dark green indicates an underripe fruit, while yellow signals a fruit past its prime. In addition to fresh apples, you will find them dried, canned as applesauce or slices, and as juice. Because of the variety of apples available you should select those best suited to your planned use. The ones most commonly found in the markets are listed below with a note about their characteristics.

Varieties

Cortland—Firm with slightly tart flavor makes it a good all-purpose apple for eating and for pies and baking. Its very white flesh doesn't brown easily, so it is a good choice for salads. When ripe it is primarily red with a green background.

Crispin-Mutsu—A cross between Golden Delicious and a Japanese variety, Indo, it is a relative newcomer to the American market and is known by one or the other name depending on the region. This variety is grown in much of the Far West. It is a good firm eating apple with a green-russet skin.

Empire—Named for New York State, where it was developed as a cross between the Red Delicious and the McIntosh and introduced in 1966. It has a deep red color with a crisp texture and excellent keeping qualities. A good all-purpose apple, it has the same qualities as the McIntosh except it has a firmer flesh.

Golden Delicious—Originated in West Virginia, it has a light gold color when ripe. In the older varieties the skin tends to be dull gold with a pink blush, while those developed later are somewhat greener in color and have a smoother, glossier skin. These are more common in the markets, but the older ones have the fuller flavor. This is an excellent apple for open tarts, since it retains its shape through cooking and for this reason it is not as good for applesauce. It resists browning, making a good choice for slices served with cheese, dips, or in salads.

Granny Smith—One of newer introductions that has met with unexpected success because the conventional wisdom in apple marketing had it that a solid green apple would never make it. Discovered in Australia in 1868 by Mrs. Thomas Smith, the first of these apples to appear in our markets came from South Africa and New Zealand as early as the mid-1950s. Although slow to catch on at first, they are now grown in quantity in this country and are distributed nationwide. In the 1980s they became the darling of food stylists, and bowls and baskets of Granny Smiths appeared in every home magazine. For many it has become the apple of choice for recipes specifying a firm, tart apple and

for those who prefer a very hard apple for eating out of hand.

McIntosh—Discovery of John McIntosh in Ontario, Canada, it has been important not only in its own right but as the parent to many other varieties. When ripe it is red with a green background. This is a best choice for applesauce since it retains a good flavor but breaks down when cooked. It's good in combination with a firmer variety for closed apple pies. For those preferring a less crisp eating apple it has an excellent flavor.

Newtown Pippin—An eighteenth-century variety reputed to have been a favorite of George Washington, and was also grown by Thomas Jefferson. By mid-century it was introduced to England by Benjamin Franklin. This has a greenish-yellow skin with a yellow tinge to the flesh. It's a good keeper, and its tart flavor makes it a fine selection for cooking and serving raw.

Red Delicious—Discovered on the farm of Jesse Hiatt in the 1870s near Peru, Iowa, it was brought to the attention of the Stark Brothers Nursery at a fruit fair in Louisiana. It was they who named it the "Delicious." Primarily an eating apple, it is deep red, distinguished by its shape—tall, with wide shoulders at the stem end that taper down to five distinct knobs at the blossom end. It has been overdeveloped into a huge, shiny red, tasteless fruit used more for show than eating. Beware of these apples in late spring and summer, since they can look gorgeous on the outside and be brown and mealy inside. However, there are some growers who produce a smaller, firm, sweet, and truly delectable eating apple, and still a very pretty fruit. Many in this category are organically grown.

Winesap—There is no clear place or date of origin, but it was used in the early nineteenth century in New Jersey for cider-making. This variety has a dark red skin with background streaks of yellow, and can have a dark red overlay verging on purple. The flesh is tinted with yellow and often has red streaks. It's a crisp, all-purpose apple with a distinctive tangy taste. Before present-day storage techniques it was especially valued for its keeping qualities, since it could be held for very nearly year-round use.

Northern Spy—Another versatile apple that is good for all cooking purposes as well as eating out of hand. It is large with bright red striping over yellow and a moderately tart flavor that makes it useful for canned slices.

New varieties keep showing up, many as imports such as the Royal Gala and Braeburn (both excellent eating apples) from New Zealand, and the Japanese Fujis, which are being planted on the West Coast.

Equivalents	
1 pound usually	= 4 small apples
	= 3 medium
	= 2 large
1 pound sliced	= 2 ¾ cups
1 pound diced	= 3 cups
2 medium grated	= 1 cup

STORAGE
✢ AND PREPARATION ✢

Apples may be kept up to six weeks in the refrigerator or an unheated pantry, but make sure the temperature is above freezing. They will deteriorate rapidly if kept at room temperature. Apples may be sliced and frozen.

Apples may be peeled with a sharp paring knife, however we prefer a swivel-blade vegetable peeler because it removes a thinner skin. Starting at the top, remove peel in a continuous spiral.

For slices, cut in half lengthwise, from stem to blossom end, then cut in quarters. Remove core with paring knife, being sure to remove all the small particles of shell surrounding the pips. The quarters can then be sliced into desired thickness. If you are not using immediately drop cut fruit into water with lemon juice added to prevent browning.

For baking apples whole, it is easiest to use an apple corer, but you can also use a paring knife. Before peeling, insert point in stem end, push toward (but not through, if you plan to fill) the base, and withdraw the cylinder containing the core and seeds. For large quantities of fruit you might consider a mechanical peeler, either hand or electrically operated.

✢ ✢

Apples are one of the most adaptable of all fruits. You can start your day with a dish of applesauce or an apple compote for breakfast, have a raw apple at morning break, apples with soup or salad for lunch, apple cake for tea, and apples with fish, meat, or poultry for dinner, not to mention the dozens of delectable apple desserts. Nearly every spice and condiment can be used in dishes from soup through dessert. Apples work as well with onions and garlic in a vegetable dish or entree as they do with nutmeg and cinnamon in a pie. Poach apples in a light syrup flavored with lemon as a dessert, sauté in butter, or braise in lime juice to accompany an entree, or bake in a pie flavored with cinnamon, nutmeg, and lemon juice. Serve raw in salads combined with other fruits and nuts in a mayonnaise dressing, or try whole slices with a curry dip. Cheddar cheese may be served with raw slices or with a wedge of hot apple pie, American style.

Curry Dip with Delicious Apple Slices

Yields 1 cup

For an attractive presentation use both Golden and Red Delicious apple slices. Other fruits such as pears and bananas are also good but should be sprinkled with lemon juice to prevent discoloration.

1 *cup (1 8-ounce carton) sour cream*
2 *tablespoons curry powder, preferably Madras*
2 *tablespoons chopped preserved ginger*
2 *tablespoons chopped mango chutney (optional)*
4 *medium Delicious apples (1–1½ pounds total)*

Mix sour cream, curry powder, ginger, and chutney until well combined. Allow at least 30 minutes for flavors to blend. Core but do not peel apples, then cut into slices slightly thicker than ¼ inch. Place bowl of dip in the center of a tray and surround with fruit slices.

Danish Herring Salad with Apples

Yields 7 cups

This is an old family recipe. It will keep for some weeks in the refrigerator, but usually disappears so quickly that our main concern is having an ample supply on hand.

1 *(32-ounce) jar Party Snacks herring in wine sauce*
¼ *cup plus 2 tablespoons sugar*
3 *tablespoons canola or other vegetable oil*
1 *large Granny Smith apple (½ pound), diced*
½ *cup diced onion*
1 *cup diced kosher baby dill cucumbers*
1 *cup cider vinegar*
½ *teaspoon Dijon mustard*
1¼ *cups tomato puree*

Drain all the liquid from the jar of herring. In a large bowl, mix the remaining ingredients with the herring. Cover and refrigerate for several days before serving. During this period, stir and mix well at least once.

Curried Butternut Squash and Apple Soup

Serves 6–8

The taste of the curry and the tartness of the apples provide a wonderfully complex flavor to the humble butternut squash.

> 2 *tablespoons canola or other vegetable oil*
> 1 *cup finely chopped onion*
> 1 *garlic clove, minced*
> 1 *tablespoon medium curry powder*
> 1 *teaspoon ground cumin*
>   *Pinch of cayenne pepper*
> 5 *cups chicken stock*
> 2½ *pounds butternut squash, peeled and diced*
> 3 *medium-tart Granny Smith apples (¾–1 pound total), peeled, cored, quartered, and diced*

In a large saucepan, heat the oil. Add the onion and cook over moderate heat until golden brown. Add the garlic, curry powder, cumin, and cayenne and cook, stirring constantly, for about 30 seconds. Add the stock, squash, and apples. Bring to a boil and simmer, covered, for about 30 minutes, or until both the squash and apples are tender. Puree the mixture in a blender or food processor in batches. Reheat to serve.

NOTE: The soup may be refrigerated for up to 5 days, or frozen for 2 months. If desired, a spoonful of chopped chives mixed into plain yogurt may be added.

Apple and Celeriac Salad

Serves 4–6

In this recipe, the celeriac is immediately immersed in orange juice to prevent discoloration and the mixture is brought to a boil for only a minute. The result is crisp but without the raw taste that is so often associated with this vegetable.

> 1–1½ *pounds celeriac (celery root), peeled and julienned*
> ½ *cup orange juice*
> 1 *tablespoon Dijon mustard*
> ¼ *cup mayonnaise*
> ¼ *cup plain low-fat yogurt*
>   *Freshly ground black pepper to taste*
>   *Pinch of cayenne pepper*
> 3 *medium Granny Smith apples (¾–1 pound total), cored, unpeeled, and cut into ¼-inch cubes*

Place the julienned celeriac in a nonreactive saucepan with the orange juice and boil for 1 minute. Remove from heat, stir in the mustard, and set aside to cool. In a large bowl, mix the mayonnaise, yogurt, and peppers. Carefully add the diced apples and finally the celeriac and orange juice mixture. Toss, cover, and chill until ready to serve. This salad will hold in the refrigerator for 2 days, retaining both flavor and texture.

Scandinavian Beet Salad

Serves 6–8

For best appearance all the vegetables in this salad should be diced the same size—about ½ to ¾ inches.

1½   cups diced cooked potatoes
1   cup diced cooked carrots
1   medium onion, diced
1   large tart apple (8 ounces), peeled, cored, and diced

CREAM SALAD DRESSING

1   teaspoon Dijon mustard
1   teaspoon sugar
1   tablespoon vinegar
    Salt and freshly ground pepper to taste
¾   cup whipping cream

2   cups diced cooked beets

Combine potatoes, carrots, onion, and apple. Mix mustard and sugar for dressing. Beat in the vinegar and season with salt and pepper. Lightly whip the cream and fold into vinegar mixture. Add beets to potato mixture and fold in cream dressing.

Acorn Squash Stuffed with Apples and Prunes

Serves 4

8   large pitted prunes, cut into small pieces
½   cup Port wine
2   acorn squash (12–16 ounces)
4   tablespoons (½ stick) lightly salted butter
2   tablespoons chopped onion
4   small apples such as McIntosh (1 pound total), chopped into ½-inch cubes
¼   cup coarsely broken pecans

Preheat the oven to 350° F.

Macerate the prunes in the Port wine until swollen. Cut squash in half, remove seeds, and place cut side down in a baking dish with about ¾ inch water. Bake in center of oven for 20 to 30 minutes or until flesh is tender when pierced with a fork.

In a medium skillet, melt 3 tablespoons of the butter, add the onion, and cook until tender. Add apples and sauté lightly (the apples should not get too soft). Remove squash from oven and turn halves over; pierce inside in several places. Drain the prunes and spoon about 1 tablespoon of the drained wine over each squash half. Mix nuts and prunes with apple mixture, stirring well, and pile into squash centers. Spoon the remaining wine over filling, dot with remaining butter and return to oven for 30 minutes.

Apple and Sauerkraut Casserole

Serves 4

Delicious served together with grilled sausages such as knockwurst or bratwurst. A baked potato completes the course.

    1 tablespoon unsalted butter or margarine
    1 large garlic clove, minced
    1 medium onion, thinly sliced
    2 medium Cortland apples (¾ pound
       total), unpeeled, cut into ½-inch cubes
    1 (16-ounce) jar kosher-style sauerkraut,
       drained and rinsed
    1 cup chicken stock, or more as needed
    1 teaspoon dark brown sugar
       Pinch of cayenne pepper
    1 teaspoon caraway seeds

Preheat the oven to 350° F.

In a nonreactive skillet melt the butter, add the garlic and onion, and sauté until soft but not brown. Add the apples and stir well. Add the sauerkraut, stock, and brown sugar. Transfer the mixture to a casserole, cover, and bake for 40 minutes. Stir occasionally to ensure that the mixture does not stick to the pan. If it appears a little dry, stir in additional stock. Remove from oven and season with cayenne and caraway seeds. Serve directly from the casserole. This dish may be refrigerated for several days, then reheated before serving.

NOTE: If sausages are to be served as part of the dish, they can be sliced into 1-inch-thick rounds and added to the casserole. Sauté for a few minutes after cooking the onion.

Apple, Onion, and Potato Casserole

Serves 6

Accompanied by a green salad, this casserole may be eaten as a light meal. It also blends well with the flavors of roast beef, chicken, or pork.

        2 tablespoons (¼ stick) unsalted butter
           or margarine
        3 medium onions, thinly sliced
        1 large garlic clove, minced
 1¼–1½ pounds all-purpose potatoes (4 large)
        4 medium Cortland apples (1–1¼
           pounds total)
       ¼ teaspoon ground nutmeg
           Freshly ground pepper to taste
       ¼ cup light cream
       ¼ cup grated low-moisture part-skim
           mozzarella cheese

Preheat the oven to 375° F. Grease an ovenproof 9-inch square or round casserole dish with 2-inch sides.

In a large skillet melt the butter and sauté the onions and garlic until soft but not brown. Set aside. Peel and cut the potatoes into ⅛-inch round slices. Peel, core, and slice the apples into quarters, then cut each quarter into thirds, then slice again crosswise.

Arrange the potatoes evenly to cover the bottom of the dish. Follow with a layer of onions and then with apples. Sprinkle with nutmeg and pepper. Repeat this process, ending with a layer of apples. Drizzle the cream over the mixture and sprinkle with the cheese. Cover with a lid or aluminum foil and bake for 25 minutes. Uncover, increase the oven temperature to 400° F. and continue baking for another 25 minutes or until the top is slightly golden brown in color. Remove from oven and serve.

Himmel und Erde (Heaven and Earth)

Serves 4

A German peasant dish of pureed apples and potatoes that Dorrit remembers from her childhood. It's traditionally served with sausages and fried onions.

2 *large Idaho or Russet potatoes, suitable for mashing (1 pound)*
2 *tablespoons (¼ stick) unsalted butter or margarine*
2 *large, firm Cortland or Granny Smith apples (1 pound), peeled, cored, and sliced into eighths*
5 *tablespoons low-fat milk, or more if needed*
Salt and freshly ground pepper to taste
2 *teaspoons lemon juice*
3 *tablespoons chopped fresh chives or parsley*

Peel and slice the potatoes. Place in a saucepan, cover with water, and cook until tender, about 15 minutes. Remove from heat, drain, and set aside.

Melt the butter in a saucepan and sauté the sliced apples for about 5 minutes, stirring occasionally, until softened.

Using an electric mixer with a paddle attachment, combine the potatoes, apples, milk, salt, pepper, and lemon juice and beat until well mixed and smooth. Return the puree of apples and potatoes to the saucepan and cook over low heat, stirring constantly, until very hot. Add a little extra milk if necessary to retain a smooth consistency. Sprinkle with chives or parsley. Serve immediately.

NOTE: A masher or ricer, or even a fork, is a perfectly acceptable alternative to the electric mixer. Don't use a food processor for mixing; the result is pasty and gluelike.

Apples with Beets

Serves 6

For contrast in texture, make the beets just a little smoother than the apples, but neither should be of baby-food consistency.

4 *tablespoons (½ stick) lightly salted butter or margarine*
1 *cup chopped onion*
1 *(16-ounce) can whole beets*
5 *McIntosh apples (1½ pounds total), peeled, cored, and coarsely chopped*
½ *teaspoon sugar*
½ *teaspoon salt*
2 *tablespoons balsamic vinegar or dry red wine*

Melt 2 tablespoons of the butter in a saucepan, add the onion, and cook, covered, until soft and lightly colored. Place with beets in a blender or food processor and chop but do not puree. Melt the remaining 2 tablespoons butter in the saucepan and add the apples, sugar, salt, and vinegar; cook until the apples are tender but still hold their shape. Stir in beet mixture, taste for seasoning, and heat through but do not boil, then serve.

Mixed Fruit and Vegetable Casserole

Serves 4–6 as a main course

A recipe adapted from West Africa; the combination of ingredients is unusual, but the taste is delicious.

    1   cup dried bean soup mixture, or dried
         navy beans
  2½   cups chicken stock
    2   large all-purpose potatoes (1 pound to-
         tal), peeled and sliced, then sliced again
         crosswise
   ½   pound green beans, washed and cut in
         half
    3   Granny Smith apples (about 1½ pounds
         total), peeled, cored, and sliced
    1   Anjou pear (about 8 ounces), peeled and
         sliced
    2   large carrots, scraped and cut into ¼-
         inch slices
    1   teaspoon lemon juice
         Freshly ground pepper to taste
    1   (7-ounce) can corn, drained
    6   whole red cabbage leaves, for serving
         Orange slices, for garnish

Soak the beans in water overnight, then drain.

In a large saucepan, simmer the stock and beans for 1 hour, stirring occasionally. Add the remaining ingredients except the corn and garnishes and cook for a further 35 minutes. Mix in the corn. Serve each portion on a red cabbage leaf and garnish with sliced orange.

Bluefish with Apples

Serves 4

Although bluefish combines beautifully with the apple and mustard flavors, if it's not available another fish such as pollock will do.

    4   bluefish fillets, about 6 ounces each
    6   tablespoons (¾ stick) lightly salted butter
    1   small onion, thinly sliced
    2   tart apples (1 pound total), peeled and
         sliced ¼ inch thick

SAUCE

    1   cup fish stock or rich vegetable or chicken
         stock
    2   tablespoons coarse-grained mustard
   ⅓   cup whipping cream

         Parsley, for garnish

Preheat the broiler.

Dot the fish with 1 tablespoon butter, then place in broiler about 4 inches from heat and grill until the top is lightly browned and fish is cooked through. Transfer to heated serving platter. Heat the remaining 5 tablespoons butter in a wide skillet, add the onion, and cook until soft. Add the apple slices and sauté until lightly colored but still firm. Place apples over and around the fillets, and keep warm while making the sauce.

Boil the fish stock in a small saucepan until reduced to ½ cup. Add the stock to the sauté pan, whisk in the mustard, and reduce the sauce to a syrupy consistency. Add the cream and reduce until the sauce is thick enough to coat a spoon. Spoon the sauce over the fish and apples, then garnish with parsley.

Braised Red Cabbage with Apples and Pork

Serves 4

Come winter, this is the dish our families entreat us to prepare.

  4   center-cut boneless pork cutlets, 5 ounces each
  2   tablespoons canola or other vegetable oil
  2   medium onions, thinly sliced
  1   head red cabbage (about 1½ pounds), finely shredded
  2   large tart apples (1 pound total), peeled, cored, and sliced
  ⅓   cup red currant jelly
  1   bay leaf
  ½   teaspoon ground cloves
  1   cup beef stock, or more as needed
  3   tablespoons red wine vinegar
  1   cup unsweetened apple juice
  1   teaspoon lemon juice
       Salt and freshly ground pepper to taste

Preheat the oven to 325° F.

In a heavy ovenproof skillet, brown the pork in the oil for 4 to 5 minutes on each side and set aside. In the same pan, sauté the onions until soft but not brown. Add the remaining ingredients, then return the chops to the cabbage mixture. Cover tightly, place in oven, and bake for 1½ hours, stirring occasionally. If necessary, add a small quantity of extra stock to prevent sticking.

Cornish Game Hens with Apples

Serves 4

The apples provide an interesting and flavorsome variation to the always popular Cornish game hens.

  1   tablespoon canola or other vegetable oil
  2   Cornish game hens (each about 1¼ pounds), split and backbone removed
  1   medium onion, chopped
  1   garlic clove, minced
  ¾   cup dry white wine
  1   cup unsweetened apple juice
  1   tablespoon cornstarch
  1   cup plain nonfat yogurt
  2   large apples (1 pound total), Granny Smith or Northern Spy, peeled, cored, and sliced
  2   teaspoons light brown sugar
  ¼   teaspoon ground nutmeg
       Salt and freshly ground pepper to taste

Preheat the oven to 375°F.

Heat the oil in a large saucepan and brown the hens on both sides over medium-high heat until golden brown. Remove to an ovenproof baking dish, arrange the hens skin side up, and set aside. Using the same pan, sauté the onion and garlic for a few minutes until soft. Add the wine and apple juice, scraping up any particles from the bottom and sides of the pan, and cook over medium-high heat until the liquid is reduced to 1 cup, stirring occasionally. Stir the cornstarch into the yogurt to prevent it from separating on contact with heat, then add to the pan to-

(continued on next page)

gether with the apples, brown sugar, nutmeg, salt, and pepper. Mix well.

Pour over the hens and bake for 25 minutes. Baste with the apple mixture. Increase the oven temperature to 425° F. and bake for 10 minutes more, until golden-brown. Remove from oven and serve.

Breasts of Duck à la Normande

Serves 4

A dish that the duck lover will surely appreciate. The rich flavor of the duck is nicely balanced by the fresh taste of the apples.

- 1 *tablespoon unsalted butter*
- 1 *tablespoon olive oil*
- 4 *large shallots, chopped*
- 3 *medium Granny Smith apples (1 pound total), peeled, cored, and sliced into eighths*
- 2 *tablespoons honey*
- ½ *cup Calvados or apple brandy*
- 1 *cup chicken stock*
- 2 *whole duck breasts, skin removed and split*
   Freshly ground pepper to taste

Preheat the oven to 450° F.

In a large skillet over medium-high heat, heat the butter and oil and sauté the shallots for 4 to 5 minutes until soft but not brown. Lower the heat to medium, add the apples and honey, and continue cooking, stirring, for another 5 minutes. Add the remaining ingredients except for the duck and pepper, increase the heat, and reduce the sauce for 5

to 8 minutes until slightly thick. Season to taste, remove from heat, and keep warm.

Place the duck breasts on a rack in an ovenproof pan filled with ½ inch water (this prevents the meat from drying during the roasting process). Roast for about 8 minutes each side, then remove to a cutting surface and cover to keep warm while reheating the sauce.

To serve, cut the duck into ¼-inch slices on the diagonal and arrange on a large platter or on individual serving plates. Spoon the sauce over the meat and serve immediately.

Sauté of Apples with Chicken Breasts

Serves 4

Serve this elegant dish with small new potatoes and snow peas.

- 2 *tablespoons flour*
   Freshly ground pepper to taste
- 2 *whole boned and skinned chicken breasts (1¼ pounds), halved and pounded flat*
- 2 *tablespoons (¼ stick) unsalted butter*
- 1 *tablespoon olive oil*
- 3 *shallots, finely chopped*
- 3 *Granny Smith apples (1 pound total), unpeeled, cored, quartered, and sliced into 12 to 16 pieces*
- ¼ *cup cognac*
- 1 *cup natural apple cider or unsweetened apple juice*
- ½ *cup chicken stock*
- 1 *heaping teaspoon cornstarch*
- ½ *cup light cream*
   Salt to taste
   Several sprigs of fresh tarragon

Preheat the oven to 200° F.

Mix the flour and pepper in a bag and dredge the chicken pieces in it, shaking off the excess. Heat the butter and oil in a large skillet over medium-high heat and cook the chicken for 5 minutes on each side or until golden in color and springy to the touch. Transfer to a flat dish, cover, and place in warm oven.

In the same skillet, scrape the bottom and sides of the pan, add the shallots, and sauté, stirring constantly for 2 to 3 minutes. Then add the apples, deglaze with the cognac, and cook for an additional 4 minutes. Add the cider and stock and cook for about 7 minutes over medium-high heat. Mix the cornstarch into the cream, add to the apple mixture, and continue cooking until slightly thickened. Season with salt and pepper.

To serve, place the chicken on a large warmed platter or on individual serving plates. Arrange the apples around the meat and cover with the sauce. Sprinkle with several snips of fresh tarragon.

❧   ❧

Applesauce

Yields 2 cups

Any variety of apple can be used for applesauce, but while those that hold their shape when cooked are a better choice for poaching, those that break down readily—notably, the McIntosh—are ideal for sauce. A combination of the two will yield a chunky sauce. Salt here is optional but just a few grains can bring out the flavor and lesson the amount of sugar needed.

3 *medium McIntosh apples (1 pound total), peeled, cored, and quartered*
1 *tablespoon sugar, or to taste*
   Pinch of salt
1 *teaspoon lemon juice (optional)*

Place the apples in a heavy nonreactive saucepan with just enough water to coat the bottom and prevent scorching. Cover and start cooking over medium-high heat to boiling point, then reduce heat to keep just at a simmer. Cook for about 15 minutes, stirring once or twice. Remove lid and stir in sugar and salt; continue cooking until apples are soft and almost all the water has evaporated. If not sweet enough, stir in more sugar and cook until dissolved. The amount of sugar depends on sweetness of apples and personal taste. The lemon juice may be added at any point in the cooking, best used if apples are bland.

VARIATION: Follow all directions and amounts as above but do not peel the apples. When cooking is completed, put through a food mill or press through a sieve. The peels will give the sauce a slightly pink color and added flavor. The sauce will be very smooth.

NOTE: The sauce may be flavored with a sprinkling of cinnamon or a few grains of nutmeg. Hot applesauce can be enriched with a bit of butter.

Oven Baked Apples

Serves 4

We have decided to include recipes for baked apples that utilize both the conventional oven and the microwave oven. Apples prepared either way are transformed into a very special dessert. Baked apples can be served warm or at room temperature, plain or with a low-fat frozen yogurt. They may also be refrigerated for several days and used as needed.

> 4 *firm large Cortland or Granny Smith apples (about 8 ounces each)*
> ½ *teaspoon ground cinnamon*
> 2 *tablespoons sugar*
> ¼ *cup mixed dark and golden raisins*

Preheat the oven to 375° F.

Wash and core the apples. Prick the skin all over with a sharp knife. Mix the cinnamon and sugar. Place apples in an ovenproof dish just large enough to hold them comfortably. Fill the cavities with the raisins and cinnamon-sugar mixture. Pour sufficient water into the dish to measure about ½ inch deep. Place in oven and bake for 15 minutes, then reduce the temperature to 300° F. and continue for another hour or until the apples are soft to the touch but still hold their shape. Baste with the liquid in the dish at intervals, spooning some into the cavities and over the apples. Remove from oven, and cool a little before serving.

Microwave Stuffed Apples

Serves 4–6

The skins of apples prepared in a microwave oven will remain a natural clear color. Do not expect them to brown and caramelize because they won't. We frequently buy Golden Delicious or Cortland apples in "family-size" packages because the apples are smaller, about 3 to 4 ounces each, and when baked they make a refreshing snack. They can be stored in the refrigerator for a few days.

> 6 *small Golden Delicious or Cortland apples (approximately 4 ounces each)*
> 1 *lemon wedge*
> ⅓ *cup raisins*
> ¼ *cup chopped dates*
> 3 *tablespoons honey*
> 3 *tablespoons dry white wine*
> 3 *tablespoons orange juice*

Core the apples, trying not to cut through the bottoms. Peel a strip around the top, about 1 inch, and rub with lemon to avoid discoloration. Stand the apples in an 8- or 9-inch round or square baking dish with at least ½-inch sides. Stuff the apples with the raisins, dates, and honey. Pour the wine and orange juice over the apples and cover with plastic wrap, pierced for air to escape. Microwave on high for 7 minutes, then check for doneness. If the apples still appear to be hard, microwave for another minute or so. Allow to stand for 10 minutes before serving.

American Apple Pie

Yields one 9-inch pie

This is a traditional apple pie that can be varied in flavor according to personal taste with more or less sugar, using only cinnamon or nutmeg, or adding a tablespoon of lemon juice. Serve it hot or cold, plain, with ice cream or with a wedge of cheddar cheese.

PASTRY

2 cups all-purpose flour
1 teaspoon salt
²/₃ cup plus 1 tablespoon solid vegetable shortening
4 tablespoons cold water
1 teaspoon vinegar

FILLING

7 cups ¼-inch-thick apple slices (use 3 pounds firm, tart apples)
³/₄–1 cup sugar, depending on tartness of apples
¼ teaspoon ground nutmeg
½ teaspoon ground cinnamon
1 tablespoon lemon juice (optional)
2 tablespoons (¼ stick) lightly salted butter

Prepare crust. Measure flour into a mixing bowl with the salt. With a pastry blender, cut in the shortening until mixture resembles coarse meal. Sprinkle with the water and vinegar, a tablespoon at a time, mixing with a fork. Gather dough together in a ball with fingers and roll around so it cleans the bowl.

Preheat the oven to 450° F.

Divide ball of dough in half and roll out on a well-floured board about 1 inch larger than pie pan. Line a 9-inch pie pan with pastry, leaving a 1-inch overhang.

Prepare filling. Place apples in a large bowl; mix the sugar, nutmeg, and cinnamon and stir lightly into the apple slices. If apples are bland, add lemon juice with sugar and spices. Heap into prepared shell, dot with butter, and cover with top crust. Dampen bottom edges, press top and bottom together along rim to seal, then fold overhang over entire edge and crimp together decoratively. Make slits in top crust to allow steam to escape. Bake for 10 minutes at 450° F., then lower to 350° F. and bake 35 minutes longer or until the top crust is golden brown. Even if serving hot, allow to sit for 20 minutes to make cutting easier.

Tarte Tatin

Serves 8–12

On a trip through the Loire Valley some years ago Dorrit was served tarte tatin—the caramelized upside down apple tart originally created by the two Tatin sisters. This recipe is an adaptation and about as foolproof as we know.

PÂTE BRISÉE

- 1 cup all-purpose flour
- 1 teaspoon sugar
- ⅛ teaspoon salt
  Grated lemon rind from ½ lemon
- 4 tablespoons (½ stick) chilled unsalted butter, cut in very small pieces
- 2 tablespoons solid vegetable shortening
- 3–4 tablespoons ice water
- 1 teaspoon lemon juice

FILLING

- 9–10 large firm Golden Delicious, Granny Smith, or Cortland apples (4 pounds total)
- ⅓ cup sugar
- 3 tablespoons lemon juice
  Grated rind of 1 lemon

CARAMEL

- 1 cup sugar
- 5 tablespoons unsalted butter

In the bowl of an electric mixer or food processor, combine the flour, sugar, salt, and lemon rind. Mix for a few seconds, then add the butter and shortening and mix until it has the appearance of coarse meal. Add the ice water mixed with the lemon juice a tablespoon at a time until the dough holds together almost in a ball. Roll out about ¼ inch thick, place in wax paper or plastic wrap, and refrigerate. (The dough may be made ahead and either frozen or refrigerated.)

Peel, quarter, and core the apples. Cut each quarter lengthwise in half so that you have eighths. Toss in a bowl with the sugar, lemon juice, and grated rind. Leave for 30 minutes, mixing occasionally. Drain off the excess juice.

Preheat the oven to 400° F. For this recipe you will need a 9- or 10-inch cast-iron or heavy nonstick skillet that is usable both on top of the stove and in the oven. In the skillet, caramelize the sugar with the butter over medium-high heat until sugar is dissolved and mixture begins to turn golden brown. Remove from heat.

Arrange a layer of apples in concentric circles on the bottom of the pan. Fill the dish with the remaining apples, closely packed. Return the skillet to the stovetop, and over medium-high heat, cook the apples for 10 minutes, covered. Uncover and cook for a further 10 minutes to allow much of the liquid to evaporate; the remaining juices should appear syrupy. Drain off any excess liquid into a small saucepan to be reduced and drizzled over the apples for a glaze after the tart has been baked. (Depending on the apples, there may be as much as ⅔ cup liquid.)

While the apples are cooking, roll out the pastry on a lightly floured surface to a thickness of ⅛ inch. Cut into a circle 1 inch larger than the dish. Place it over the apples and fold the excess dough inward to form a thick outer rim. Prick evenly to allow steam to escape. Bake for 45 minutes in lower third of oven. Remove and invert onto a serving dish.

Over medium-high heat, reduce the excess juice in the small saucepan to ¼ cup, stirring occasionally. Spoon over the apples evenly to glaze. Keep warm and serve with whipped cream if desired.

❧ ❧

Viennese Apple Tart

Yields one 10-inch tart

This tart is from the Viennese cooking sessions conducted by Martha Stasa for members of Harvard Neighbors, a group affiliated with Harvard University. It is really very simple to make and worth every calorie! But be sure to use only butter in the pastry.

PASTRY

2⅔ *cups all-purpose flour*
½ *cup sugar*
   Pinch of salt
2 *large egg yolks*
¾ *cup plus 2 tablespoons (1¾ sticks) chilled unsalted butter, cut into pieces*

FILLING

½ *cup dry white wine*
½ *cup golden raisins*
4 *large Golden Delicious apples (2 pounds total), peeled, cored, and sliced ¼ inch thick*
   Juice and rind of 1 large lemon
1 *teaspoon ground cinnamon*
3 *tablespoons sugar*
½ *cup whipping cream*

Combine the flour, sugar, and salt in a large mixing bowl. Make a well in the center and drop in the egg yolks, stir with a fork, then work in the butter by hand, rubbing the flour and pieces of butter together quickly and lightly until mixture resembles coarse meal. Work the mixture to a smooth paste with your hands and shape into a ball. Wrap and chill for 30 minutes.

Butter a 10-inch springform pan on the bottom and about 1 inch up the sides.

Place the wine and raisins in a small saucepan, bring to a simmer, and let stand until cool. Mix the apple slices with the lemon juice and lemon rind; set aside.

Press the chilled dough evenly on the bottom and up the sides of the pan. Arrange the apples, starting at the outer edge, with curved edge against pan side, continuing in circles toward the center, forming a pattern like the petals of a rose. Drain the raisins (discard wine), and spoon over the apples. Combine the cinnamon and sugar and sprinkle over fruit. Chill about 1 hour (if pressed for time, place in freezer for 20 minutes).

Preheat the oven to 375° F.

Bake on middle rack of the oven for about 50 minutes or until crust is golden and apples have released their juices. Serve warm or cooled, in true Viennese style with whipped cream.

Apple Crisp

Serves 6–8

No matter how much of this dessert we make, there is never anything left over. It is served at Skipjack's in Boston, where it is known as Dorrit's Apple Crisp. The recipe is foolproof and can easily be adjusted for different quantities and various size dishes and pans.

5–7 *large apples (about 3 pounds total), Granny Smith, Cortlands, Northern Spy, or even a mixture of varieties*
1 *tablespoon lemon juice*
2 *tablespoons granulated sugar*
½ *cup (1 stick) softened unsalted butter or margarine*
1 *cup dark brown sugar*
1 *cup all-purpose flour*
¾ *cup coarsely chopped pecans*
2 *teaspoons ground cinnamon*
¼ *teaspoon ground ginger*

Preheat the oven to 375° F. Grease and flour a 9- or 10-inch square or round pan.

Peel, core, quarter, and then slice the apples approximately ⅛ inch thick. Arrange half the apples in the prepared pan, then sprinkle with a little lemon juice and granulated sugar. (Keep the remaining juice and sugar for the top when all the apples have been used.)

Combine the butter, brown sugar, flour, nuts, cinnamon, and ginger in a bowl and mix well. Place over the apples, then press down lightly. Sprinkle with remaining lemon juice and sugar. Bake for 45 to 60 minutes, until golden brown, crisp, and bubbly. Re-move to a rack and bring to room temperature before serving.

This dessert may be covered and refrigerated for several days, then brought back to room temperature and warmed in the oven before serving. It may also be frozen for up to 6 weeks.

Apple Cake

Yields one 8-inch cake

Easy to make and great to have on hand for snacks or to pack in a picnic basket.

2 *cups coarsely chopped apples (about ¾ pound total)*
1 *cup sugar*
⅓ *cup corn oil*
½ *teaspoon vanilla extract*
1 *large egg, beaten*
1½ *cups all-purpose flour*
1 *teaspoon baking powder*
1 *teaspoon baking soda*
½ *teaspoon ground cinnamon*
½ *teaspoon ground nutmeg*
½ *teaspoon salt*
½ *cup coarsely chopped pecans*

Preheat the oven to 350° F. Grease and flour an 8-inch square pan.

Combine the apples and sugar in a mixing bowl and let stand 15 minutes. Blend the oil, vanilla, and egg with the apples. Mix the dry ingredients and combine with the apple mixture, then add the pecans. Spread evenly in prepared pan and bake 35 to 40 minutes. May be served warm or dust with confectioners' sugar when cool.

Apple Cobbler

Serves 8

If available, use a combination of tart, sweet, firm, and soft apples. For example, combine Granny Smith or Golden Delicious, Rome, and McIntosh. Try serving this warm with half-and-half or crème fraîche.

FILLING

2 teaspoons ground cinnamon
1/4 cup granulated sugar
3 pounds mixed apples, peeled and cut into 1/2-inch slices
1/4 cup dark brown sugar
1 tablespoon lemon juice
1 teaspoon grated lemon rind
1 1/2 tablespoons lightly salted butter, cut into pieces

TOPPING

2 cups all-purpose flour
3 tablespoons sugar
1 tablespoon baking powder
5 tablespoons solid vegetable shortening
3/4 cup milk

Preheat the oven to 425° F. Butter a 2-quart baking dish that is 3 inches deep.

Mix the cinnamon and granulated sugar, then toss together with apples, brown sugar, lemon juice, and grated rind and turn into prepared baking dish. Dot with butter and set aside.

Mix the flour, sugar, and baking powder in a large bowl; cut in shortening a tablespoon at a time until mixture has the consistency of coarse meal. Stir in the milk with a fork just until absorbed and gather dough into a ball. Press into a flattened disk on a floured board and, with a floured rolling pin, roll a 1/2-inch-thick circle slightly larger than circumference of dish. Cut vent in center and place over apples. Bake for 10 minutes, then reduce temperature to 350° F. and bake until the crust is golden brown and the apples are soft (use a cake tester through center vent), about 40 minutes more. Serve slightly cooled or at room temperature, with or without cream.

Note: The biscuit topping can be brushed with milk and lightly sprinkled with sugar before placing in oven.

A·P·R·I·C·O·T·S

Chilled Apricot Soup

Sweet Potato with Apricots

Hot Curried Fruit Casserole

Baked Chicken with Apricots

Cold Curried Fish in Apricot Sauce

Bobotie

Danish Fruit Soup

Apricot Whip

Apricot Sauce and Rice Pudding

Chocolate-Dipped Apricots

Apricot Sorbet

Ginger Apricot Muffins

Apricot Farfel Squares

Homemade Apricot Preserves

Among the most delicious and distinctly flavored fruits, apricots, like their relatives almonds and peaches, belong to the genus *Prunus*. The species from which the finest cultivated varieties have been developed is *P. armeniaca,* not, as the name suggests a native of Armenia, but from China, where apricots still grow wild in the mountains.

As with other fruits originating in the Far East, the apricot followed trade routes to the West. Apricots came to the United States by way of the Spaniards, and reached California via the mission 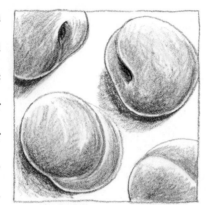 fathers early in the eighteenth century. Although Captain John Smith reported that apricots were thriving in Virginia in 1629, the apricot has never proved well suited to the eastern United States for market production.

Commercial growing of apricots in California started in 1792 in an orchard in the town of Santa Clara, near San Jose. California is now the largest producer of apricots in the world and is responsible for about 96 percent of production in the United States. Outside of this country only Australia, South Africa, Syria, and Iran produce apricots in any considerable quantity. However, we now receive small winter shipments (in January) of fresh apricots from Chile; this fruit has a lovely typical "apricot" color with a slight blush but unfortunately tends to be dry and the flavor has no character.

Fully ripe fresh apricots are not readily available in markets outside of California. Because their growing season is brief and the soft fruit does not travel well, those found in eastern markets often lack the uniquely pungent flavor for which the apricot is prized. Happily, canned apricots make a reasonably good substitute in most dishes, and the dried fruit can add an intensity of flavor. The apricot juice, usually called apricot nectar, is useful both as a beverage and for additional flavor in frozen desserts, soups, and sauces.

☙ HOME CULTIVATION ☙

There are few fruits more delicious than a tree-ripened apricot; therefore if your climate permits it, the apricot is a worthwhile tree to add to the garden and its cloud of white blossoms in early spring is a most welcome sight. The apricot will thrive in areas free from the effects of damaging late-spring frosts. As with other fruit trees, a dwarf variety will take less room and will make harvesting easier. Because of their very specific needs you should consult a local nursery for varieties that have been successfully grown in your area.

☙ NUTRITION ☙

Apricots are a particularly valuable source of vitamin A, potassium, and fiber, plus a lesser amount of vitamin C and some iron. Three fresh medium-size apricots contain 55 calories; 2 ounces (¼ cup) dried have 140 calories.

☙ SELECTION ☙

When buying fresh apricots select well-formed, plump, and fairly firm fruit. The color will vary slightly with the variety but look for a deep yellow or orange apricot. Fruit tinged with green or of a very pale yellow color will not ripen further after purchase. Dried apricots are available either sulfur-treated to retain the rich, orange color or without the use of sulfur, usually in health

food stores. Those treated with sulfur tend to be somewhat softer and have the characteristic apricot color, but the flavor in both is about the same.

Apricots are rarely sold by varietal name, and until recently, they were mostly a single variety called Blenheim. These are being supplanted by the Patterson, which though blander in flavor yields a heavier crop and ships well. Two other varieties mentioned by the growers are Castlebrite and Early Cot. The Castlebrite produces a relatively sweet, jumbo-size, yellow-orange fruit.

> EQUIVALENTS
> 1 pound = 3 cups sliced
> 1 pound large = about 12–14 apricots
> 4 ounces = ½ cup dried apricots

STORAGE
☙ AND PREPARATION ☙

Fresh apricots can be kept for several days stored in the refrigerator, but for best flavor bring them to room temperature before eating.

Apricots need little preparation, since they are usually cooked or eaten fresh without removing the peel. The skins slip off easily if they are immersed in boiling water for 1 minute, then in cold water to make handling easier. When cut in half, the pit is easily lifted out.

Dried apricots should be stored in an airtight container, however if they have become overly dry and hard they may be softened by either of the following methods sent to us by the California Apricot Advisory Board.

If using a microwave oven, spread 2 cups apricots in a glass baking pan. Sprinkle approximately ¼ cup water over fruit and cover. Heat 2 to 2½ minutes at 700 watts. For a more conventional, steam method, bring water to a boil in a large pot. Put 2 cups apricots in a colander or strainer and lower into pot (water should not reach apricots). Cover and allow water to continue boiling for 5 to 6 minutes.

⊹   ⊹

Apricots are truly an across-the-menu fruit, from soup through dessert. Their punchy flavor can pick up a dried fruit compote, give a surprising tang to sweet potatoes, or sharpen a chicken stuffing. Sauces can be tart and spicy for fish, meat, and poultry, or sweet and tangy for desserts. Lemon, lime, or orange juice are often included in apricot recipes, but for the most part this fruit can stand alone. Apricot glaze is indispensable for open fruit tarts, and a puree made from either fresh or dried fruit serves as a flavor-filled base for sauces, soufflés, and pastry fillings. Delicious preserves can be created and, if you are one of the fortunate few who have a good source for ripe fresh fruit, consider freezing some for later use.

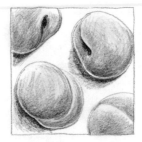

Chilled Apricot Soup

Serves 4

You can substitute very ripe fresh apricots (about 1 pound) for the canned in this recipe. If you do, add an extra 1 or 2 tablespoons of sugar.

  1 (8-ounce) *can apricot halves*
 ½ *cup dried apricots*
1½ *cups orange juice*
 ½ *cup whole milk*
  1 *tablespoon dry sherry*
 ½ *cup chilled soda water*
  4 *tablespoons sour cream*
     Freshly grated nutmeg (optional)

Place apricot halves and dried apricots, orange juice, milk, and sherry in a blender or food processor, and puree until smooth. Chill soup for 1 hour or more. Just before serving stir in the soda water. Swirl 1 tablespoon of sour cream in a decorative pattern into each serving; sprinkle just a bit of nutmeg over top if desired.

Sweet Potato with Apricots

Serves 4

The apricots add a pleasant tang to the sweet potatoes in this excellent side dish for pork, ham, or anything barbecued.

 10 *dried apricots, chopped*
1½ *pounds sweet potatoes*
  2 *tablespoons (¼ stick) lightly salted butter, or more if needed*
  2 *tablespoons light cream, or more if needed*
     Salt to taste

Soak the apricots in hot water just to cover until plumped and then drain. Boil the sweet potatoes until tender. Peel, cut in chunks, and place in a blender or food processor with apricots, butter, cream, and salt. Process just until smooth. If desired, additional butter may be added, or if too dry, a bit more cream.

Hot Curried Fruit Casserole

Serves 6–8

This is a variation of a recipe that came to us from Dallas, where Rolce's sister-in-law, Vilma Redard, serves it as a brunch dish. It is also an excellent accompaniment to barbecued poultry and meats. The use of canned fruit makes this a year-round dish.

1 *(16-ounce) can apricot halves*
1 *(16-ounce) can pear halves*
1 *(16-ounce) can peach halves*
1 *(16-ounce) can pineapple chunks or spears*
1 *large banana, cut in thick slices*
⅓ *cup lightly salted butter, melted*
¼ *cup dark brown sugar*
3 *tablespoons curry powder*

Preheat the oven to 325° F.
Drain the fruit and pat dry with paper towels. Place in a 9 × 13-inch baking dish. Mix the melted butter, brown sugar, and curry powder; pour evenly over the fruit. Bake uncovered on center rack of oven for 1 hour. Serve hot.

Baked Chicken with Apricots

Serves 4

A light, tangy recipe to make when fresh apricots are at the height of their season, luscious and flavorsome.

8 *ounces fresh apricots*
⅓ *cup chopped dried apricots*
3 *tablespoons chopped onion*
¼ *cup fresh orange juice*
2 *tablespoons honey*
½ *teaspoon ground ginger*
½ *teaspoon Dijon mustard*
2 *pounds split chicken breasts, with skin remaining*
   Salt and freshly ground pepper to taste
2 *tablespoons chopped scallions (including some green)*

Wash the fresh apricots, remove the pits, and quarter. Place in a saucepan with the dried apricots, onion, orange juice, honey, ginger, and mustard. Bring to a boil, lower the heat, and simmer for 10 minutes. Remove from heat and cool.
Preheat the oven to 350° F.
Wash the chicken, pat dry with towels, and season with salt and pepper. In an ovenproof dish sufficiently large to contain the chicken in a single layer, place skin side down and spread the apricot mixture over the top. Bake for 15 minutes, then turn and baste with the sauce. Increase the temperature to 425° F. and bake for an additional 15 minutes. Remove from the oven, sprinkle with the scallions, and serve directly from the dish.

Cold Curried Fish in Apricot Sauce

Serves 6–8

For the full flavor to develop, prepare this dish a day ahead and refrigerate. It will keep for several days and taste as wonderful as ever. It is best served at room temperature, so remove it from the refrigerator at least 30 minutes before serving.

- ¼ cup all-purpose flour
- ¼ cup bread crumbs
  Freshly ground pepper to taste
- 2 pounds firm white fish such as haddock or halibut, cut into steaks or fillets (4–5 ounces each)
- 2 tablespoons (¼ stick) unsalted butter
- 2 tablespoons canola or other vegetable oil
- 5 ginger cookies, finely ground
- 1¾ cups water
- 1 (17-ounce) can apricots in syrup
- ¾ cup cider vinegar
- 1 cinnamon stick
- 1½ teaspoons medium curry powder
- 1 medium onion, thinly sliced
- ½ cup raisins
- 3 tablespoons tomato sauce
  Salt

Mix the flour, bread crumbs, and some pepper in a plastic bag. Dredge the fish in this mixture, shaking off the excess. In a large skillet, heat 1 tablespoon each of the butter and oil, add the fish in batches if necessary, and cook over medium-high heat for about 4 to 5 minutes on each side or until light golden. Add the remaining butter and oil as required to complete cooking the fish. Remove fish from the heat and place on paper towels to drain. Arrange the fish in a shallow serving dish and keep warm while preparing the sauce.

Soak the ground ginger cookies in ¾ cup water and mix to form a paste. Set aside. Drain the apricots and put only the juice (about 1 cup) in a saucepan together with the remaining 1 cup water, vinegar, cinnamon stick, curry powder, sliced onion, raisins, and tomato sauce. Bring to a boil and cook over medium heat for 5 minutes. Remove the cinnamon stick from the mixture, and stir in the ginger cookie paste, and season to taste. Cook for about 2 minutes, stirring, until the sauce has thickened. Put the apricot halves into the sauce, remove from heat, and pour the hot sauce over the fish. Allow to cool at room temperature for 30 minutes before covering with plastic wrap and refrigerating. Serve chilled.

Bobotie

Serves 8–10

A delicate dish of Malay origin, Bobotie was allegedly cooked by travelers in an oven made from antheaps in the ground. It is really just an exotic form of baked curried chopped meat. Toward the end of the cooking period as with moussaka, an egg mixture is poured over the top and browned. Accompanied by chutney this is a fine meal when served with a bowl of turmeric-flavored rice and a green salad.

  1 *tablespoon canola or other vegetable oil*
  1 *large onion, thinly sliced*
2½ *pounds lean ground beef*
  ¼ *cup milk*
  1 *large egg*
  2 *slices white bread, crusts removed and cubed*
  ½ *cup finely chopped dried apricots*
  1 *large apple (8 ounces), peeled, cored, and grated*
  ¼ *cup raisins*
  ¼ *cup blanched almonds*
  2 *tablespoons sugar*
  2 *tablespoons medium curry powder*
  3 *tablespoons lemon juice*
  2 *teaspoons salt*
  ½ *teaspoon freshly ground pepper*
  4 *bay leaves*

TOPPING

  2 *large eggs*
  1 *cup milk*
  ½ *teaspoon turmeric*

Preheat the oven to 350° F.

In a heavy skillet, heat the oil and sauté the onion until soft and golden. Add the meat and stir until no longer red. Remove from pan and set aside. In a large bowl combine the milk, egg, and bread cubes. Add the apricots, apple, raisins, almonds, sugar, curry powder, lemon juice, salt, and pepper, and mix until well blended. Stir in the meat mixture. Turn into a lightly greased ovenproof dish and press the bay leaves on top of the mixture. Bake, uncovered, for 30 minutes.

Beat the eggs, milk, and turmeric lightly, then pour over meat mixture. Return to the oven and bake 10 to 15 minutes, or until the topping has set and is bubbly and golden brown. Remove from oven, cover, and leave for about 30 minutes before serving. This dish may be covered and refrigerated for several days or frozen for up to 6 weeks.

Danish Fruit Soup

Serves 6

Recipes for Danish fruit soups abound; this is a typical one with a nice tart-sweet flavor. We consider this a dessert soup, which may be served plain or with sour cream, or with lightly whipped sweet cream dusted with cinnamon or nutmeg.

     1½   cups dried apricots
       1   cup pitted prunes
     ⅔   cup sugar
       5   cups water
     ¼   cup dark raisins
     ½   lemon, sliced
       1   cinnamon stick
       8   whole cloves
       3   tablespoons cornstarch
       1   cup Chablis wine

Combine the apricots, prunes, sugar, water, raisins, lemon slices, cinnamon stick, and cloves in a saucepan. Heat to boiling, then simmer uncovered for 5 minutes (not longer or fruit will disintegrate), stirring once or twice. Blend the cornstarch with the wine until smooth, then slowly add to the fruit, stirring constantly. Cook until the mixture thickens and starts to boil, then remove from heat and discard cinnamon stick and cloves. May be served at room temperature or chill to serve cold, plain or with cream.

Apricot Whip

Serves 8

A traditional whip is a light gelatin-based dessert that contains whipped cream or stiffly beaten egg whites. This dessert contains no gelatin but relies solely on beating the egg whites until really stiff for its lightness. Leaving it in the oven for a few extra minutes at the end of the baking time minimizes the shrinkage normally associated with many baked desserts with similar ingredients.

       1   cup dried apricots
     ½   cup plus 2 tablespoons sugar
       5   large egg whites

Preheat the oven to 275° F. Grease a 2-quart ovenproof baking or soufflé dish.

Place the apricots in a small bowl, cover with boiling water, and soak overnight. Drain, reserving 2 tablespoons of the juice. (The remaining juice may be refrigerated or frozen for other uses.) Using either a food processor or blender, puree the apricots along with the 2 tablespoons juice and ¼ cup plus 1 tablespoon of the sugar. Set aside.

In the bowl of an electric mixer, beat the egg whites on high, gradually adding the remaining sugar. Beat until stiff and able to hold peaks. Carefully add the apricot puree and fold until completely integrated. Pour into the prepared dish and bake for about 35 minutes or until set and golden and puffy. Turn off the oven, open the oven door slightly, and cool in the oven for an additional 10 minutes. Remove, bring to room temperature, then place in refrigerator to chill.

Apricot Sauce and Rice Pudding

Serves 6

We developed this apricot sauce especially to serve with rice pudding. It has a tart yet sweet flavor and is equally pleasing as a topping for ice cream and custard.

½ cup dried apricots
1 (8-ounce) can apricot halves in syrup
2 tablespoons sugar, or to taste
2 tablespoons cognac or other brandy

Rice Pudding

⅓ cup long-grain white rice
1 quart whole milk
¼ cup sugar
⅛ teaspoon salt
1 teaspoon vanilla extract
¼ teaspoon ground nutmeg
    Ground cinnamon, to sprinkle over the
    top

Soak the dried apricots in water to cover for 24 hours. Transfer the fruit and liquid to a saucepan, bring to a boil, cover, and cook over medium heat for 15 minutes. Add the apricot halves and the juice from the can. Stir in the sugar and cook uncovered for 20 minutes. Remove from heat and add the cognac; stir to blend, and cool for 30 minutes.

Place the apricot mixture in a blender or food processor and puree until smooth. (You will have about 1⅓ cups.) The sauce may be served at room temperature or chilled. If desired, place in an airtight container and freeze for up to 3 months; thaw before serving.

Preheat the oven to 325° F. Grease a 1½-quart baking dish.

Put the rice and milk in the baking dish and soak for 30 minutes. (This allows the rice to absorb some of the liquid even before the cooking begins.) Stir in the sugar and salt, and bake uncovered for 2 hours, stirring at intervals. Mix in the vanilla and nutmeg and continue cooking for an additional 1 to 1½ hours, or until the rice has swollen and the mixture is tender, smooth, and creamy. Remove from oven and sprinkle with cinnamon. Rice pudding may be served warm or cold and refrigerates successfully for several days. A successful rice pudding is the result of a long, slow cooking period.

✢ ✢

Chocolate-Dipped Apricots

Yields about 30 pieces

These are wonderful with after-dinner coffee. For an elegant look serve them on a silver tray lined with a fancy paper doily. We use one of the dark Swiss chocolates.

3 ounces good-quality semisweet chocolate
1½ tablespoons brandy or fruit liqueur
1 cup dried apricots

Break the chocolate into pieces, combine with the brandy in the top of a double boiler, and heat until melted. Dip half of each apricot into the chocolate and place on wax paper. Refrigerate until chocolate has hardened, then store, covered, in a cool place.

Apricot Sorbet

Yields 1 pint

May be served with one or two other fruit sorbets of contrasting colors and flavors, or center the apricot sorbet on a puree of fresh or frozen blueberries with a mint leaf or two for a wonderful flavor combination. Sorbets such as this one can be put together in less than 30 minutes using an ice cream machine (with chilled ingredients).

      1 *(17-ounce) can apricot halves, chilled*
      3 *tablespoons lemon juice*
      1 *tablespoon orange liqueur such as*
         Cointreau
      2 *tablespoons sugar*
      1 *tablespoon water*

Puree the apricot halves in a blender or food processor, then add the lemon juice, liqueur, sugar, and water and process to blend thoroughly. The flavor is a bit more intense if the apricots are not made silken smooth. Freeze in an ice cream maker, following manufacturer's directions, and pack in a freezer carton, or pour into a flat pan (the wider the pan the faster mixture will freeze) and place in the freezer. When mixture is frozen, spoon into a chilled bowl and beat with an electric or hand rotary beater until light and smooth. Pack lightly in the freezer carton and return to freezer. Soften slightly to serve.

Ginger Apricot Muffins

Yields 12 muffins

Fruit muffins are always a breakfast treat but they are also an excellent hot bread to serve with a salad lunch.

    ¾ *cup chopped dried apricots*
    ¼ *cup sweet sherry*
   1¾ *cups all-purpose flour*
    3 *tablespoons sugar*
   2½ *teaspoons baking powder*
    ½ *teaspoon ground ginger*
    ¼ *teaspoon salt*
    1 *large egg*
    ⅓ *cup lightly salted butter, melted*
    ¾ *cup milk*
   1½ *teaspoons grated lemon rind*

Macerate the chopped apricots in the sherry for 30 minutes, then drain and discard the liquid.

Preheat the oven to 400° F. Grease the bottoms only of twelve 2½-inch muffin cups.

Place the flour, sugar, baking powder, ginger, and salt in large mixing bowl. In another bowl beat the egg and add the butter and milk with the drained apricots and lemon rind. Pour this mixture into the dry ingredients and mix just to moisten. Do not beat; batter should be stiff and lumpy. Fill the muffin cups two-thirds full and bake for 25 minutes or until lightly browned. Remove from tins to wire rack and serve while hot.

Apricot Farfel Squares

Yields 20 squares

Farfel is an egg-noodle dough that is grated or minced and usually eaten in soups. In this recipe the act of grating the dough to cover the apricot filling is reminiscent of farfel noodle dough, hence the name.

- ½ *cup (1 stick) softened unsalted butter or margarine*
- ½ *cup sugar*
- 1 *tablespoon canola or other vegetable oil*
- 1 *large egg, well beaten*
- 2 *teaspoons vanilla extract*
- 2 *cups all-purpose flour*
- 2 *teaspoons baking powder*
  Pinch of salt
- 9 *ounces apricot preserves, either home-made or purchased*

In a large bowl, cream the butter, sugar, and oil. Add the egg and vanilla. In another bowl, mix the dry ingredients for about 30 seconds to aerate. Add to the egg mixture and mix until dough begins to form a ball; the mixture should feel quite firm. Wrap in wax paper and freeze for about 30 minutes.

Preheat the oven to 350° F. Grease a 10 × 7-inch pan.

Press half the mixture evenly onto the bottom of the pan. Spread with the apricot preserves. Grate the remaining dough evenly over the layer of preserves. Bake for 40 minutes or until the top is golden brown and the sides have pulled away from the pan. Remove from oven, place on a rack, and immediately run a knife around the edge of the pan to facilitate the removal of the squares. Cool for 20 minutes, then cut. Store in an airtight container for up to 1 week, or freeze for up to 3 months.

Homemade Apricot Preserves

Yields 1½ cups

Even though a store-bought preserve is an acceptable substitute, the one you make yourself has more tartness and flavor. This recipe is simple to make and can be used for glazes, fillings for cookies, and when diluted with either water or wine, as a wonderful marmalade finish to baked chicken or fish.

- 2 *cups water*
- 1 *cup sugar*
- 1½ *cups chopped dried apricots*
- 1 *teaspoon fresh lemon juice*

Combine the water, sugar, apricots, and lemon juice in a heavy saucepan. Cover and cook over low heat for about 10 minutes until sugar has dissolved. Increase the heat to medium-high and cook for about 15 minutes, stirring occasionally to prevent burning, until the mixture has become really thick and all the liquid has been absorbed. Remove from heat and cool. Preserves should be stored in an airtight container and refrigerated. They will keep for 2 to 3 months.

A·V·O·C·A·D·O·S

Guacamole

Avocado Sauce

Potato Avocado Soup

Avocado Potato Salad

Eggs Mexican Style

Pita Sandwich of Pureed Avocado and Chicken

Salmon Steaks with Avocado Horseradish Puree

Angel Hair Pasta with Avocado and Salmon

Shrimp and Avocado Gratinée

Tuna with Avocado and Grapefruit

Sliced Smoked Turkey with Avocado, Tomato, and Thousand Island Sauce

The avocado, a genuine native American, is also known as the alligator pear, perhaps because of its rough skin and pear shape. The name avocado is an Anglicization for the Aztec *ahuacatl*, which becomes *aguacate* in Spanish and *abacate* in Portuguese. Because the avocado doesn't have the sweet flavor that we usually associate with fruit, it is sometimes thought of as a vegetable; nevertheless, as a seed surrounded by a fleshy pulp, it fits the botanical description of a fruit. In other parts of the world as far removed from each other as South Africa and Hawaii, it is served with sugar and lemon or  lime juice as a common dessert or breakfast food.

A native of the high- lands of Mexico and Central America, the avocado has been an important food in that area for thousands of years. It was taken to Spain in 1601, to Jamaica about 1650, and to Asia around 1850. The first recorded avocado in the United States dates from 1833 in Florida. Although California's first plantings were made in 1848, true commercial efforts did not start until the early 1920s. Today it is a major crop in both California and Florida. It is grown in nearly all tropical and subtropical countries of the world, although the most important production is in the Western Hemisphere.

There are three basic categories of avocado: the Mexican, Guatemalan, and West Indian. The more hardy Mexican type is grown in California, the West Indian can be grown only in southern Florida, and the intermediate Guatemalan is raised in both states. These three groups have been crossed to produce fruits of different sizes and seasons, so that we can enjoy avocados year round.

A highly nutritious fruit, the avocado has long been a staple food and common dooryard tree in many parts of tropical America. The trees, which are naturally long lived, grow to thirty feet or more, with leaves that are elliptical in shape and four to twelve inches in length. The fruit is variable in size, shape, and color. Some of the Mexican varieties are no larger than hens' eggs, while those of other types may weigh three or four pounds. The form varies from round to pear shape, and the color from green to dark purple. The skin is sometimes no thicker than a pear's, or can be coarse and woody in texture. The greenish or yellow flesh has a buttery consistency with a rich nutty flavor.

HOME CULTIVATION

An avocado can easily be grown from the pit as a houseplant with interesting foliage, but it will not bear fruit. Avocados can be grown outdoors only in subtropical climates such as Florida and California. If the large size of the tree is no problem, select a tree from a local nursery to obtain the right variety for your location.

NUTRITION

Avocados are a highly nutritious fruit rich in vitamin A (beta-carotene), and a good source of vitamin C, folic acid, niacin, and vitamin E, and with smaller amounts of the other B vitamins. They are an especially good source of potassium, with lesser amounts of phosphorus, magnesium, calcium, and iron, and traces of zinc, copper, and manganese. Three ounces of a California avocado has 177 calories, three ounces of one from Florida has 112 calories. Avocados contain from 7 to 23 per-

cent fat (depending on type) but no cholesterol.

SELECTION

Avocados do not soften until after they leave the tree, but are not usable until softening has taken place. In some markets they are pre-softened and are labeled as ready to use. Avocados are ripe when they yield to gentle pressure. Plan on two to three days for a firm fruit to ripen at room temperature.

California varieties are usually smaller and creamier than those from Florida. The pebbly-skinned Hass normally comprises about 75 percent of California's avocado crop and is available all year, with a peak season from February to October. Other California varieties with overlapping harvest times are Fuerte, Bacon, Zutano, Pinkerton, and Reed.

Florida varieties tend to be larger with a lighter green, shiny skin, and a higher water content. Some of these very large fruits have huge seeds leaving no more usable flesh than the smaller ones. The Florida avocado season runs from July to February, with a peak in October. The varieties are Booth, Lula, Hill, and Hickson.

> EQUIVALENTS
> One 11-ounce avocado = 1 cup mashed pulp

STORAGE AND PREPARATION

A firm avocado will ripen at room temperature, but it can take several days. (Ripening can sometimes be hastened if you put the avocado in a closed paper bag with an apple.) Never use fruit that is hard, as it will be devoid of flavor and difficult to peel. Once ripe, avocados can be stored in the refrigerator for up to a week.

To prepare an avocado, cut lengthwise around the seed and rotate the halves to separate. Remove the seed with the tip of a knife, being careful to hold the fruit gently because it mashes easily. After you've removed the seed, using either a knife or your fingers pull back the skin, which usually comes off quite easily in large sections. Once cut, the exposed flesh will darken, but you can sprinkle it with lemon or lime juice to preserve the color. Very soft avocados are best for mashing, as for guacamole or soup; slightly firmer ones should be used for slicing, cutting into chunks, or using as shells.

The avocado has long lost its status as an exotic novelty. Now in the mainstream, it is a salad ingredient of first importance. Its smooth buttery texture, delicate coloring, and subtle flavor team beautifully with oranges and grapefruit drizzled with a lemon vinaigrette dressing. Add cold roasted chicken slices or cooked shrimp and you have a full-meal salad. A spicy guacamole can be added to a pita bread sandwich, top a baked potato, or serve as a dip for corn chips or crudités. Crisp bacon, smooth avocado, and tangy tomatoes make a great salad or sandwich combination. Once the pit is removed, the halves form a natural shell that can be filled with a spicy dressing, or heaped with a chicken or seafood salad. Try an avocado for breakfast—sprinkle with lemon or lime juice and just a bit of sugar.

Guacamole

Yields 1½ cups

There are many different versions of this popular appetizer. Corn chips are a natural for dipping and those made with blue cornmeal are especially nice. Guacamole is also a great filling for a simple omelet, a topping for a baked potato, or a stuffing with cheese, bacon, and lettuce for a pita bread sandwich.

2   ripe medium avocados
1   small onion, chopped
1   medium tomato, seeded and chopped in
     ¼-inch cubes
1   garlic clove, finely minced
1   tablespoon coarsely chopped cilantro
     (fresh coriander), plus additional (op-
     tional) for garnish
½   teaspoon salt
2   tablespoons finely chopped green chile, or
     1 small pickled jalapeño, finely chopped
2   teaspoons lemon or lime juice

Mash the avocados, and stir in the onion, tomato, garlic, cilantro, salt, and chile. Blend well and pour the lemon juice on top to keep the avocado from darkening. Stir only just before serving. Additional chopped cilantro may be sprinkled on top.

Avocado Sauce

Yields 2 cups

A versatile sauce served as a dip, with steamed or fried fish, or spooned on cold shrimp or lobster.

2   ripe medium avocados, peeled and
     coarsely chopped
2   cups plain low-fat yogurt
3   tablespoons lemon juice
     Pinch of cayenne pepper
1   teaspoon sugar
     Salt and freshly ground black pepper to
     taste

Blend all the ingredients together in a food processor or blender. Cover and chill.

❧ ❧

Potato Avocado Soup

Serves 4

This soup has the most gorgeous pale green color. Serve it before a seafood salad for a great summer meal.

2   bacon slices, fried crisp and well drained
1   tablespoon lightly salted butter, or more
     as needed
⅓   cup chopped onion
2   medium potatoes (about 8 ounces),
     cubed
3   cups chicken stock
2   medium avocados, cubed (reserve ¼
     avocado for garnish)
½   teaspoon salt
     Freshly ground pepper to taste
½   cup sour cream

Fry the bacon until crisp enough to crumble easily, drain on paper towels, and set aside. In a saucepan melt the butter and sauté the onion until soft. Add the potatoes and stock to the onion and heat to boiling, then simmer until the potatoes are tender. Remove from heat, add the avocado, and puree in a blender or food processor until smooth. Return to the saucepan just to heat through, taking care not to boil. Remove from heat, add salt and pepper, and stir in the sour cream. Spoon the soup into 4 individual bowls. Cut 8 thin slices lengthwise from the reserved avocado and place 2 slices on each serving with curves forming an oval. Center with a sprinkling of crumbled bacon.

Avocado Potato Salad

Serves 4

Serve as a main course for lunch or a light supper with warm asparagus.

- 1 *pound all-purpose potatoes, cooked and cut into ¾-inch cubes*
- 2 *hard-boiled eggs, coarsely chopped*
- 2 *tablespoons lemon juice*
- ½ *cup mayonnaise*
- 6 *thin, lean bacon slices*
- 2 *scallions, including about 2 inches of green, sliced*
- 2 *medium avocados, cubed*

Place the hot potatoes in a salad bowl with the eggs. Mix the lemon juice and mayonnaise and stir into potatoes. Sauté the bacon until crisp, drain well, and crumble over potato mixture. Add the scallions and gently mix in the cubed avocado. Serve while still warm or at room temperature.

Eggs Mexican Style

Serves 4

Good any time you have a ripe avocado and want a quickly prepared meal. More hot pepper flakes may be added for a spicier sauce, and a sprinkling of grated Monterey Jack cheese can be added.

- 1 *tablespoon olive oil*
- 1 *medium onion, chopped*
- 1 *garlic clove, minced*
- ½ *medium green bell pepper, chopped*
- 1 *pound fresh tomatoes, or 1 (16-ounce) can, chopped*
- ¼ *teaspoon crushed red pepper flakes*
- ½ *teaspoon sugar*
- 3–4 *fresh basil leaves, torn into pieces*
- ½ *teaspoon salt*
- 4 *corn or flour tortillas, or halves of English muffins*
- 4 *large eggs, poached with 1 tablespoon vinegar*
- 2 *ripe medium avocados, peeled and sliced*

Heat the oil in a skillet and add the onion, garlic, and pepper; cook until soft and the onion is transparent. Add the tomatoes and cook until soft, then add the pepper flakes, sugar, basil, and salt and simmer until thickened.

Heat tortillas, or if using English muffins, toast halves. Poach the eggs in water to which the tablespoon of vinegar has been added to keep eggs from spreading.

On each plate, place a tortilla or muffin half, top with well-drained poached egg, place slices of avocado attractively to one side, and pour the sauce over the eggs.

Pita Sandwich of Pureed Avocado and Chicken

Serves 4

Avocados can be used for many last-minute meals—this sandwich is just one example. Experiment and create other combinations for yourself.

2   *medium avocados*
    Juice of ½ lemon
2   *tablespoons low-fat mayonnaise*
    Salt and freshly ground pepper to taste
4   *pita rounds, opened but not completely split*
2   *skinless and boneless chicken breasts (6 ounces each), either broiled or sautéed*
1   *medium tomato, thinly sliced*
1   *medium cucumber, washed and thinly sliced*
½   *sweet onion, thinly sliced*
1   *cup alfalfa sprouts*

In a small bowl, mash the avocado and puree with the lemon juice and mayonnaise. Season with salt and pepper. Divide the puree evenly and spread on each inner side of the pita rounds. Layer with the chicken, sliced tomato, cucumber, onion, and sprouts. Close the pita and press firmly.

Salmon Steaks with Avocado Horseradish Puree

Serves 4

The mild taste, satiny texture, and soft green color of the avocado are combined here with horseradish and a touch of cayenne pepper to create a unique dish.

SALMON

¾   *cup dry white wine*
1½ *cups water*
2   *bay leaves*
1   *teaspoon dried thyme*
4   *black peppercorns*
1   *celery stalk, trimmed and cut into 2-inch pieces*
4   *salmon steaks (about 6 ounces each)*
½   *teaspoon salt*
    Freshly ground pepper to taste

AVOCADO PUREE

1   *ripe medium avocado*
3   *tablespoons lemon juice*
¼   *cup low-fat mayonnaise*
1½ *teaspoons prepared white horseradish*
½   *teaspoon sugar*
    Pinch of cayenne pepper

In a large saucepan, combine all the ingredients but the salmon and salt and pepper. Bring to a boil and simmer for about 10 minutes. Wash the fish, pat dry with paper towels, and season with salt and pepper. Place in the court bouillon, cover, bring to a simmer, and cook until firm. A rule of thumb for poaching fish is 10 minutes per inch of thickness. Remove the pan from the heat, keep covered, and allow the salmon to cool in the liquid.

Halve, peel, and pit the avocado. Place in a food processor together with the remaining ingredients and puree until smooth. Adjust the seasonings, put in a small serving bowl, and chill. Spoon over the salmon when ready to serve and pass the remainder separately.

❧   ❧

Angel Hair Pasta with Avocado and Salmon

Serves 4

An unusual combination of delicate flavors and textures with a most pleasing final result.

½ *cup dry white wine*
½ *cup chicken stock*
2 *tablespoons finely chopped shallots*
4 *tablespoons (½ stick) unsalted butter*
1 *teaspoon cornstarch*
1 *cup plain low-fat yogurt*
1 *teaspoon Dijon mustard*
2 *tablespoons grated Parmesan cheese*
  Salt and freshly ground pepper to taste
12 *ounces fresh salmon, poached, boned, and skinned*
2 *ripe medium avocados*
  Juice of 1 lemon
12 *ounces fresh broccoli*
8 *ounces angel hair pasta*
3 *tablespoons chopped scallions, including about 2 inches of green*

Combine the wine, stock, and shallots in a saucepan. Bring to a boil and cook over medium heat for 10 minutes. Remove from heat and whisk in the butter, a tablespoon at a time, until completely blended. Mix the cornstarch with the yogurt, add to the wine mixture, and cook over low heat for about 4 minutes. Stir in the mustard and Parmesan cheese, season to taste, and cook for 3 more minutes. Set aside and keep warm.

Cut the salmon into bite-size pieces and set aside. Peel, seed, and cut the avocados into julienne strips. Immediately coat with lemon juice to prevent discoloration and set aside. Steam or microwave the broccoli until almost tender and set aside. Cook the pasta in 2 quarts of boiling water until al dente and drain.

Heat the sauce. In a large bowl, gently mix the hot pasta with the sauce, broccoli, and salmon. Carefully blend in the scallions and avocados and serve immediately.

Shrimp and Avocado Gratinée

Serves 4

Avocado and seafood match well. And this dish is particularly good served over white rice.

- 2 *ripe medium avocados, sliced*
- 4 *tablespoons lime juice*
- ½ *cup shredded cheddar cheese*
- ¼ *cup freshly toasted bread crumbs*
- 2 *tablespoons (¼ stick) unsalted butter*
- 1 *large garlic clove, minced*
- 24 *large shrimp (about 1 pound total), deveined, peeled, with tails intact*
- 2 *tablespoons chopped scallions, including about 2 inches of green*

Arrange the avocado slices evenly in a shallow ovenproof dish and coat all over with the lime juice. Set aside. Mix the cheese and bread crumbs in a small bowl and also set aside.

In a large skillet, melt the butter, add the garlic and shrimp, and cook over medium-high heat until the shrimp turn pink, about 4 minutes. Stir in the scallions and remove from the heat.

Preheat the broiler.

Place the shrimp on top of the avocados, and sprinkle the cheese–bread crumb mixture over them. Broil until the topping is melted and golden brown. Serve immediately over a bed of rice.

Tuna with Avocado and Grapefruit

Serves 4

The flavors of avocado and grapefruit go well with tuna, bluefish, or other similar, slightly oily fishes.

- 1 *ripe medium avocado*
- ½ *cup fresh grapefruit juice*
- ½ *large grapefruit*
  Salt and freshly ground pepper to taste
- 4 *fillets of tuna or bluefish (4–6 ounces each), skin left on*
- 2 *tablespoons (¼ stick) unsalted butter or margarine*

Preheat the oven to 400° F.

Cut, peel, and mash the avocado. Immediately mix with ¼ cup of the grapefruit juice. Set aside. Peel and remove as much of the pith as possible from the grapefruit, then cut into 4 slices and divide each slice into quarters. Season the fish and cut a vertical slit running almost the entire length along the top to make a pocket. (Be careful not to tear the lower skin.)

In an ovenproof pan large enough to contain the fish in a single layer, melt the butter, add the fish, and coat on both sides. Turn the fish skin side down, then fill the pocket with the avocado mixture and spread the rest over the top. Arrange the grapefruit pieces in between and around the fish. Adjust the seasonings. Pour the remaining ¼ cup grapefruit juice over the fish, baste with the liquid in the pan, and bake for 8 to 10 minutes, or until the fish begins to flake. Do not overcook. Serve immediately.

Sliced Smoked Turkey with Avocado, Tomato, and Thousand Island Sauce

Serves 4

The presentation of this quick-to-prepare salad is especially pretty. The sauce is served in hollowed-out red and yellow peppers. Serve it for lunch with fresh crisp bread.

DRESSING

- ⅔ cup low-fat mayonnaise
- ⅓ cup low-fat yogurt
- 1 teaspoon tomato paste
- 6 stuffed green olives, finely chopped
- 1 tablespoon chopped fresh parsley
- ½ teaspoon paprika
- ¼ teaspoon sugar
  Salt and freshly ground pepper to taste

SALAD

- 1 medium red bell pepper
- 1 medium yellow bell pepper
- 3 ripe medium, firm tomatoes
- 2 ripe medium avocados
- 1 tablespoon fresh lemon juice
  Mixed loose-head lettuce, to line the platter
- 12 ounces sliced smoked turkey
  Fresh parsley, for garnish

Prepare the dressing. Combine the mayonnaise, yogurt, tomato paste, olives, parsley, paprika, and sugar. Add the seasonings.

Mix well and chill until ready to serve. This will yield 1 cup of salad dressing.

Cut off the top-third of each pepper, making a lid. (If the peppers are large, use only one.) Remove all the seeds, clean the inside of any flesh, and decorate the top edges with grooves if desired. Set aside. Wash and slice the tomatoes. Halve, peel, and remove the seeds from the avocados. Cut into thin slices and immediately coat with lemon juice to prevent the fruit from darkening.

Line a large serving platter with the lettuce. Fill the peppers with the dressing and place toward one side of the platter. Arrange the sliced tomatoes in a band on top of the lettuce. Moving toward the center of the platter, place the avocado slices in 2 rows forming 2 incomplete circles; the position of the peppers blocks the completion of the circle. Arrange the sliced meat in the middle of the platter and garnish with parsley. Preferably, serve immediately; otherwise, cover tightly with plastic wrap and refrigerate for no more than 1 hour, since after this time the avocado will begin to discolor.

B·A·N·A·N·A·S

Bacon-Wrapped Banana Hors d'Oeuvre

Banana Fritters

Banana Soup with Curry

Banana Chutney

Baked Bananas

Fruit and Lentil Curry

Belizean Kingfish with Lime-Braised Bananas

Outeniqua Sandwich

Banana Stuffing

Lamb Curry with Bananas

Bananas in Yogurt

Banana Bran Muffins

Sliced Banana Cheesecake

Chocolate-Covered Bananas

Banana Pecan Ice Cream

Banana Lassi

We Americans consume more than twenty-five pounds of bananas per person each year! This is more than any other kind of fruit, and somewhat surprising for a tropical fruit raised in Central America, but not native to this continent. It is believed that the banana's origins were in India and the jungles of Malaysia because so many varieties are found there. Early records place it in India at the time of Alexander's conquest in 327 B.C.

The banana began its journey with traders who carried it from the Far East to eastern Africa, and from  there the slave and ivory traders took it with them to the west coast of Africa. The Portuguese continued its journey, taking it northward to the Canary Islands, where bananas are still grown commercially. A Spaniard, Friar Tomas de Berlanga, brought the first root stocks to the Western Hemisphere when he sailed to the Caribbean in 1516, where the banana roots he planted flourished in the rich, moist soil of the tropics.

Bananas reached the east coast of the United States via clipper ships as early as 1850, where they remained a rare luxury until the advent of the steamship and refrigeration. Since no bananas are commercially grown in the United States, the improvement in transportation was paramount in providing us with a plentiful year-round supply at a reasonable cost.

Although treelike in appearance, the banana is actually a gigantic herb, springing from an underground stem, or rhizome. The stalk, formed of large overlapping leaves, can attain a height of twenty-five feet, making the banana the largest plant in existence without a woody trunk. This stalk is crowned with a rosette of ten to twenty oblong leaves, from which a large flower spike on a single stem emerges. As the flowers develop, each blossom becomes an individual fruit, known as a finger. The whole group of up to twenty bananas growing together is known as a hand. As these fruits develop the stem bends downward to become the bunch of seven to nine hands. Within nine to twelve months the stem, weighing eighty-five to one hundred pounds, is ready for harvesting, which takes place while the fruit is still green. Even when used in the local areas where they are grown, bananas are picked green, since the texture and flavor is impaired if left to turn yellow on the tree. Once the plants have fruited they die and are replaced by others, which arise from the underground stem. The banana plant thrives in tropical weather with an average temperature of 80° F.

Bananas are now displayed by the hand on produce shelves, but some of us can remember when a whole bunch, on display in the grocer's window, was suspended from the ceiling just as it hung on the tree, with each finger pointing skyward. Highly nutritious, bananas are an important food source in countries where they are grown.

❧ HOME CULTIVATION ❧

A dwarf form of the banana, growing to about eight feet tall and with a five-foot spread of leaves, can be grown in a large warm greenhouse, either set directly in the ground or in a large pot. It may also be grown outdoors in Florida or California, where temperatures do not drop below 50° F. Temperature is crucial to the setting of fruit.

❧ NUTRITION ❧

Although bananas are regarded as a rich fruit, they are 98.5 percent fat free with no cholesterol, but because they are high in carbohydrates they are an excellent energy food. They are a superior source of potassium, B vitamins, especially B_6, as well as vitamins A and C. Other minerals include calcium, magnesium, manganese, phosphorus, and 100 percent-available iron. They are an excellent source of fiber, including crude fiber, nondigestible fiber, and pectin. One 4¼-ounce banana has 100 calories.

❧ SELECTION ❧

Since bananas are ripened off the tree, you can buy totally green fruit and let it ripen at home. If it's to be used at once, select according to your planned use (see next page). Avoid bananas that have large brown areas on an otherwise yellow fruit; this indicates bruising. If the skin has an overall gray look it's a sign of cold damage, and further ripening will not occur.

Although there are more than a hundred varieties of bananas known, the large yellow type used in our recipes is the best known and most readily available. As red bananas have become more plentiful their quality has greatly improved. The flesh has a pink cast and the flavor is sweet and slightly tangy. We have seen a nice quality in those from Ecuador. The small finger bananas found only occasionally are especially nice for a quick snack. Plantains, which are less sweet, are used throughout the Caribbean as a starch vegetable.

EQUIVALENTS
3 medium bananas = about 1 pound
1 sliced banana = ⅔ cup
2 diced bananas = 1 cup
3 mashed bananas = 1 cup

STORAGE
❧ AND PREPARATION ❧

When a banana has reached the skin color appropriate for your use, it can be stored in the refrigerator until needed. Even though the skin turns dark, the pulp will stay at the desired ripeness. In fact you can even freeze bananas in the skin—the pulp will be of a creamy consistency when it thaws. Green-tipped bananas are best used in cooked entrees or vegetable dishes. Completely yellow bananas are excellent for eating out of hand, in salads, or on cereal. Brown spotted bananas are best for baking breads and muffins. As the fruit ripens, the skin darkens and the starch in the fruit turns to sugar, which causes the fruit to taste sweeter.

Bananas require little preparation beyond removing the peel. If they are not to be used immediately, once peeled, sprinkle with lemon juice to prevent discoloration.

❧   ❧

A banana is undoubtedly one of the simplest foods to eat. It is easy to peel, requires nothing added to make it palatable, and makes no mess, making it perfect for picnics. Because of its naturally sweet, soft flesh and high nutritional content, the banana has become a prime choice for baby's first solid food. Its distinctive flavor can dominate or blend beautifully in fruit salads, especially with citrus and tropical fruits. Fried in a light batter it can accompany an entree, or give it the same treatment but add a chocolate or butterscotch sauce and you have a great dessert. Bananas take as well to curried poultry and fish as they do to ginger and cinnamon-flavored pies and puddings. The banana's creamy texture can be appreciated in a chilled soup, ice cream, or thick milkshake. For an easy-to-make, wonderful-to-eat treat, dip sections in chocolate and freeze.

Bacon-Wrapped Banana Hors d'Oeuvre

Yields 16 pieces

These are easy to prepare ahead of time and pop under the broiler at the last minute. Plan on two to three pieces per person.

> 6 *bacon slices, each cut into 3 pieces*
> 1 *8-inch banana, cut into 1-inch slices*
> 1 *tablespoon lemon juice*
> 1–2 *drops hot pepper sauce*

Preheat the broiler.

Fry the bacon over low heat until partly cooked but still soft enough to wrap around banana pieces. Cut each banana slice in half. Mix lemon juice and hot pepper sauce, and roll banana pieces in the juice to coat on all sides. Wrap bacon around the banana, secure with a toothpick, and place on broiler pan. An infra-red broiler will take about 5 minutes to finish cooking the bacon and bake bananas. A regular broiler will take a bit longer. These could also be finished over coals on an outside grill.

Banana Fritters

Yields 8 servings

This recipe yields two pieces per serving as an accompaniment to a main course poultry, fish, or meat dish.

> *Oil for deep-frying*
> 4 *medium bananas, yellow but not brown-flecked, each about 6 inches long*
> 2 *large eggs*
> 1/2 *cup milk*
> 1 *cup all-purpose flour*
> 1 *teaspoon baking powder*
> 1 *teaspoon salt*
> 1 *teaspoon canola or other vegetable oil*

Heat oil for deep-frying to 375° F.

Cut the bananas in half crosswise, then halve lengthwise. In a shallow bowl, combine the eggs, milk, flour, baking powder, salt, and vegetable oil and mix well. Dip banana sections in the batter and fry until golden brown, drain on absorbent paper, and serve hot.

VARIATION: For dessert fritters, add 1 teaspoon sugar to batter. Cut bananas into 1-inch chunks and fry as above. Serve dusted with confectioners' sugar or a hot fruit or chocolate sauce.

Banana Soup with Curry

Serves 6

Serve this soup with thin slices of Virginia baked ham, biscuits, and a watercress salad for a delectable lunch.

- 2 tablespoons (¼ stick) *lightly salted butter or margarine*
- ¼ cup coarsely chopped onion
- 1 medium garlic clove, minced
- 1 tablespoon curry powder
- ¼ cup white rice
- 6 cups chicken stock
- 2 cups light cream
- 1 cup thickly sliced ripe bananas (about 2 medium)
- 2 tablespoons lemon juice
- ½ teaspoon salt
- ⅛ teaspoon cayenne pepper or few drops hot pepper sauce
  Cubed cantaloupe or blueberries, for garnish (optional)

Melt the butter in a heavy saucepan. Add the onion and sauté until soft. Add the garlic, cook for about 1 minute, then stir in the curry powder and cook 3 minutes. Stir in the rice, add stock, and bring to a boil. Lower heat, cover, and cook until the rice is very soft, about 20 minutes.

Place the soup in a blender or food processor, add the cream, bananas, lemon juice, salt, and cayenne pepper. Puree until fairly smooth. Chill for at least 2 hours. Garnish with cantaloupe or blueberries, if desired.

Banana Chutney

Yields 7–8 cups

This chutney's pungent fruity flavor is marvelous with broiled fish as well as poultry and meat dishes.

- 2 medium onions, chopped
- 2 large garlic cloves, minced
- 1 cup dark brown sugar
- 6 large bananas, ripe but firm, peeled and cut into ¼-inch slices
- ½ cup cider vinegar
- 1 (8-ounce) can crushed unsweetened pineapple, including juice
- ½ cup raisins
- 3 ounces crystallized ginger, chopped
- 1 medium Italian pepper, finely diced
- ¼ cup lime juice
- 1 teaspoon salt
- 3 whole cloves
  Freshly ground black pepper to taste
  Few drops hot pepper sauce or more for spicier flavor

In a medium size pot, place all the ingredients except for the freshly ground black pepper and hot pepper sauce. Bring the mixture to a boil, then lower the heat to medium-low and cook for 20 minutes, stirring occasionally to prevent sticking. Season with the black pepper and hot pepper sauce. Remove from heat and cool to room temperature, then bottle. Store in the refrigerator for up to 8 weeks.

Baked Bananas

Serves 4

Baked bananas are traditionally served as a dessert, alone or with a scoop of ice cream or a dollop of whipped cream. In the South they are a breakfast delicacy. They may also be served in place of a vegetable with certain meat courses, especially those flavored with curry, since the sweetness of the bananas enhances the curry. Bananas also combine well with simply prepared broiled chicken.

>   3   *tablespoons unsalted butter, melted*
>   4   *tablespoons dark brown sugar*
>   2   *tablespoons lime juice*
>   2   *tablespoons light rum (optional)*
>   4   *large ripe but firm bananas with a green tinge*

Preheat the oven to 375° F.

Put the butter, brown sugar, lime juice, and rum in a baking dish sufficiently large to contain the bananas and place in the oven for about 3 minutes to allow the sugar to dissolve. Remove and stir a few times to mix.

Peel and slice the bananas into half lengthwise; carefully place them in the dish and coat them all over with the syrup. Arrange them cut side down so that they do not overlap. Bake for 15 minutes, remove from the oven, and serve immediately.

Fruit and Lentil Curry

Serves 4

This can be a main-course vegetarian dish or a side dish with meat, poultry, or fish. Here we use white rice, but brown rice could be substituted.

>   1   *cup lentils*
>   2   *medium onions, chopped*
>   1   *tablespoon canola or other vegetable oil*
>   1   *tablespoon butter*
>   1   *tablespoon curry powder, or to taste*
>   2   *large firm apples such as Granny Smith, chopped coarsely*
>   2   *medium bananas, cut into medium chunks*
>   1/3   *cup raisins*
>   2   *teaspoons lemon or lime juice*
>   1   *cup long-grain rice*
>   2   *cups water*
>   2   *tablespoons finely chopped chutney, such as Major Grey*
>   1/4   *cup shredded coconut*

Place the lentils in a saucepan with water to cover about 1 inch. Bring to a boil, then lower heat to simmer and cook until tender, 30 to 40 minutes. Sauté the onions in the oil and butter until golden, then stir in curry powder and cook for 2 minutes. Add the chopped apples and sauté lightly, just until slightly colored but not soft. Add this mixture to the cooked lentils along with the bananas, raisins, and lemon juice, mixing well. Set aside.

Place rice in a saucepan with water and bring to a boil, then lower heat and cook until the water is absorbed and the rice is done, about 20 minutes. (Brown rice will take longer.)

Heat the lentil mixture and allow to simmer over very low heat for 10 minutes, adding more water if needed to keep moist. When rice is cooked, stir in the chutney and coconut. To serve, mound lentil mixture in the center of a serving platter and surround with rice.

Belizean Kingfish with Lime-Braised Bananas

Serves 4

This dish is an adaptation of a meal served at Maruba Resort in Belize. A few slices of baked sweet potato are a pleasing accompaniment.

1½   pounds firm white fish such as kingfish, cod, or pollack
3   tablespoons teriyaki sauce, homemade or purchased
3   tablespoons flour
3   tablespoons cornmeal
2   tablespoons canola or corn oil
2   tablespoons dark brown sugar
¼   cup water
3   tablespoons sugar
4   small bananas
¼   cup lime juice
    Lime wedges, for garnish

Cut the fish into serving pieces, place in a flat dish, and pour teriyaki sauce over, turning fish to coat on all sides. Allow to marinate 30 minutes to 1 hour. Blot with paper towels, then dust well with flour, followed by cornmeal—pat onto fish to make it cling.

Heat the oil in a wide nonstick skillet (if using other than nonstick you may need more oil) over medium-high heat. Sauté fish pieces until lightly browned, then turn and sprinkle browned side with brown sugar; when second side is brown, turn over onto sugared side, lower heat, and cook until fish is done and flakes easily with a fork.

While fish is cooking, mix water with sugar in a second skillet wide enough to hold bananas in one layer. Bring to a boil, then lower the heat and place bananas cut side down and cook about 3 minutes. Turn to other side, pour lime juice over fruit, and continue to cook until slightly transparent but still firm enough to handle. When fish is done lift pieces with spatula to a serving platter and surround with the cooked bananas. Garnish with wedges of lime.

Outeniqua Sandwich

Serves 1

This open-faced luncheon sandwich made with whole wheat bread was served to us on a trip to the Outeniqua mountains in Africa.

1   slice whole wheat or other health bread
2   tablespoons low-fat cottage cheese
1   medium ripe banana, peeled and sliced into rounds
1   tablespoon honey, or to taste
1   tablespoon toasted sliced almonds

Spread the bread generously with the cottage cheese. Place the banana rounds on top of the cheese, overlapping the slices. Drizzle the honey evenly over the bananas. Sprinkle with toasted almonds.

Banana Stuffing

Yields 3½ cups

This stuffing is an interesting variation on the usual one made with just bread. It absorbs a lot of juice from the bird, which brings out both the flavor of the banana and makes the stuffing wonderfully moist.

> 3 *large ripe bananas, coarsely mashed*
> 2 *tablespoons lemon juice*
> 5 *pieces day-old bread*
> 2 *tablespoons canola or other vegetable oil*
> 2 *tablespoons (¼ stick) unsalted butter*
> ⅓ *cup chopped scallions, including about 2 inches of green*
> ⅓ *cup trimmed and chopped celery*
> ¼ *teaspoon peeled and minced fresh ginger*
> ⅛ *teaspoon ground nutmeg*
>   *Freshly ground pepper to taste*

Coarsely chop the bananas and mix with the lemon juice. Remove the crusts from the bread and cut into approximately ¼-inch cubes.

In a large skillet, heat the oil and butter. Add the bread and sauté over medium heat until lightly browned. Add the remaining ingredients and cook, stirring until thoroughly mixed. Remove from heat. Adjust seasonings. The stuffing may be prepared several hours ahead and refrigerated.

Lamb Curry with Bananas

Serves 4

Lamb curry remains a most popular dish in India. In this recipe the fruit becomes incorporated into the sauce. Serve it over rice with a fruit chutney or relish. Our Date and Onion Salad (see recipe page 95) is a particularly fine accompaniment.

> 1½–1¾ *pounds lean boneless lamb, cut into 1-inch cubes*
> 1 *tablespoon unsalted butter*
> 1 *tablespoon canola or other vegetable oil*
> 1 *large onion, thinly sliced*
> 1 *garlic clove, minced*
> 1 *teaspoon peeled and minced fresh ginger*
> 1 *teaspoon ground cumin*
> 1 *teaspoon ground turmeric*
> 1 *teaspoon ground coriander*
> 1 *teaspoon ground cardamom*
> ½ *teaspoon ground cloves*
> ½ *teaspoon ground cinnamon*
> ½ *teaspoon sugar*
> ½ *teaspoon salt*
> ½ *teaspoon freshly ground black pepper*
> 1 *Granny Smith apple, peeled, cored, and cut into 1-inch cubes*
> 2 *large bananas, slightly underripe, peeled and sliced ½ inch thick*
> 1½ *cups chicken stock*
> 1 *tablespoon cider vinegar*
>   *Dash of cayenne pepper or Tabasco*

Remove any fat on the meat. Set aside.

In a large saucepan, heat the butter and oil. Add the onion, garlic, and ginger and cook over medium-high heat for 5 to 7 minutes, stirring to prevent any burning or sticking on the bottom of the pan. Add all the spices and sugar, stir into the onion mixture, then add the lamb and cook for 10 to 12 minutes, stirring occasionally to even the browning. Should a large amount of juice accumulate, raise the heat to high briefly to help some of the liquid evaporate. Add the apple and bananas, mix well, then blend in the stock and vinegar. Bring to a boil, lower the heat, and simmer for 1 hour or until the lamb is tender and the liquid has thickened to a sauce. Add the cayenne pepper and adjust the seasonings as desired. Serve immediately or refrigerate for up to 3 days. This dish may be frozen for up to 6 months.

NOTE: If individual spices are unavailable, substitute 1½ tablespoons medium curry powder.

✤ ✤

Bananas in Yogurt

Serves 6

Serve this delicious cool relish with any curried fish or meat, or with grilled chicken.

½ *cup plain low-fat yogurt*
2 *tablespoons lime juice*
2 *teaspoons sugar*
1 *teaspoon ground cumin*
   Dash of cayenne pepper (optional)
   Salt and freshly ground black pepper to taste
3 *large ripe bananas, peeled and sliced into eighths*

In a bowl combine the yogurt with the lime juice, sugar, cumin, cayenne pepper, salt, and black pepper. Mix in the bananas.

Banana Bran Muffins

Yields 12 muffins

These muffins are wonderful for breakfast or brunch. They're so moist you don't even need butter to enjoy them.

¾ *cup whole bran cereal*
¼ *cup milk*
1½ *cups mashed bananas (3 brown-flecked medium)*
1 *large egg*
¼ *cup molasses*
2 *tablespoons canola or other vegetable oil*
1 *cup all-purpose flour*
1 *teaspoon baking soda*
¼ *teaspoon salt*
¾ *cup raisins*

Preheat the oven to 375° F. Grease twelve 2½-inch muffin cups.

Mix cereal into milk to soften. Puree the bananas in a blender or food processor, then add the egg, molasses, and oil and blend well. Add bran and milk just to blend. Combine the flour, baking soda, and salt in a medium bowl. Stir in the banana mixture until just moistened. Fold in raisins. Spoon into greased cups and bake on middle rack of oven for 25 to 30 minutes. Best served immediately but will keep, wrapped in foil, for several days.

Sliced Banana Cheesecake

Serves 10–12

A cheesecake that has become one of the favorite dessert items at Skipjack's in Boston. It is a dish for indulgence, not for calorie counting.

    4 tablespoons (½ stick) unsalted butter or
       margarine
    1 cup ground chocolate wafers (about 20
       Nabisco Famous), plus 3–4 crushed for
       garnish
    1 cup plus 2 tablespoons sugar
    2 large ripe bananas
    3 tablespoons fresh lemon juice
 1½ pounds cream cheese
    3 large eggs
 1½ teaspoons vanilla extract
  ¼ teaspoon salt
 1½ cups sour cream
    1 tablespoon cornstarch
  ⅓ cup miniature chocolate chips (optional)

Grease a round 8 × 3-inch pan on the bottom and sides, and line the bottom with wax paper. You may use a springform pan, but wrap the outside with foil to prevent seepage.

Melt the butter, then blend with the ground wafers and 2 tablespoons of the sugar. Press evenly to cover the bottom of the pan and extend slightly up the sides. Place in refrigerator to chill.

Preheat the oven to 350° F.

Slice the bananas into ⅛-inch rounds, combine with the lemon juice, and set aside. In the large bowl of an electric mixer, beat the cream cheese and remaining cup of sugar for

about 3 minutes at medium speed. Add the eggs, one at a time, beating after each addition until smooth. Add the vanilla and salt, and beat until blended, then add the sour cream and cornstarch. Carefully fold in the sliced banana mixture. Then, if you are using chocolate chips, add them by hand.

Pour the batter into the prepared pan. Set it in a larger pan filled with 1 inch of very hot water. Bake on the middle rack for 45 minutes. Turn off the oven without opening the door and leave for an additional hour. Remove to a rack and cool to room temperature. When completely cool, cover with plastic wrap and refrigerate for at least 6 hours before serving.

Run a knife around the sides of the cake and invert onto a plate. Remove the parchment and reinvert onto the serving plate. If using a springform pan, release the sides of the pan before inverting. Sprinkle the top with the crushed chocolate wafers, cover, and refrigerate until serving. This cheesecake may be refrigerated for 1 week or frozen up to 2 months.

NOTE: Placing a pan on a burner over low heat and moving it around for 10 to 30 seconds will help release any custard-style cake or baked food from the pan when inverted.

Chocolate-Covered Bananas

Yields 8

After several hours in the freezer, bananas undergo a magical transformation. Pureed in either a blender or food processor, they emerge as thick and smooth as ice cream.

Dipped in melted chocolate, a previously frozen banana becomes an elegant dessert. Insert a thin wooden stick into the fruit as a handle and you have a banana popsicle. And remember, the calories are only a fraction of many other frozen desserts.

> 4 *medium bananas, ripe but firm*
> 2 *tablespoons fresh lime or lemon juice*
> 4 *ounces semisweet chocolate, melted*

Peel the bananas, slice in half crosswise, coat with the lime juice, wrap in wax paper, and freeze for at least 3 hours. Place the chocolate in the top of a double boiler making sure the bottom of the top pot does not touch the water. Stir until chocolate is melted and smooth. Coat each piece of banana with chocolate, place on a wax paper–lined tray, and place in the refrigerator to cool and harden. Either serve as is or rewrap in plastic and freeze until needed.

Banana Pecan Ice Cream

Yields 3 cups

Since frozen bananas develop a marvelously creamy consistency, this ice cream doesn't require the traditional addition of heavy cream.

> 1/4 *cup toasted pecans*
> 1 *cup mashed bananas (2 medium)*
> 1/2 *cup sugar*
> 1/2 *cup light cream*
> 1/2 *cup whipping cream*
> 1/2 *cup milk*

Toast pecans in 350° F. oven for about 5 minutes, allow to cool, then break into large pieces. Mix bananas with sugar. Add cream and milk to banana mixture and blend. Stir in broken pecans. Pour into an ice cream maker and freeze according to manufacturer's directions, or place in wide, shallow metal pan and put in freezer compartment. When edges are frozen and center is nearly so, spoon into chilled bowl and beat with rotary or electric beater until light and smooth. Pack in freezer carton and return to freezer.

Banana Lassi

Serves 2

Lassi traditionally is a yogurt drink commonly served throughout India and now enjoyed by many in Indian restaurants all over the world. In texture it is somewhat similar to a frappe.

> 1 1/2 *cups plain yogurt*
> 1 *large very ripe banana, peeled and cut into 4 pieces*
> 1/2 *cup fresh orange juice*
> 1/2 *teaspoon vanilla extract*
> 1 *tablespoon sugar, or to taste*
> 2 *ice cubes*

Combine all the ingredients in a blender or food processor and process until well mixed and smooth. Divide between 2 glasses and serve immediately.

B·L·A·C·K·B·E·R·R·I·E·S
and
R·A·S·P·B·E·R·R·I·E·S

Rosé Raspberry Soup

Pea Pods with Raspberries

Roast Game Hens with Fresh Raspberries

Blackberry Cobbler

Raspberry Lemon Tarts

Summer Pudding

Fresh Raspberry Sauce

Raspberry Sorbet

Raspberry Bavarian Cream

Raspberry Vinegar

Anyone who has picked blackberries or raspberries can readily believe their botanical relationship with the thorny rose. Their other name, bramble berries, refers to their prickly canes. For centuries they have been gathered in the wild in temperate climates all over the world and are found in nearly every region of the United States.

While in Europe cultivated raspberries are derived from just one species, North America provides several varieties: the red raspberry, the eastern black raspberry, and the western black rasp-  berry are all common. Lately a purple berry and a striking golden yellow one have become available. The red berry dominates the commercial plantings in Oregon and Washington, Michigan, Minnesota, and western New York. There is no more fragile fruit than the raspberry; they must be handled very gently since they crush easily and in humid weather are most vulnerable to mold. Rain at harvest time can devastate an entire crop. Because of this delicacy about 80 percent of the crop is marketed as frozen berries. The black, purple, and the increasingly popular golden berries are usually found only in local farmers markets or farmstands.

The most notable difference between raspberries and blackberries is the little hollow cup found only in the raspberry, regardless of its color. When ripe the raspberry lifts easily away from the white core, which remains on the stem, leaving the familiar hollow, whereas the blackberry retains the core when picked. Both berries leave behind their stems and sepals (the little green caps at the base of the stem) when ripe.

Blackberries, while always black, encompass a larger variety of species, which can lead to some confusion of names. Among these are the youngberry, boysenberry, ollalie berry, and the creeping dewberry. The loganberry has all the other characteristics of the blackberry, but is dark red when ripe, with a slightly acidic taste. Discovered in California, it is thought to be a hybrid between a blackberry and a raspberry. Boysenberries are a three-way cross among the black, logan, and raspberry, which produces a large, red-black berry. Ollalie berries, a cross between a youngberry and a logan, are a black, sweet type grown in California. There is some commercial production of blackberries but, perhaps because they are so readily available in the wild, it is not a huge industry.

HOME CULTIVATION

Raspberries and blackberries can be grown in nearly all states if planted in a sunny location, with a light, well-drained soil. They can be trained onto wires or rails, but because of their rampant growth cannot be considered an attractive addition to the landscape. Pruning is essential to growing these berries, both to obtain abundant crops and to maintain some order in the plants. When the canes become long enough they will arch over, and when the tips touch the ground they will take root, creating a new plant. If not kept tidy you will have your own Bre'r Rabbit briar patch. Thornless types of blackberries have been developed that make pruning and harvesting less of a hazard to body and clothing.

NUTRITION

Red raspberries are rich in vitamins A and C plus potassium and some calcium. Black raspberries supply vitamin C, but only a negligible amount of vitamin A. Blackberries contribute an unusual amount of calcium for a fruit, plus potassium and vitamins A and C. All berries are high in fiber content. Three-quarters of a cup (five ounces) of blackberries has 65 calories; three-quarters of a cup (three ounces) of raspberries has 53 calories.

SELECTION

Look for berries that are plump and fully colored for their type. Check for any staining of the baskets as they may indicate crushed or overripe berries. Look for signs of mold, small whitish-gray spots, especially on raspberries. Except for the loganberry, blackberries should be a shiny black, with no red color. In our northeastern markets all these berries are usually sold in the small, half-pint containers.

Raspberries are rarely marketed by named varieties, simply by color. The lesser known gold are usually large and of very good flavor. The black are found growing wild and sometimes sold in farm markets. The purple berries are a cross between the red and black. Each has a flavor slightly different but also a distinctively raspberry taste. They start appearing in the markets in late May until November for those domestically grown. Because they require hand picking, during the season you will see farms that advertise pick-your-own fruit. You can obtain choice berries for less money, but it is not easy work!

Blackberries are not readily available in supermarkets, and only briefly in the farm markets. They are in season from mid-June through August. In New England it's a fruit of late summer, and is often found in the country in sunny fields and along abandoned railroads.

```
┌─────────────────────────────────────┐
│            EQUIVALENTS                │
│      ½ pint berries = 1 cup           │
└─────────────────────────────────────┘
```

STORAGE AND
❧ PREPARATION ❧

All berries should be refrigerated and used within a day of purchase. Check them first for any spoiled berries and rinse (gently) only when you're ready to use them. All types may be frozen after carefully picking over to remove imperfect fruit and stems. It is best to freeze them on trays in a single layer, then place the frozen berries in cartons or bags.

❧ ❧

All fresh berries are delicious served with cream and are an excellent addition to breakfast cereals. Chocolate and the sharp decisive flavor of the raspberry are made for each other. Try a fresh raspberry sauce with a wedge of rich chocolate cake, or line a meringue shell with chocolate, fill with fresh raspberries, and top with a dollop of whipped cream. To really appreciate blackberries bake them in a pie or cobbler, lightly dusted with cinnamon and just a hint of lemon juice. Add sparkle to your meal with the bright flavor and color of raspberries in a chilled soup, sprinkled in a salad, or frozen in a sorbet. Although you may wish to remove the seeds, both fruits make excellent jams.

Rosé Raspberry Soup

Serves 4

This is a light, delicately flavored soup that is not too sweet for a first course.

    2   cups raspberries (reserve 12 raspberries
        for garnish)
    5   tablespoons sugar
    1   tablespoon lemon juice
    ½   cup sour cream
    1½ cups water
    1   cup rosé wine

Work the raspberries through a fine sieve. Combine the puree with the sugar, lemon juice, sour cream, water, and wine. Chill for at least 1 hour. Garnish with reserved raspberries, 3 to a bowl.

NOTE: If you don't object to the seeds or do not have a sieve, puree the berries in a blender or food processor, then proceed as above.

Pea Pods with Raspberries

Serves 4–6

This unusual pairing is visually spectacular with a refreshingly different flavor. A great color and taste accent for a chicken salad, this recipe works equally well with grilled fish or poultry.

    ½   pound snow pea pods
    1   tablespoon balsamic vinegar
    2   tablespoons olive oil
    ¼   teaspoon salt
        Freshly ground pepper to taste
    ¾   cup raspberries

Wash and remove tips and strings from pea pods. Bring a large saucepan of water to a rapid boil, add the pea pods, and after water returns to a full boil, cook for just 3 minutes. Drain well in a colander, then toss in a serving bowl with vinegar, oil, salt, and pepper until well coated. Gently stir in the raspberries, taking care not to mash them. Serve warm.

Roast Game Hens with Fresh Raspberries

Serves 4

The hens are first placed in a marinade including both raspberry vinegar and pureed raspberries. They are then oven-roasted and coated with a light sauce studded with lovely fresh raspberries. Serve this colorful and tasty dish with tiny new potatoes or rice and a combination of quickly sautéed snow peas and julienned zucchini.

6 *ounces fresh raspberries*
7 *tablespoons raspberry vinegar*
2 *teaspoons Dijon mustard*
7 *tablespoons canola or other vegetable oil*
  Salt and freshly ground pepper to taste
2 *Cornish game hens (1¼ pounds each, including necks and giblets)*
2 *tablespoons shallots, peeled and finely chopped*
1 *cup chicken broth*
1 *cup white wine*
2 *teaspoons sugar*
1 *teaspoon cornstarch*
2 *teaspoons water*

In the bowl of a food processor, puree half the raspberries. Add 4 tablespoons of the raspberry vinegar, the mustard, and 6 tablespoons of the oil. Process briefly until well blended. Season with salt and pepper, then place the marinade in a flat dish large enough to hold both the hens.

Remove any fat from inside the cavities of the hens, reserving the neck and giblets for the sauce. Rinse well and pat dry with paper towels. Place the hens in the dish with the marinade, turning so that the entire surface of the birds is well coated. Cover and refrigerate for 12 to 24 hours. During this time turn the hens twice.

Preheat the oven to 400° F.

Transfer the hens and the marinade to a roasting pan and place them breast side down. Roast for 25 minutes, baste, then turn the birds so that the breast side is up and roast for 20 minutes more. Baste again. Increase the oven temperature to 450° F. and cook for another 5 to 7 minutes. The hens will be a wonderfully rich mahogany color when done.

While the hens are roasting, prepare the sauce. In a medium-sized saucepan, heat the remaining tablespoon of oil, add the shallots, necks, and giblets and cook over medium-high heat for about 4 minutes, or until the shallots are softened but not brown. Lower the heat to medium, add the remaining 3 tablespoons of raspberry vinegar, the chicken broth, wine, and sugar. Cook for about 35 minutes. Strain the sauce, return to the saucepan, and season with salt and pepper. Mix the cornstarch with water and stir into the sauce. Bring to a boil for just a minute until the mixture thickens, then set aside.

When the hens are cooked, remove them from the roasting pan to a cutting surface and halve each bird lengthwise. Pour the pan drippings into the sauce, bring to a boil, and cook briefly just to heat through. Add the remaining whole raspberries and swirl them around in the sauce for just a few seconds. Place each half hen on individual serving plates, spoon some sauce over each portion, and serve immediately.

Blackberry Cobbler

Serves 6–9

This is an old summertime favorite, recalling vacations on Martha's Vineyard and the White Mountains of New Hampshire. Armed with an assortment of containers we would seek out the nearest berry patch, then head home with our loot. This dessert is incredibly delicious for something that takes so little time and effort. A good vanilla ice cream, lightly whipped cream, or crème fraîche are equally good toppings.

2/3 cup sugar
1   tablespoon cornstarch
1   cup boiling water
3   cups blackberries
1 1/2 teaspoons lightly salted butter
1/2 teaspoon ground cinnamon
1   cup all-purpose flour
1   tablespoon sugar
1/2 teaspoon salt
1 1/2 teaspoons baking powder
3   tablespoons solid vegetable shortening
1/2 cup milk

Preheat the oven to 400° F. Butter an 8-inch square baking dish.

Mix the sugar and cornstarch in a saucepan, then gradually stir in boiling water. Boil 1 minute, stirring constantly, then add berries. Pour into the baking dish, dot with butter, and sprinkle with cinnamon. Mix the flour, tablespoon of sugar, salt, and baking powder in a bowl. Cut in shortening with a pastry blender or 2 knives until finely blended, then stir in the milk just to moisten. Drop by tablespoons evenly over the fruit. Leave spaces since the dough will spread as

it bakes. Bake about 30 minutes, or until top is golden brown and fruit is bubbling.

NOTE: To make with any canned fruit, use 2 1/2 cups drained fruit. Use the juice in place of sugar and water. Because canned syrups vary so much in sweetness, taste to see if you need to add any sugar.

Raspberry Lemon Tarts

Serves 8

These tarts are easily assembled at the last minute. The tart shells can be made the day before, and the lemon curd a week or more ahead.

SHELLS

1 3/4 cups all-purpose flour
1/4 teaspoon salt
1   teaspoon sugar
1/2 cup (1 stick) lightly salted butter, cut in bits
1   large egg yolk
4   tablespoons cold water, approximately

FILLING

2   cups Lemon Curd (page 133)
2   cups fresh raspberries
1   cup whipping cream, whipped

Mix the flour, salt, and sugar in a medium bowl. Add the butter and blend with fingertips until the mixture resembles coarse meal. Make a well in the center, drop in the yolk and about half the water, and mix with fingers just until dough comes together. If dough is slightly crumbly, add just enough water to make dough form a ball. Form into 2 flattened disks, wrap in plastic, and place in refrigerator for 30 minutes.

Preheat the oven to 350° F.

To roll dough out, flour a board well, sprinkle flour on top of pastry disk, and flour the rolling pin. Roll dough ¼ inch thick, then cut into circles of desired size. A 4-inch custard cup may be used for baking and as a guide, cutting dough about 1 inch larger, then fitting inside. Prick shells with a fork and place pie weights, dried beans, or rice inside to weight the pastry and bake for 15 minutes. Remove weights and return shells to oven for about 10 minutes or until bottoms are golden brown.

To assemble, put 4 tablespoons Lemon Curd in each of the shells, then top with fresh raspberries and a dollop of whipped cream. Place cream in the center to let the raspberries show around the edges.

Summer Pudding

Serves 6

Summer pudding is a traditional English dessert. It always includes bread and is made with a variety of berries. Almost any fruit in season can be used, provided there is enough juice to color and hide the bread.

7–10 thin slices white bread, crusts removed
  2 pounds mixed fresh berries such as raspberries, blackberries, blueberries, red currants, and strawberries
  ¼ cup water
½–¾ cup sugar
     Whipped cream or Crème Anglaise (page 247), for serving

Grease a 1½-quart mold or dish.

Flatten each slice of bread with a rolling pin, to make the bread more pliable. Line the sides and bottom of a mold or dish with some of the bread, overlapping the slices. Use your fingers to press the pieces together so there are no gaps. If necessary, trim the top to make it even. Make sure you reserve enough bread to cover the mold once it is filled.

Wash the berries and remove any stems. In a saucepan, combine the fruit and sugar with the water, bring to a boil, and cook over medium-high heat for 4 to 5 minutes. (For tart berries or fruit, use the greater amount of sugar.) With a slotted spoon, fill the lined mold with the fruit and top with remaining bread. Pour the remaining juice all over and allow it to trickle down the sides. Cover with a round of wax paper cut to fit the mold, place a plate over the paper, and put a 1- to 2-pound weight on the plate to press down the pudding. Refrigerate at least overnight.

When ready to serve, run a knife around the inside edge of the mold to loosen the pudding and turn it out onto a serving platter. Serve with whipped cream or Crème Anglaise. If any berries remain, sprinkle over the top. This dessert may be frozen, covered for 6 months, then thawed slowly in the refrigerator before unmolding.

Fresh Raspberry Sauce

Yields 2½ cups

The sweetness of the sugar modifies the fresh slightly tart taste of the raspberries. Together, the striking color and enlivening taste give a sauce that graces a rich chocolate cake and turns an ordinary scoop of ice cream into a delectable treat.

12 ounces fresh or frozen raspberries, thawed
4 tablespoons superfine sugar
1 tablespoon fresh lemon juice
2 tablespoons cognac

Combine all ingredients in a blender or food processor and process until pureed. Strain through a sieve to remove the seeds. Store in the refrigerator in an airtight container until ready to serve. The sauce will keep for up to 1 week; the color may darken somewhat but the taste will remain unchanged.

Raspberry Sorbet

Yields 1½ pints

The dark red color and intense raspberry flavor of this sorbet contrast beautifully with other lighter sorbets such as pear, pineapple, or peach. Try serving three on one plate.

⅓ cup sugar
⅓ cup water
1½ cups fresh raspberries
1½ tablespoons lemon juice
1 cup ginger ale

Boil the sugar and water for 6 minutes. Set aside to cool. Puree the raspberries in a blender and stir into the cooled syrup along with the lemon juice and ginger ale. Freeze in an ice cream maker, following the manufacturer's directions, and pack in a freezer carton, or pour into flat pan (the wider the pan, the faster mixture will freeze) and place in freezer. When frozen place in chilled bowl and beat with electric or hand rotary beater until light and smooth. Spoon lightly into freezer carton and return to freezer.

Raspberry Bavarian Cream

Serves 4

Bavarian creams were popular summertime desserts in the days when a cold dessert was made in an old-fashioned ice box. Those creams were usually made with egg custard, but you can eliminate the eggs and use only gelatin as we've done here.

1   *pint fresh raspberries*
1/2 *cup sugar*
2   *teaspoons gelatin*
3   *tablespoons water*
3   *tablespoons boiling water*
2   *teaspoons lemon juice*
1   *cup whipping cream, whipped*

Puree the berries in a blender of food processor, then press through a sieve to remove seeds, forcing through as much of the pulp as possible. Add sugar to the raspberry puree and let stand for 30 minutes. Soak the gelatin in the water to soften, then dissolve it in the boiling water. Stir the gelatin mixture and lemon juice into the raspberry puree. Place in the refrigerator until mixture becomes thick and syrupy. Remove from the refrigerator, stir in the whipped cream and blend thoroughly. The dessert may be poured into a wet mold to be turned out for serving or spooned from a serving bowl.

NOTE: It will take about 10 to 15 minutes for the gelatin to reach the syrupy stage. Watch this timing carefully; if it hardens there will be small gelatinous lumps in your finished dessert. It will still taste fine, but a smooth and creamy consistency makes a more appealing dessert.

Raspberry Vinegar

Yields 2 cups

The tartness and distinctive refreshing flavor of this vinegar adds a spark when used in salad dressings or in sauces and glazes for poultry, game, and smoked meats. With a little sugar added, it makes a lively summer drink when added to mineral water or to a glass filled with ice cubes.

12 *ounces fresh raspberries*
2   *cups well-flavored white wine vinegar*
2   *tablespoons sugar*
6   *whole fresh raspberries*

In a bowl combine the 12 ounces of raspberries, vinegar, and sugar. Cover tightly and allow the mixture to stand for 3 days. Strain the mixture through a sieve and pour into an airtight jar or bottle, adding the reserved raspberries for decoration. The vinegar will keep indefinitely, stored in a cool, preferably dark place.

B·L·U·E·B·E·R·R·I·E·S

Chilled Blueberry Soup

Blueberry Pancakes

Blueberry Pie

Blueberry Flummery

Wild Blueberry Lemon Muffins

Blueberry Kuchen

Blueberry Syrup

The blueberry is one of our native fruits, long utilized by the American Indians in several unique ways. In addition to eating the fresh fruit in season, they dried the berries for use during the winter months as a seasoning for soups, stews, and meat. In their journal Lewis and Clark describe a meal with the Indians that consisted of venison cured by pounding blueberries into the flesh and smoke-drying. The Indians also made blueberry tea from the roots, and they used a blueberry syrup for coughs.

The North American blueberry, genus *Vaccinium*, is sometimes mistakenly called a huckleberry. (The huckleberry, *Gaylussacia*, is blackish, and has ten stony seeds, whereas the blueberry seeds may number up to sixty-five, but are so small as to go unnoticed.) The British species, *V. myrtillus*, called the bilberry (also, whortleberry and blaeberry), bears its fruit singly, in contrast to the many-fruited clusters of the American blueberry.

Blueberries are classified as lowbush and highbush species. The lowbush type grows wild on the rocky blueberry barrens of northern New England and maritime Canada. These plants reach a height of only one to two feet and spread by underground stems. In Maine the harvesting, formerly done by the MicMac Indians, is now done increasingly by mechanical gatherers as the demand for these flavorful berries becomes worldwide. Much of the crop is canned, frozen, or dehydrated for later use. These berries have become very popular in Europe, where they are combined with the more acidic European strains for jam and juice making. In our country, they may be blended with less flavorsome cultivated berries for baking, jam, and syrup. So valuable has the wild crop become that Maine has been plagued with blueberry rustlers who skim off the best and easiest picked berries to be sold to canneries. In 1989 it was reported that a good night's haul could pay as much as $700. Landowners now hire guards to patrol the barrens, and laws have been passed to make it a punishable offense.

Most cultivated berries are derived from two native highbush species, the common highbush blueberry, *V. corymbosum* (four to twelve feet high), and the rabbit-eye blueberry of the South, *V. ashei* (eight to sixteen feet high). The highbush is the principal type cultivated in the major blueberry-producing states—Michigan, New Jersey, North Carolina, Washington, and Oregon. The berries are large and firm with a good, tart flavor. They have a thick bloom—the waxy coating that gives them their characteristic light blue color. The rabbit-eye berries are more heat and drought tolerant, with fruit that is almost black. More than 60 percent of all North American blueberries are harvested during the peak season, from mid-June to mid-August. Very recently Florida has been sending a small quantity to northern markets as early as May. These berries are of good size and flavor but extremely expensive.

❧ HOME CULTIVATION ❧

Blueberries are an attractive shrub for the home garden with pretty white blooms in spring, berries in the summer, and vivid red fall color. They can be very effective in the landscape when grown in a planting with azaleas, which require the same well-drained, moist, acid soil. Blueberries thrive all along the Atlantic Seaboard from Florida to Maine and west to Michigan. Since cross-pollination

is necessary for fruit-bearing, two or more varieties are needed. Because birds are particularly fond of these berries, some bird lovers plant a few bushes as food for their friends, but to protect fruit for your own use, cover the plants with netting.

❧ NUTRITION ❧

Blueberries are an excellent source of vitamin A and a good source of vitamin C; among the important minerals provided are calcium, iron, phosphorus, and potassium. And in common with other fruits, they provide natural fiber. A half-cup serving is 41 calories.

❧ SELECTION ❧

Blueberries are almost always sold in pint baskets with cellophane covers (occasionally you'll find them in quarts). The specific varieties are of note only for growing purposes, since blueberries are rarely marketed by name. The small wild berries, though less available fresh, can be found in cans and are an excellent choice for baking. The flavor is superior and they don't leave hollow spots in baked goods as the larger berries are apt to. There is a growing interest in new blueberry products such as juice and wine, in addition to the old standbys of muffin and pancake mixes, pie fillings, and pancake syrup.

EQUIVALENTS
1 pint = 2½ cups
16-ounce can = 1 cup, drained
frozen, 12-ounce package = 2½ cups

STORAGE
✧ AND PREPARATION ✧   ✧ ✧

Since fresh blueberries are perishable, pick them over—discard any soft or dried berries—then refrigerate them without washing. (Only wash berries just before you use them.) Once chilled, they will last at peak flavor for up to two weeks.

If you wish to freeze blueberries, two methods are recommended by the North American Blueberry Council. The simplest way is to remove the cellophane covering and completely overwrap the container with plastic wrap. Make sure that you cover the air holes at the bottom of the container. Berries should be completely dry before freezing. Do *not* wash until ready to use. The second method is to place a layer of berries on a baking sheet or other shallow metal pan and put directly into the freezer. As soon as the berries are hard and frozen, they can be packed in plastic bags or containers.

Blueberries are a pleasure to prepare—no peeling and no pitting; simply wash and use.

Blueberries are a traditional American breakfast food, served over cereal, baked in muffins, added to pancake batter, or simply served fresh with cream. At the height of the blueberry season, dessert menus abound with old-time favorites: cobblers, pies, and sauces. For a burst of spicy flavor and color contrast, toss a few with cut-up cantaloupe or honeydew melon, add them to a salad of fresh peaches, or serve them alongside a helping of lemon sherbet.

Lemon juice and cinnamon are commonly used as flavor enhancers for blueberries. The dark blue of the whole berries turns a rich royal purple when they are crushed or cooked in sauces or pies. (A stain from this vivid juice on your best linen tablecloth, or white blouse, can disappear like magic with a few drops of lemon juice.) When the huge cultivated berries are in good supply, use some to make syrup and preserves, and don't forget—they freeze easily and well.

Chilled Blueberry Soup

Serves 4

Serve this summer soup in white china bowls to set off its spectacular color. The peach garnish provides a contrast of color, texture, and flavor, but cubes of cantaloupe or other melon could also serve this purpose.

2½ cups fresh blueberries
2½ cups water
  2 tablespoons lemon juice
  2 teaspoons grated lemon rind
  ¼ cup sugar
  ½ cup orange juice
  ¼ teaspoon ground cinnamon
  ½ cup dry red wine, such as Burgundy
  ¾ cup sour cream
  1 large ripe fresh peach, chopped in ½-inch cubes

In a nonreactive saucepan, combine the blueberries, water, lemon juice, lemon rind, sugar, orange juice, and cinnamon. Bring to a boil, then lower heat and simmer for 10 minutes, stirring occasionally. Puree in a blender or food processor, add wine, and chill for at least 1 hour. Just before serving stir in the sour cream, then garnish each serving with the chopped peach.

Blueberry Pancakes

Yields sixteen 4-inch pancakes

Serve hot with butter and a sprinkle of sugar or warmed maple syrup.

1¼ cups all-purpose flour
  2 teaspoons sugar
  1 teaspoon baking powder
  ½ teaspoon salt
  1 large egg
1¼ cups soured milk or buttermilk
  ½ teaspoon baking soda
  2 tablespoons (¼ stick) lightly salted butter, melted and cooled
  ¾ cup blueberries

Mix the flour, sugar, baking powder, and salt; set aside. Beat the egg in a medium mixing bowl and stir in the milk and baking soda. With a rotary beater or whisk, blend in the flour mixture until smooth. Stir in the melted butter and blueberries. Pour the batter with a ladle onto a hot, lightly oiled griddle. When top begins to bubble, turn and brown on the other side. Keep pancakes hot until all are done. Serve with butter or syrup.

Blueberry Pie

Yields one 9-inch 2-crust pie

A large pie bursting with deep blue, ripe, firm, and juicy blueberries. The bottom crust is pre-baked for a brief period, permitting a shorter baking time after the blueberries have been added. Thus they remain plump and retain their juice.

PASTRY

2 cups all-purpose flour
⅛ teaspoon salt
2 tablespoons sugar
½ cup (1 stick) lightly salted butter
1 large egg yolk
4 tablespoons cold water, as needed

FILLING

5 cups fresh blueberries
¼ cup all-purpose flour
1 cup sugar
  Pinch of salt
1 tablespoon lemon juice
1–2 tablespoons milk, for brushing top of dough
1–2 tablespoons sugar, for sprinkling top of dough

In a medium bowl, mix the flour, salt, and sugar. Add the butter and blend with your fingertips until the mixture resembles coarse meal. Make a well in the center, drop in the yolk and half of the water, and mix with fingers just until dough comes together. If dough is slightly crumbly, add only enough water to make the dough form a ball. Shape into 2 flattened disks, wrap in plastic, and place in refrigerator for 30 minutes while preparing the filling.

Pick through the blueberries, discarding any leaves, twigs, overripe, or shriveled berries. Rinse and place in a large bowl. Sift together the flour, sugar, and salt. Stir this mixture into the blueberries and mix well to distribute evenly. Blend in the lemon juice and set aside.

Preheat the oven to 425° F. Grease and flour a 9-inch round pie dish. Shake out any surplus flour.

On a lightly floured surface, roll out half the dough until ⅛ inch thick. Fit the dough into the pan, allowing 1½ inches extra for it to fit easily in the pan and to fold back for an edge. Cover with foil, or place an aluminum pie plate over the dough, add pie weights, dry rice, or beans, and bake for 8 minutes. Remove from oven, take out the weights and foil, and cool for 5 minutes. Roll out the remaining dough as for the bottom crust.

Pile the blueberries into the partly baked crust and carefully place the dough for the top crust over the berries. Fold the excess dough to form a rim around the edge, then press it down with a fork or the back of a knife to seal to the bottom crust. If necessary, trim with a pair of scissors. Brush the top with a little milk and sprinkle with sugar. Using the tip of a knife, pierce the dough to make several steam vents. Place on a shallow baking pan and bake for 25 minutes or until the top crust is a light golden color. Remove from oven and leave for about 30 minutes before serving.

NOTE: Frozen blueberries may be substituted; the flavor will be equally good but the berries will be less firm.

Blueberry Flummery

Serves 6

A flummery is one of those easy-to-make, age-old desserts. Some recipes are made with oatmeal or cornstarch as a thickener; this one uses strips of bread. While the bread does thicken the fruit juice, it also adds a special texture and flavor.

    4 cups blueberries
    3/4 cup sugar
    2 tablespoons lemon juice
    1 teaspoon lemon rind
    1 teaspoon ground nutmeg
    1/4 cup water
    1/2 cup (1 stick) lightly salted butter
    8 slices oatmeal bread or white bread,
       from standard size, soft type loaf

Preheat the oven to 350° F. Butter well a 1½-quart baking dish.

In a nonreactive saucepan, mix the blueberries, sugar, lemon juice and rind, nutmeg, and water. Stir over medium heat until sugar dissolves and the mixture begins to bubble; allow to simmer for 10 minutes.

Melt butter in a small saucepan. Remove crusts from bread, cut each slice into 3 strips, and dip the strips to coat with butter. Line the baking dish with a layer of the bread. Pour half the hot berries over the bread, add another layer of bread, and cover with the remaining berries. If your dish is narrow and deep, it may need to be done in 3 layers; just be sure to finish with a layer of berries. Bake on the middle rack of the oven for 20 minutes. This dessert is excellent served hot but may be cooled to room temperature.

Wild Blueberry Lemon Muffins

Yields 12 medium muffins

Fresh wild blueberries can be used in this recipe if you can find them. If you use the usual large cultivated berries the flavor will still be good, but they leave holes where cooking has caused them to collapse.

    2 cups all-purpose flour
    1/2 cup sugar
    2 teaspoons baking powder
    1/4 teaspoon salt
    1 large egg, lightly beaten
    1/4 cup canola or other vegetable oil
    1/2 cup milk
    2 teaspoons grated lemon rind
    1 cup canned wild blueberries, rinsed and
       drained thoroughly

Preheat the oven to 375° F. Thoroughly grease a dozen 2½-inch muffin cups or use paper liners.

Combine the flour, sugar, baking powder, and salt in a large mixing bowl and set aside. Blend the egg with the oil, milk, and lemon rind, then stir into the flour mixture just until ingredients are moistened. Fold in the blueberries, and fill muffin cups about three-fourths full. Bake until lightly colored and a tester inserted in center comes out clean.

NOTE: For tea cakes, combine ¼ teaspoon grated rind with 2 tablespoons sugar and sprinkle over tops before baking.

Blueberry Kuchen

Serves 8–10

The batter for this cake is one of the most versatile we know. We use it in several ways: with fresh blueberries only, with blueberries and nectarines, and with a combination of fresh fruits such as blueberries, apricots, nectarines, Italian prune plums, and peaches. A heavy hand with the cinnamon does no harm. It can be baked at short notice or prepared ahead and frozen for up to six weeks.

> ½ cup (1 stick) unsalted butter or margarine
> 1 cup plus 2 teaspoons sugar
> 2 large eggs
> 1 cup all-purpose flour
> 1 teaspoon baking powder
> Pinch of salt
> 2½ cups blueberries
> 1 tablespoon ground cinnamon
> 1–2 teaspoons lemon juice, depending on tartness of berries

Preheat the oven to 350° F. Grease and flour a 9-inch springform pan.

In the bowl of an electric mixer, beat the butter and 1 cup sugar until light and creamy. Add the eggs and beat until well mixed. Blend the flour, baking powder, and salt, then stir into the egg mixture. Spoon the batter into the pan and place the blueberries on top. Sprinkle with the remaining sugar, cinnamon, and lemon juice. Bake in the middle of the oven for 50 to 60 minutes, or until the top is puffy and the sides begin to come away from the pan. Transfer to a rack and cool a little before serving. Remove the sides of the pan. This cake is best served warm.

NOTE: A 9- or 10-inch round or rectangular pie plate or glass baking dish may be used as an alternative to a springform pan. The only difference is that the cake may bake somewhat higher in the pan. Serve directly from the pie plate or dish.

Blueberry Syrup

Yields 2 cups

This syrup can be served warm or cold to pour over pancakes or French toast, or it can be the base for a thicker sauce by heating and adding a ½ cup of whole blueberries to 1 cup of syrup. The flavor can be varied with the addition of more lemon juice, rum, or orange liqueur.

> ½ cup water
> ½ cup sugar
> 2 cups fresh blueberries
> 1 ½-inch-thick slice lemon, with rind
> ⅛ teaspoon ground cinnamon

Bring the water and sugar to a boil in a nonreactive saucepan, then add the blueberries, lemon, and cinnamon. Simmer for 10 minutes, stirring occasionally. Pour into a blender or food processor and puree until smooth. Pour into a sterile pint jar and seal. Store in refrigerator for a month or more.

C·H·E·R·R·I·E·S

Cherry Soup with Red Wine

Roast Duck with Cherries

Barbecued Quail with Fresh Cherry Sauce

Pork Tenderloin with Dried Cherry Sauce

Fresh Sweet Cherry Pie

Cherry Clafouti

Double Chocolate Sour Cherry Dessert

Cherry Sauce

Cherries Jubilee

Dried Cherry Oat Muffins

The visual perfection and palate-pleasing flavor of cherries has delighted us for millennia. As early as the first century B.C., Roman agriculturist Marcus Terentius Varro describes the grafting of cherries, and other sources indicate that this was an established practice even in the time of the Etruscans. In the same period, Pliny the Elder listed ten varieties of cherries grown in Italy. The Romans carried this highly prized fruit along the routes of their conquests throughout Europe and England.

Cherries arrived in America with the very first settlers along the Eastern Seaboard and with French colonists to the north, along the Saint Lawrence River and into the Great Lakes. Records indicate that red Kentish cherries from England were being cultivated by 1629 in Massachusetts. By 1847 the trees had made it to Oregon, transported by employees of the Hudson's Bay Company.

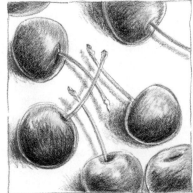

Cherries are grown in all areas of the world where winter temperatures are not too severe. The two most important fruit-producing species are the sweet cherry, *Prunus avium*, and the sour cherry, *Prunus cerasus*. Sweet cherry trees are broad and can grow to a height of thirty-five feet. The fruit may be heart-shaped or round, about an inch in diameter, with skin that is yellow, mahogany red, or nearly black in color and a succulent, sweet flesh that varies from yellow to dark red. Sour cherries grow on trees seldom more than fifteen feet tall with fruit that is light or dark red in color, and so acidic that they are rarely eaten fresh.

The United States is the leading country in the production of cherries, with over half of that crop in sour cherries. The major growing areas for tart cherries are Michigan, New York, and Wisconsin, while Washington, Oregon, and California are the producers for sweet cherries. Although all European countries grow cherries, the heaviest production is in West Germany, Italy, and Switzerland. Two European cherry products familiar to us are kirsch or kirschwasser and maraschino. Kirsch is made from the small, wild black cherries found in the Black Forest. It is distilled from a mash consisting of the cherries with their stones, resulting in a clear, colorless liqueur with a slight almond taste. It is an important liqueur for macerating a variety of fresh fruits. Maraschino is not to be confused with our red maraschino cherries, but is a strong, clear liqueur made from marasca cherries of Dalmatia, Yugoslavia, and may be bottled as a sweet or dry liquor.

The sweet cherry that fits the ideal cherry description—glossy, firm, dark red, and succulent—is also the one with a recognizable name, the Bing cherry. It was developed in 1875 by Seth Lewelling, a grower in Milwaukie, Oregon, and the name was that of a Chinese workman in his orchards. This has become the main variety grown in California and Washington.

The three principal varieties of tart or sour cherries cultivated in the United States are the English Morello, which is a dark red with reddish juice, the Early Richmond, and the Montmorency, both of which are lighter in color and less acidic than the Morello, and produce a colorless juice. Of these three, Montmorency is the dominant variety grown.

Because sweet cherries are marketed with stems intact, harvesting is still primarily done by hand, but tart cherries can be machine picked, since the crop is used principally for canning. The high cost of hand picking and the scarcity of migrant labor has led to the use of a machine that shakes the trunk of the tree, loosening the fruit with a few firm movements. The cherries then fall into inclined frames, roll onto conveyor belts, and are carried to tanks of cold water. Less than an hour after harvest, the cherries are resting in ice and water in a cooling station.

Sweet cherries are used to produce the familiar bright red maraschino cherries that top an ice cream sundae, and for the candied cherries used in baked goods.

To create them, the fruit is subjected to the following tortured process, the origins of which are shrouded in mystery. If you love candied or maraschino cherries you may not care to know how they got that way! First, the cherries are washed, then placed in vats of sulfur dioxide and other chemicals that firm and bleach them. This process takes four to six weeks, after which a second bleaching may take place with yet other bleaching agents. The colorless cherries are next leached to remove the chemicals and are then ready to be dyed a brilliant red or, in some cases, bright green. Next, they are heated in a sugar syrup and flavoring is added. For candied fruit the process is essentially the same, but before the flavoring is added there is a longer sugar buildup, after which drying takes place.

Sour cherries are canned or frozen without sugar, or with sugar and thickener for ready-to-use pie filling. A smaller amount is made into a puree for the production of jam, ice cream, toppings, and frozen desserts, because the flavor and color are more easily preserved in this way with pulpy fruits.

✧ HOME CULTIVATION ✧

Sweet cherries are more vulnerable to early spring frosts than sour cherries, a major consideration in your decision to grow them. Because variety is very important to local adaptability, you should consult a local nursery to help make an appropriate selection. Standard sweet cherries require a large sunny area but, unlike some other fruits, dwarf varieties do not produce satisfactory crops. While sour cherries are self-pollinizers, sweet cherries require a second tree to be fruitful.

Before you make a firm decision to grow your own sweet cherry tree, just one more point—it is a well-known fact that the day before the cherries are ripe enough for human consumption, the birds will swoop down and harvest your entire crop. You may be left an untouched handful!

❧ NUTRITION ❧

One cup of cherries contains 82 calories, largely as carbohydrate, with some protein and negligible fat. They are a good source of dietary fiber. The sour cherry has a somewhat higher vitamin A content; both are good sources of vitamin C and of minerals, particularly calcium, phosphorus, magnesium, and potassium.

❧ SELECTION ❧

Sweet cherries have a very limited season, and where they are not grown locally they sometimes seem to disappear before our very eyes. Look for firm, plump fruit with green stems. If stems are dry and brown the fruit is not as fresh; without stems, it does not keep well. There should be no brown color around the base of the stem. Sour cherries rarely appear in the produce markets as fresh fruit. They are mostly available in cans, either packed in water or with sugar and thickener as prepared pie filling, and in some markets you may find them frozen. Sweet cherries are also sold canned and sometimes frozen. There are now dried sweet and tart cherries that can be used like other dried fruits, eaten out of hand, in baking, and for sauces.

EQUIVALENTS
1 pound = 80 cherries = 3 cups sliced

STORAGE
❧ AND PREPARATION ❧

Cherries are highly perishable and should not be washed until they are to be used. They can be kept two to three days in the refrigerator.

Cherries can be pitted by pushing the pit through the fruit with a skewer or similar object, but the most efficient method is to use a cherry pitter. It pushes the pit through the cherry, leaving a small hole—quick and neat. Although slightly more expensive, get the one that has a stop to prevent the cherry from being flattened in the operation.

❧   ❧

Ripe, fresh sweet cherries are a special treat to tuck into a lunchbox, add to a hiker's pack, or to present any time in a beautiful bowl. Usually we use the canned cherries for sauces and baking, but a fresh sweet cherry pie, with only a bit of sugar added, has a wonderful flavor and a gorgeous color. Use them to create a dessert sauce to go over cake, ice cream, or puddings; a fresh cherry clafouti is a French tradition well worth emulating. Both sweet and sour cherries, fresh or canned, make excellent sauces for poultry (especially duck) and pork, and can be turned into superb preserves, jams, and conserves.

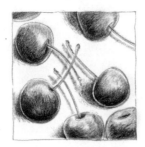

Cherry Soup with Red Wine

Serves 4

This is a Hungarian-style soup that can be served hot or cold. If you have access to fresh cherries, simply replace the canned fruit with two cups of fresh fruit stewed with the ¼ cup of sugar.

- 1 *(1 pound) can water-packed pitted sour cherries*
- ¼ *cup sugar*
- 2 *teaspoons cornstarch*
- ¼ *teaspoon salt*
- ¼ *teaspoon ground cinnamon*
- 2 *3-inch strips orange zest, finely minced*
- ½ *cup orange juice*
- ½ *cup Burgundy or any other good, dry red wine*
- ½ *cup whipping cream, whipped*

Reserve a few whole cherries for garnish, then place cherries with liquid, sugar, cornstarch, salt, cinnamon, orange zest, and orange juice in the container of a blender or food processor; blend until smooth. Pour into a nonreactive saucepan and cook over medium heat until the mixture comes to a boil. Lower heat and continue to cook, stirring constantly, until slightly thickened. Remove from heat and stir in the wine. Reheat to serve hot, or chill for 2 hours or more to serve cold. Before serving add reserved cherries, and garnish with unsweetened whipped cream.

Roast Duck with Cherries

Serves 4

The cherries here are cooked together with the duck during the bird's last thirty minutes. The result is wonderfully moist meat with a slightly glazed finish. Serve with rice, pureed spinach, or tiny green peas and a mixed salad.

- 1 *duck, about 4–5 pounds*
  Salt and freshly ground pepper to taste
- ½ *teaspoon ground ginger*
- ⅓ *cup red wine vinegar*
- 1 *(16½-ounce) can pitted dark sweet cherries*
- ½ *cup Port wine*
- ½ *cup dry red wine*
- 2 *tablespoons red currant jelly*
- 1 *cup chicken or duck stock*
- 2 *teaspoons cornstarch*
- 2 *tablespoons water*

Preheat the oven to 425° F.

Wash the duck, remove any extra loose fat from the cavity areas, and prick the skin all over with a fork. Season with salt, pepper, and ginger, then pour the vinegar over the entire surface and inside the cavity. Place the duck breast side up on a rack in a roasting pan containing about 1 inch of water. This will prevent smoking from the fat and also ensures that the meat remains moist. Roast for 45 minutes. Reduce the oven temperature to 375° F., turn the duck, and continue roasting for 45 minutes. Remove from the oven, drain on brown paper, then cut into serving portions.

While the duck is roasting, make the sauce. Drain the juice from the cherries into a saucepan; put the cherries in a small bowl and set aside. Add the wines, jelly, and stock to the cherry juice and bring to a boil. Lower the heat to medium and cook for 10 minutes. Set aside.

Place the duck in a clean, shallow oven-proof serving dish, pour the sauce over, and roast in the oven for 30 minutes more, basting occasionally. Remove the duck to a serving platter. Return the liquid to a saucepan. Mix the cornstarch with the water, stir into the sauce, and cook over medium heat for about 4 minutes or until thickened. Add the cherries and blend into the sauce. Pour over the duck and serve.

NOTE: If unable to serve immediately, cover duck lightly with foil and keep in a warm oven. If you wish, put the dish under the broiler for a minute before serving, watching very carefully to avoid any burning.

Barbecued Quail with Fresh Cherry Sauce

Serves 4

Quail are simple to cook, and there are few dishes more elegant and festive than a plate with quail covered by a glistening sauce of fresh cherries. Serve with rice or sautéed slices of potato, asparagus, tiny fresh peas, or string beans.

    2 tablespoons cognac
    4 tablespoons ruby Port wine
    3 tablespoons red currant jelly
    ½ cup fresh orange juice
    ⅛ teaspoon ground cinnamon
    ⅛ teaspoon ground allspice
    1 tablespoon fresh lemon juice
    ¼ teaspoon Dijon mustard
    1 pound fresh cherries, pitted (about 3
       cups)
    1 teaspoon cornstarch
    1 tablespoon water
    3 tablespoons unsalted butter
       Salt and freshly ground pepper
    8 ready-to-cook partly boned quail (about
       2½ pounds)

In a medium saucepan, combine the cognac, Port, jelly, orange juice, cinnamon, and allspice. Bring to a boil, lower the heat to medium, and cook for 15 minutes. Add the lemon juice, stir in the mustard until completely blended, then add the cherries. Cook for a further 5 minutes. Mix the cornstarch with the water and add to the sauce. Bring to a boil and cook for 2 minutes, stirring. Swirl in 1 tablespoon of the butter, season to taste,

(continued on next page)

and if using immediately, keep warm. The sauce may be prepared ahead and refrigerated for 2 days, or if the cornstarch and butter are omitted in the initial preparation, it may be frozen for several weeks. In this event, thaw, reheat, and then add the cornstarch and the butter.

Rub the quail with the remaining 2 tablespoons of butter and season with pepper. Prepare the grill and oil the rack. Cook the quail about 4 inches from the coals for 5 minutes on each side, or until done. Transfer to a large serving platter. Heat the cherry sauce, spoon over the quail, and serve immediately.

NOTE: Quail are available from specialty butchers. They may be purchased either fresh or frozen, in packages containing 4 birds, and are ready for cooking.

Pork Tenderloin with Dried Cherry Sauce

Serves 4

We have recently discovered a wonderful tart dried cherry, the tangy Montmorency. It comes in a vacuum pack, is about the size of a large raisin, and is superb as a snack, or as used here for a cherry sauce.

> 1   tablespoon unsalted butter
> 1   tablespoon canola or other vegetable oil
> 1   pound boneless lean pork tenderloin
> 1   cup dried tart cherries
> 1   cup dry red wine
> ½   cup Port wine
> ½   cup chicken stock
> 1   teaspoon Dijon mustard
>   Salt and freshly ground pepper to taste

Preheat the oven to 400° F.

In a heavy skillet melt half the butter and the tablespoon oil, coat the meat on all sides, then place in the oven and roast for 20 minutes. An instant meat thermometer should record 140° F. when meat is done. Remove from oven, place the meat on a plate, and cover lightly to keep warm while preparing the sauce. Set skillet aside, retaining cooking particles in skillet.

Combine the cherries, wines, stock, and mustard in a saucepan. Bring to a boil, lower the heat, and cook over medium heat for about 10 minutes. Place half the sauce in a blender or food processor and puree, then return to the saucepan with the remaining sauce. Keep hot.

Put the sauce into the roasting skillet over medium-high heat and scrape the particles from the bottom. Add the remaining butter, season to taste, and stir the sauce for about 3 minutes or until completely heated through. Slice the pork on the diagonal and arrange on individual serving plates in a fan shape. Spoon on the sauce. Serve with small new potatoes and sautéed spinach.

✢ ✢

Fresh Sweet Cherry Pie

Yields one 8-inch pie

A classic cherry pie that needs no spice other than lemon juice to let the wonderful flavor of fresh cherries come through. The filling is a luscious sparkling red.

PASTRY

1½ *cups all-purpose flour*
 ½ *teaspoon salt*
 ½ *cup plus 1 tablespoon solid vegetable
      shortening*
  1 *teaspoon vinegar*
  4 *tablespoons cold water*

FILLING

  2 *cups pitted fresh dark sweet cherries*
 ½ *cup sugar*
  2 *tablespoons cornstarch*
1½ *teaspoons lemon juice*
  1 *tablespoon lightly salted butter*

Preheat the oven to 425° F.

Combine the flour and salt in a mixing bowl. Cut in the shortening with a pastry blender until the mixture resembles coarse meal, then sprinkle with the vinegar and water a tablespoon at a time, mixing with a fork until all the flour is moistened. Gather together with fingers until dough cleans the bowl. Press into a ball, then divide in half and roll out each half onto a well-floured board into 2 circles slightly larger than pie pan. Line 8-inch pie pan with 1 pastry circle, leaving about ½-inch overhang.

Combine the cherries, sugar, cornstarch, and lemon juice. Fill pastry with cherry mixture and dot with butter. Cover with top crust, fold overhang over top edge, press to seal, and flute edges. With a fork or knife, make vent holes in the top crust. Place on the middle rack of oven and bake for about 40 minutes, until the fruit is bubbling and the crust is golden brown. Allow to cool at least 30 minutes before cutting.

Cherry Clafouti

Serves 4–6

Clafouti, a French creation, is a simple custard dessert. Cherries are traditional, but fresh plums or peaches may also be prepared in this manner.

 ¼ *cup sugar plus 1 tablespoon*
  2 *cups pitted sweet cherries*
  2 *large eggs*
 ¾ *cup milk*
 ¾ *cup light cream*
 ¾ *cup all-purpose flour*
 ¼ *teaspoon salt*
  1 *teaspoon vanilla extract*
      Confectioners' sugar, for dusting
      Whipping cream, whipped (optional)

Preheat the oven to 375° F. Generously butter a shallow baking dish such as a 10-inch glass or pottery pie plate or quiche dish.

Sprinkle the tablespoon of sugar evenly over the bottom of the baking dish. Distribute the pitted cherries over the sugar. Beat the eggs lightly with a rotary beater, then add the milk, cream, flour, salt, remaining sugar, and vanilla and beat just until smooth. Pour over cherries and bake in center of oven until puffed and lightly browned, about 45 to 50 minutes. Dust with confectioners' sugar and serve warm. If you like, top each serving with whipped cream.

Double Chocolate Sour Cherry Dessert

Serves 8

This delicious moist tart may be served with whipped cream spiked with a little kirsch or just sprinkle the top with confectioners' sugar. The chocolate wafer crust makes it all the more festive.

    12 tablespoons (1½ sticks) unsalted butter
        or margarine, melted
     1 cup ground chocolate wafers (about 20
        Nabisco Famous)
     1 cup plus 2 tablespoons sugar
     2 large eggs
    ½   teaspoon vanilla extract
    ½   cup plus 2 tablespoons all-purpose flour
     3 tablespoons unsweetened cocoa powder
     1 teaspoon baking powder
    ½   cup finely chopped pecans or walnuts
     1 (16-ounce) can pitted tart red cherries in
        water, well drained

Preheat the oven to 350° F. Butter and flour a 9-inch springform pan.

Melt 4 tablespoons of the butter; blend with the wafers and 2 tablespoons sugar. Press evenly to cover the bottom of the pan and to extend slightly up the sides. Place in refrigerator.

In a large mixing bowl, combine the remaining 8 tablespoons butter and 1 cup sugar, then add the eggs and beat until well blended and light, about 3 minutes. Add the vanilla. Sift together the flour, cocoa, and baking powder. Add to the egg mixture until well mixed. Carefully add the nuts to the batter and finally stir in the cherries.

Spoon the batter into the prepared pan and bake for 45 minutes or until the center springs back when slightly pressed. Cool on a wire rack until it reaches room temperature. If not serving immediately, cover or wrap in plastic. May stand at room temperature overnight, or keep in the refrigerator for up to 2 days. This dessert may also be frozen for up to 2 weeks. Return to room temperature before serving.

Cherry Sauce

Yields 2 cups

Use this sauce with blintzes, over a slice of pound cake, or as a topping for ice cream.

     2 cups pitted sweet cherries
     2 tablespoons sugar
     2 tablespoons water
     2 teaspoons cornstarch
     1 tablespoon water
        Pinch of salt
     2 tablespoons lemon juice
    ½   teaspoon grated lemon rind
     1 tablespoon kirsch

Put cherries in a saucepan with sugar and water and simmer for 4 minutes. Using a slotted spoon, remove cherries and set aside. Bring the syrup to a boil, dissolve cornstarch in water, and stir into boiling juice, stirring as it thickens. Add the salt, lemon juice, lemon rind, and kirsch and cook, stirring occasionally, for 7 minutes. Return cherries to syrup and cook for 3 minutes. Syrup may be stored in a sterile jar for 2 weeks in refrigerator.

Cherries Jubilee

Serves 4

Our version of this simple but elegant dessert classic. You decide of you want to assemble it behind-the-scenes in the kitchen or take center stage with a blazing presentation before your guests. Another option is to prepare the sauce in the day, and then simply heat it in the blazer pan and flame it at the table.

  1   (16-ounce) can pitted dark cherries
  1   tablespoon orange rind, cut into a fine julienne
¼   cup orange juice
  1   teaspoon cornstarch
  2   teaspoons sugar
  4   tablespoons kirsch (cherry brandy)
  4   tablespoons cognac or brandy
      Vanilla ice cream

    Drain the cherries, reserving the juice. Combine the orange rind, orange juice, and reserved cherry juice in the blazer pan of a chafing dish. Mix the cornstarch and sugar together, then stir into the juice mixture until smooth. Place over flame and bring to a boil, then stir and simmer until slightly thickened. Add the cherries and heat through. (The dish may be made up to this point in a skillet and stored in the refrigerator for up to 1 week. When ready to serve, place sauce in the blazer pan to warm and proceed as follows.) Heat the brandies, pour over the cherries, and ignite. When the flames begin to die down, ladle sauce over vanilla ice cream served in individual dessert dishes.

Dried Cherry Oat Muffins

Yields 12 muffins

The tartness of the dried cherries comes as a pleasant surprise in these whole-oat muffins. To enjoy the full flavor, serve them warm.

  1   cup cultured skimmed-milk buttermilk
  1   cup quick cooking oats
  1   large egg, well-beaten
½   cup dark brown sugar
  1   cup all-purpose flour
  1   teaspoon baking powder
½   teaspoon baking soda
¼   teaspoon ground cinnamon
½   teaspoon salt
⅓   cup canola or other vegetable oil
¾   cup dried red tart cherries

    Preheat oven to 400°F. Grease twelve 2½-inch muffin tins.
    Pour the buttermilk into a large bowl, add the oats, stir to mix, and allow to soak for 20 minutes or more. Make a well in the center of the mixture and drop in the beaten egg and sugar. In a separate bowl, mix the flour, baking powder, baking soda, cinnamon, and salt, and stir until well combined. Add this to the buttermilk-oats mixture. Finally, stir in the oil and the cherries until well integrated. Using a spoon, fill the muffin tins about two-thirds full. Bake for about 18 minutes. Remove from the oven and immediately turn out onto a rack to cool.

C·R·A·N·B·E·R·R·I·E·S

Small White Onions Baked with Cranberries

Fresh Cranberry Sauce

Cranberry Chutney

Roast Duck Breasts in Cranberry Sauce

Veal Shanks with Cranberries

Cranberry Pear Deep-Dish Pie

Cranberry Squares

Cranberry Nut Bread

The cranberry, *Vaccinium macrocarpon*, a native of North America, was well known to the American Indians of the East Coast. They mixed it with dried venison and fat to make pemican, the Indian's winter and trail food. Since the berries are harvested in the fall, the association of turkey and cranberries with the first Thanksgiving is probably based on fact. The early French explorers found that the Indians in Wisconsin were also using cranberries in their diet, and had an established practice of trading wild rice and cranberries for goods.

More than half the cranberries we use are harvested from the bogs of coastal Massachusetts in the area of Plymouth and Cape Cod. Wisconsin is second in production and New Jersey is third; these are the other states where the berry was found grow- 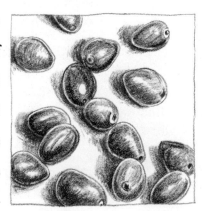 ing in the wild. Cranberries have been developed to produce larger, more uni- form fruit by selecting out and cultivating the best of the wild berries. Because the growers depend on bees for pollination, pesticides that might harm them are kept to a minimum. It is a common practice to rent hives of bees to place near the bogs when the plants are in blossom in late June and early July. The fruit ripens in early fall and harvest usually begins after Labor Day, continuing into October. Several varieties are planted, which makes for sequential ripening and prolongs the season. Ripe berries can vary in color from deep red to almost white—most are red with white streaking. None is eaten raw and only a small percentage of the crop is sold fresh. Most of our cranberry crop stays right at home, with Americans the largest consumers in the world of this native berry.

✎ HOME CULTIVATION ✎

Not feasible for the home gardener.

✎ NUTRITION ✎

Vitamin C and potassium are the principal nutrients, with traces of other minerals. One cup has 45 calories before the necessary sugar is added.

✎ SELECTION ✎

Markets usually carry cranberries in plastic bags with directions for storing and freezing printed on them. The color does not signify ripeness—the same package will have some berries that are red, some that are red and white streaked, and even, occasionally an all-white one. Berries are also sold frozen and are found made into various sauces and juices, often combined with the juice of other fruits.

EQUIVALENTS
One 12-ounce package = 3 cups

STORAGE ✎ AND PREPARATION ✎

Keep in the plastic packaging and store in the refrigerator until ready to use. They can be kept for several weeks this way, or they can be placed directly in the freezer and frozen.

Wash only when ready to use, and do not thaw frozen berries before using. Berries should be picked over before use, discarding those with soft spots. Cover when cooking to prevent spattering, since the berries burst with the heat.   ✎   ✎

Good as the traditional cranberry sauce is with the Thanksgiving turkey, next time you might try the extra spice of a cranberry chutney. Not just for the holidays, chutney can be added to a chicken sandwich or as a condiment with roast pork. With orange or lemon, cranberries make an excellent tangy sauce for duck or venison. The cranberry's tart flavor makes it a perfect fruit to add to breakfast muffins, quick coffee cakes, and tea loaves. For a dramatic effect bake a pie with a lattice top to let the brilliant red color show through, and for cobblers and compotes pair cranberries and pears flavored with lemon for a great taste sensation. It makes one of the more versatile fruit sorbets that can be served anywhere in a meal from first to last.

Small White Onions Baked with Cranberries

Serves 6

This is a pretty holiday dish served with turkey, but its piquant flavor suits other meat and poultry dishes equally well.

  1 *pound small white boiling onions (smallest available)*
  2 *tablespoons (¼ stick) lightly salted butter*
1½ *cups (6 ounces) cranberries*
  3 *tablespoons sugar*
     Salt and freshly ground pepper to taste
 ¼ *cup chicken stock*

Preheat the oven to 400° F.

Peel the onions and cut crosses into the root ends to keep them whole. Cook in butter in a wide skillet, taking care to keep them whole and turning with a wooden utensil to brown evenly. Add the cranberries; sprinkle with sugar, salt, and pepper. Stir gently, then add the stock. Transfer to a shallow glass baking dish and place on the middle rack of oven. Check at 20 minutes; the tops should be beginning to glaze. If not, move closer to the heat and bake until the onions pierce easily with a fork, about 10 more minutes.

Fresh Cranberry Sauce

Yields 2¼ cups

A simple cranberry sauce has many uses. Of course, it will always find a place of honor on the Thanksgiving table. Postholiday, it adds sparkle to the leftover turkey. The sauce can liven up smoked turkey or chicken, and a spoon of cranberry sauce on top of vanilla ice cream creates a colorful and festive dessert.

  3 *cups (12 ounces) fresh or frozen cranberries*
  1 *cup sugar*
  1 *cup water*
  1 *tablespoon fresh lemon juice*

If using fresh cranberries, pick through and discard any spoiled berries, then rinse. In a large saucepan, combine the sugar and water and bring to a boil. Add the cranberries, return to a boil, lower the heat, and cook for about 12 minutes, stirring occasionally until the berries begin to burst. Stir in the lemon juice, cook for 1 minute more, then remove from heat. Cool completely. Place in airtight containers and refrigerate. This sauce will keep for 4 months, refrigerated.

Cranberry Chutney

Yields 7 cups

The ingredients that go into this chutney make it suitable for far more than the Thanksgiving turkey. Experiment and serve it with other meats and also with hearty fish such as tuna and swordfish.

- ½ cup diced dried apricots
- 4 cups fresh or frozen cranberries (1 pound)
- 2¼ cups sugar
- ¼ cup diced crystallized ginger
- 1 lemon, peeled and diced
- 1 navel orange, peeled and diced
- ½ cup golden raisins
- ½ cup dark raisins
- ½ cup cider vinegar
- ¼ cup Madeira wine
- 1 teaspoon medium curry powder
- 1 teaspoon ground cinnamon
- ¼ teaspoon ground cloves
- ¼ teaspoon ground allspice
- ½ teaspoon peeled and grated fresh ginger
- 1¼ cups orange juice
- 2 large Granny Smith apples (1 pound), peeled and coarsely diced

In a large nonreactive saucepan, cook all ingredients except for the apples for 10 minutes over medium-high heat, stirring occasionally to prevent the mixture from sticking to the bottom and sides of the pan. Add the apples, and continue cooking for an additional 10 minutes. Cool, then pour into prepared jars. Store in refrigerator.

Roast Duck Breasts in Cranberry Sauce

Serves 4–6

The lively tart flavor of the cranberries in the sauce balances the richness of the duck. This dish is delicious when served with a combination of vegetables such as turnips, butternut squash, and tiny new potatoes cut into 1-inch pieces.

- 2 teaspoons canola or other vegetable oil
- 2 shallots, finely chopped
- 3 cups (12 ounces) fresh or frozen cranberries
- ¾ cup orange juice
- 2 tablespoons lemon juice
- ⅓ cup sugar
- 2 tablespoons Madeira or ruby Port wine
- 2 whole duck breasts, boned, split, skin removed, and reserved (about 18 ounces without the skin)

Preheat the oven to 425° F.

In a saucepan, heat the oil over moderate heat. Add the shallots and cook, stirring, until soft but not brown. Add the remaining ingredients except for the wine and the duck. Bring to a boil, then reduce the heat and continue cooking, stirring frequently for 8 to 10 minutes, until the cranberries begin to burst. Add the wine and blend into the sauce. Keep warm.

Place the duck breasts on a rack in an ovenproof pan filled with ½ inch of water (this prevents the meat from drying while roasting). Roast for about 8 minutes each side (or until done), remove to a cutting surface, and cover to keep warm while reheating the sauce. To serve, slice the duck into ¼-inch slices on the diagonal and arrange on one large platter, or on individual serving plates. Spoon the sauce over the meat and serve immediately.

❧   ❧

Veal Shanks with Cranberries

Serves 4

This is an elegant dish served with parsleyed rice and a green salad.

1 cup finely chopped onion
1 celery stalk, trimmed and finely chopped
1 medium Granny Smith apple (6 ounces), diced
2 tablespoons canola or other vegetable oil
4 veal shanks, each cut 2 inches thick
1 cup concentrated beef stock
1 cup Port wine
1 teaspoon lemon rind
2 cups fresh or frozen cranberries (8 ounces)
2 tablespoons sugar
1 teaspoon peeled and minced fresh ginger
1 teaspoon red currant jelly (optional)
Salt and freshly ground pepper to taste

Preheat the oven to 325° F.

In a nonreactive skillet, cook the onion, celery, and apple in 1 tablespoon oil over medium heat until softened but not brown. Remove and place in an ovenproof casserole. In the same skillet heat the additional tablespoon of oil, add the shanks, and brown over medium-high heat. Place the shanks in the casserole with the vegetables. Deglaze the skillet with the stock, scraping the bottom and sides to loosen the crusty particles. Add to the veal, together with the wine, lemon rind, cranberries, sugar, and ginger. Bring to a boil on top of the stove, cover, and place in the oven for 2 hours or until tender.

Remove the meat from the cranberry mixture and set aside. Over medium-high heat, reduce the sauce until 3 cups remain. Stir in jelly if desired and season with salt and pepper. If desired, puree in a food processor or blender. Return sauce and meat to casserole, heat thoroughly, and serve.

❧   ❧

Cranberry Pear Deep-Dish Pie

Serves 8

The combination of flavors and colors in this pie is a feast for palate and eye. Pears and cranberries appear together in the fall, making them a natural combination, and the slight touch of ginger brings out the flavors of both fruits.

PASTRY

2 cups all-purpose flour
⅛ teaspoon salt
2 tablespoons sugar
½ cup (1 stick) lightly salted butter
1 large egg yolk
4 tablespoons cold water, as needed

(continued on next page)

FILLING

6   *ripe but firm Bartlett pears (3 pounds), pared and cut into eighths*
2   *tablespoons lemon juice*
2   *cups cranberries (8 ounces), fresh or frozen*
½   *cup sugar*
1   *tablespoon peeled and grated or finely chopped raw ginger*
1   *tablespoon cornstarch*
2   *tablespoons butter*

Preheat the oven to 450° F. Lightly grease a 9-inch deep-pie dish or 1½- to 2-quart baking dish. Mix the flour, salt, and sugar in a medium bowl and cut in the butter with a pastry blender or 2 knives until the mixture resembles coarse meal. Whisk the yolk and water together to blend, then sprinkle over the flour mixture and stir with a fork. Add more water if necessary to make dough cling together. Form into a flattened disk, then wrap in plastic and chill for 20 minutes.

Place the pear sections in a large bowl and mix gently with the lemon juice, cranberries, sugar, ginger, and cornstarch.

Roll the pastry out on a floured board into a large, uneven circle about 4 to 5 inches larger than the circumference of the baking dish. Lay it over the dish and carefully slip it down to line the bottom and the sides, allowing the uneven edges to hang over the sides. Heap the fruit into the dish and dot with the butter, then bring the edges over the fruit, leaving an uneven opening about 3 inches in diameter in the center. Bake for 10 minutes, then lower heat to 375° F. and bake for 45 minutes more or until the filling is tender when poked with a fork and the crust is golden brown. When cool, dust with confec-

tioners' sugar and serve plain or with lightly whipped cream.

NOTE: For easy preparation the pears may be cored and cut using an 8-section circle apple and pear cutter. Check that no bits of core remain.

❧ ❧

Cranberry Squares

Yields 30 squares

The cranberry filling for these squares gives a bright splash of color. The taste is sweet but with an interesting element of tartness.

DOUGH

½   *cup (1 stick) unsalted softened butter or margarine*
½   *cup sugar*
1   *tablespoon canola or other vegetable oil*
1   *large egg, well beaten*
2   *teaspoons vanilla extract*
2   *cups all-purpose flour*
2   *teaspoons baking powder*
   Pinch of salt

FILLING

1   *cup sugar*
1   *teaspoon vanilla extract*
1   *tablespoon cornstarch*
½   *cup water*
2   *cups (8 ounces) fresh or frozen cranberries*
½   *cup raisins*

Grease and flour a 12 × 9-inch shallow baking pan.

In a large bowl, cream the butter, sugar, and oil. Add the beaten egg and vanilla. Mix the dry ingredients thoroughly in another bowl. Add to the egg mixture and mix until dough begins to form a ball; the mixture should feel quite firm. Wrap half the dough in plastic and freeze for about 30 minutes. This firms it up and makes the grating much easier. Press the remaining half of the dough evenly on the bottom of the pan.

Place all the filling ingredients in a saucepan, bring to a boil, and cook for 10 to 15 minutes, until the mixture has thickened. Remove from heat and cool. Spread with the cranberry mixture and set aside, or refrigerate for 30 minutes. Preheat the oven to 350° F.

Remove the dough from the freezer and grate over the top of the cranberry mixture. Bake for 45 minutes or until the top is golden brown and the sides have pulled away from the pan. Remove from oven, place on a rack, and immediately run a knife around the edge of the pan to facilitate the removal of the cookies. Leave for 20 minutes, then cut into squares. Cool thoroughly and pack into storage containers. These cranberry squares freeze extremely well.

Cranberry Nut Bread

Yields 1 large loaf

As with most fruit breads, this will cut easier, and have fuller flavor if it is well wrapped and allowed to stand for 24 hours.

   2 cups all-purpose flour
   1 cup sugar
1½ teaspoons baking powder
 ½ teaspoon salt
 ½ teaspoon baking soda
 ¼ cup solid vegetable shortening
   1 teaspoon grated orange rind
 ¾ cup orange juice
   1 large egg, well beaten
   2 cups fresh cranberries (8 ounces), *cut in half*
 ½ cup chopped pecans

Preheat the oven to 350° F. Grease a 9 × 5 × 3-inch loaf pan.

Sift together the flour, sugar, baking powder, salt, and baking soda. Cut in the shortening until it resembles coarse meal. Combine the orange rind, orange juice, and the egg; stir into dry ingredients, just enough to moisten. Fold in the cranberries and nuts. Turn into the prepared pan and bake on the middle rack for 60 minutes, or until a tester comes out clean. Leave in the pan for 5 minutes, then turn out onto a rack to cool. Wrap and store overnight. Keeps well for up to 2 weeks in refrigerator.

D·A·T·E·S

California Fruit with Southern Dressing

Date and Onion Salad

Date Nut Meringues

Banana Date Muffins

Old-Fashioned Date Bars

In its native North Africa, the date palm has, for thousands of years, been a welcome sight to nomadic tribes, since it not only signaled the presence of water, but its fruit was an important source of food. It is a handsome tree, eighty to one hundred feet tall, with a beautiful diamond-patterned trunk that terminates in a crown of shining feathery leaves, arching in ten- to twenty-foot fronds. A desert oasis provides the large amount of water the tree needs to flourish, with the very high temperatures and dry air necessary for fruit production.

The fruit has a  paper-thin skin with a single grooved seed. It can be round to oval, and golden to dark brown when ripe, depending on the variety. A single large bunch may hold as many as 1,000 fruits, and weigh twenty pounds or more. Dates take about six months to develop, and each tree will yield between 100 and 200 pounds annually. As they ripen the sugar content increases, and they turn from a golden yellow to brown.

Propagation can be from the seeds, but is usually done by offshoots, which arise near the base of the stem. Date palms are of two sexes and although adapted to wind pollination by nature, hand pollination has been practiced for centuries. This consists of tying the male flower to the female cluster.

Many kinds of dates are grown, but based on the texture at maturity, they are classified as soft, semidry, and dry. The most important commercial date in the United States is a semidry variety originally grown in Algeria, the Deglet Noor, Arabic for "Date of Light." Among other varieties grown here are Medjool from Morocco, and Khadrawy, Zahidi, and Halawy from Iraq. Some of the best date varieties were brought to this country by the United States Department of Agriculture in 1890. California's

Coachella Valley, 140 miles southeast of Los Angeles, was selected for experimentation because of its favorable growing conditions. This area now produces 95 percent of the total domestic crop. The only other date-growing state is Arizona. Fruit from Algeria and Tunisia is marketed in Europe, but Iraq is the leading date-producing country in the world, and supplies most of the fruit exported to other countries. Although high summer temperatures and low humidity are necessary for fruit production, the tree can be grown in any tropical and subtropical climate where prolonged temperatures below 20° F. do not occur. In these borderline areas it is grown purely for its beauty as an ornamental tree.

ᛜ HOME CULTIVATION ᛜ

In this country date trees can't be grown for fruit unless you live in the California or Arizona desert. As a guide to size, consider that in commercial date gardens the trees are allowed thirty feet in each direction—that is, nearly 1,000 square feet per tree.

ᛜ NUTRITION ᛜ

Dates are a highly nutritious food with readily accessible carbohydrates. They are also a source of calcium, iron, phosphorus, and B vitamins. Ten dates have 220 calories.

ᛜ SELECTION ᛜ

Dates are sold in several types of packaging, in boxes, plastic cups, and occasionally, in tins. Almost all are now sold without pits. In some of the ethnic produce markets they are sold in bulk, in which case look for plump fruit that has a moist appearance. All of these dates are considered fresh fruit since they are not put through any drying process once they are picked. Dried fruits such as prunes, figs, and apricots are either sun or kiln dried before packaging. Dates are also sold chopped and in blocks for use in baking.

EQUIVALENTS
7 ounces pitted dates = 1 cup

STORAGE
ᛜ AND PREPARATION ᛜ

Packaged dates are available in the markets the year round and may be kept indefinitely if stored properly. They should be kept in a tightly closed container (they tend to absorb odors from other foods) in the refrigerator, or may be frozen. Any moisture loss from overly long or improper storage can be regained by plumping with a little warm water. Pitted dates are ready to use.

ᛜ   ᛜ

Dates provide flavor and moisture when added to baked goods. Try muffins made with dates, bananas, and pecans, an orange tea loaf with dates added, or cookies with a lemon and date filling. Dates stuffed with nuts or cream cheese are an appealing addition to a tray of dried fruit as an after-dinner sweet. Blend a few into a banana milkshake for sweetening; halve them and serve as a salad with sliced oranges and onions dressed with vinegar. Make a sandwich with a whole-grain bread, banana slices, and creamed cottage cheese topped with cut-up dates. They make an excellent natural sweetener for mixed fruit salads.

California Fruit with Southern Dressing

Serves 4

Sugar and white vinegar is an old custom in southern Pennsylvania Dutch country as well as the Deep South for dressing salads. Sugar alone is often liberally sprinkled over sliced tomatoes. For this salad we like the milder rice vinegar, but white wine vinegar as well as white cider vinegar can be used.

> *Mixed salad greens, washed and dried*
> 4 *medium oranges, peeled, pith removed, sliced 1/4 inch thick*
> 12 *soft dates, halved*
> 4 *teaspoons sugar*
> 4 *tablespoons rice wine vinegar*

Tear the salad greens and line 4 individual salad plates or large salad bowl. Cut the orange slices into quarters and distribute over the greens. Scatter date halves over the oranges. First sprinkle sugar all over, then sprinkle the vinegar.

Date and Onion Salad

Serves 4

This is a typical Malaysian recipe in that it contains no oil and is really more of a relish than a salad. The spicy yet sweet flavor makes any lamb dish, chicken, broiled fish, or plate of cold cuts much more interesting. It can also be served with curries. The simple dressing of vinegar, salt, and sugar should only just moisten the onion and dates.

> 20 *pitted dates, sliced lengthwise*
> 1 *large onion, thinly sliced*
> 3 *tablespoons cider vinegar*
> 1/2 *teaspoon salt*
> 1 *teaspoon sugar*

Slice the dates and set aside. Place the onion in a bowl, pour over boiling water to cover, and leave for 20 minutes. Drain and combine with the sliced dates in a shallow serving dish. Pour over the vinegar, then sprinkle the salt and sugar over the mixture.

Date Nut Meringues

Yields 24 meringues

These are easy to make but it takes a bit of time to cut the dates and chop the nuts and they have a lengthy baking time. As with all meringues, don't undertake them in humid weather—they simply will not become dry and crisp as they should. Serve them with tea or after-dinner coffee.

>   2   *large egg whites, at room temperature*
>   *(see Note)*
> 1/2   *cup fine granulated sugar*
> 1/2   *teaspoon vanilla extract*
> 12   *dates, cut in pieces less than 1/4 inch*
> 1/2   *cup coarsely chopped pecans*

Preheat the oven to 250° F. Cover a cookie sheet with wax or parchment paper.

Beat the whites until very stiff and dry, then beat in 6 tablespoons of the sugar, a spoon at a time. Continue beating until mixture holds its shape. Add the vanilla and remaining 2 tablespoons of sugar. Fold in the dates and nuts. Shape with 2 teaspoons into 24 mounds on prepared sheet about 1½ inches apart—they do not spread. Bake 40 to 50 minutes. When done they will feel firm and dry to the touch.

NOTE: Egg whites will give better volume if slightly warm. They may be placed in a bowl over hot water until warmed through before beating.

Banana Date Muffins

Yields 12 muffins

These are a dense, moist muffin, best eaten when freshly baked. However, they may be stored in a tightly closed tin for a day or two.

>   1   *cup mashed, very ripe banana*
>   *(2 medium bananas)*
>   1   *cup pitted dates*
> 1/3   *cup buttermilk*
> 1/2   *cup packed dark brown sugar*
> 1/3   *cup lightly salted butter, melted and*
>   *cooled*
>   1   *large egg*
> 1½   *cups all-purpose flour*
> 1/2   *cup old-fashioned rolled oats*
>   2   *teaspoons baking powder*
> 1/2   *teaspoon baking soda*
> 1/4   *teaspoon salt*

Preheat the oven to 375° F. Thoroughly grease a 12-cup muffin tin.

Place the banana, dates, and buttermilk in a blender or food processor and process to chop dates coarsely. Add brown sugar, butter, and egg. Blend just to mix (dates should not be pureed); set aside. Mix the flour, oats, baking powder, baking soda, and salt in a medium bowl; add liquid ingredients, stirring just enough to moisten. Spoon into prepared pans, dividing equally. Bake on the middle rack of oven for 18 to 20 minutes, or until golden. Serve hot.

Old-Fashioned Date Bars

Yields about 2½ dozen pieces

We have cut the sugar a bit, but this is essentially the same filled snack bar that you will find in some of the oldest recipe collections. If making half this recipe use an 8-inch square pan.

    3   cups chopped pitted dates
  1½   cups water
    2   tablespoons lemon juice
   ¾   cup (1½ sticks) lightly salted butter, at
        room temperature
    1   cup firmly packed dark brown sugar
  1¾   cups all-purpose flour
   ½   teaspoon baking powder
   ½   teaspoon salt
  1½   cups rolled oats, regular or quick-
        cooking

Preheat the oven to 400° F. Butter and flour a 9 × 13-inch baking pan.

Combine the dates, water, and lemon juice in a saucepan. Cook over medium to low temperature for about 10 minutes, stirring occasionally until thickened. Set aside to cool while preparing the crust.

Cream the butter and brown sugar, either in an electric mixer or by hand. Mix the flour, baking powder, and salt together, then stir into the creamed mixture until completely blended. Stir in the oats; the mixture will be crumbly. Press half of the mixture evenly over the bottom of the prepared pan. Spread the filling over the crust and cover with the remaining crumb mixture. Press lightly in place. Bake for 25 minutes or until lightly browned. While still hot, run a thin spatula around the edges. When completely cool cut into squares or bars of desired size.

F·I·G·S

Fresh Figs and Prosciutto

Grilled Figs and Smoked Sausage Kebabs

Mission Figlets with Shrimp

Fresh Fig and Grape Salad with Toasted Chopped Pecans

Fresh Figs with Mascarpone

Fig and Ginger Ice Cream

Dried Calimyrna Fig Sauce

Fresh Figs with Ricotta Cream

Although the commercial cultivation of the fig for its edible fruits is a comparatively modern development, the tree was well known to ancient civilizations. Aristophanes, a Greek poet of the fifth century B.C., refers in his poem "The Birds" to pests encountered in the growing of figs. In the well-known reference in Genesis 3:7, the Bible tells how Adam and Eve "sewed fig leaves together, and made themselves aprons" (these well may have been some variety other than edible figs, of course). It is also said to have been Cleopatra's favorite fruit, and the asp with which she committed suicide was brought to her in a basket of figs.

The fig tree was brought to the New World by the Spanish early in the sixteenth century. The missions in Mexico document the various fruits brought from Spain to be grown in the new land, and among those listed was the fig. The year 1769 is generally accepted as the date for the first planting of fig trees in California, when the Franciscans established a mission in San Diego. The same variety was planted at missions along the coast northward to Sonoma, and thus became known as the "Mission" fig.

Although there are hundreds of known fig varieties, only three kinds of light-colored or white figs, and one black or dark-blue-skinned fig, are raised for commercial production. The dark-skinned fig, commonly called the Black Mission variety, is the fig that was planted at the coastal missions. It has a thin skin and small seeds and is eaten both fresh and dried. The White Adriatic, of medium size and high sugar content, is one of the principal drying types, popular for use in fig bars and other bakery products. A second white variety is the all-purpose Kadota.

The third important white variety is the Calimyrna fig, which is grown commercially on a large scale. The name is a combination of California and Smyrna, the ancient home of this type. After unsuccessful attempts to produce fruit on the Calimyrna trees, it was discovered that this fig required pollen from another variety known as the Caprifig. This is carried out by a tiny wasp, which lays its eggs in the Caprifig. Just before the newly developed females are ready to depart, the fruit is carried to the Calimyrna orchards, placed in small baskets or perforated bags, and hung among the branches. As each tiny wasp comes out, carrying a few of the pollen grains, she goes to a Calimyrna fig and works her way in through the eye of the fruit. Once inside she finds that, unlike the Caprifig, there is no suitable place to deposit her eggs, and leaves after brushing the pollen on the flowers of the Calimyrna. This fig is well worth the effort of pollination, since it is very large, an attractive rich yellow color, with large seeds that impart a pleasing nutlike flavor to the ripened fruit. The word *caprification* describes this method of pollinization.

For best flavor, figs should be fully ripened on the tree, but once ripe they are very fragile, which presents the grower with the dilemma of harvesting underripe fruit of inferior flavor or fuller flavor that will not survive shipping. Unfortunately, inferior flavor usually wins, leaving most fig lovers little opportunity to enjoy the unique flavor and sweetness of the truly ripe fruit. On rare occasions good fresh figs may come your way, but the season is all too brief; most of the time one must settle for dried and canned products.

✥ HOME CULTIVATION ✥

In warm western and southern states figs can be grown outdoors and it is just a matter of checking with a local nursery for suitable varieties. However, they can be grown both indoors and out as far north as Boston using special techniques to protect against frost. In Italian communities in the Northeast, they are commonly grown even on small plots in the cities. The tree is kept pruned to a size that makes it feasible to dig a trench adjacent to it, tip the tree into the trench, cover it with leaves and soil each fall, and "resurrect" it in the spring after danger of frost. It will be budded, and rapidly produce leaves and shoots. Alternatively, a tree planted in a tub in a sunny room or greenhouse will produce edible figs (the leaves drop in winter, so it is not very ornamental!). If taken outdoors in summer it will produce more fruit. Rolce has grown both Brown Turkey and white Marseilles figs using these two methods.

✥ NUTRITION ✥

Figs are higher in dietary fiber than most other common fruits, contain protein, and are a high energy food, with 91 percent of their calories coming from quickly utilized natural sugars. As with most fruits, figs have a low salt and fat content but contribute an appreciable amount of calcium and iron as well as vitamin A, C, and B complex to the diet. Two large fresh figs have 80 calories, 2 canned figs with syrup have 50 calories, 1 large dried fig has 60 calories.

↭ SELECTION ↭

When purchasing fresh figs look for plump fruits, which may be greenish (white type) or blue-purple in color. When fully ripe, they will be soft to the touch but should be handled gently, since they are extremely fragile. For good flavor a fig should be really ripe; a slightly shriveled look near the stem caused by the sun is not a reason to reject it. The dried fruits come in several different types of packaging; in this country they usually are sold in blocks of varying sizes wrapped in clear plastic, but in some ethnic markets they may be found flattened into disks with a fiber run through the center to make strings of fruit, then tied into a circle. The large Calimyrna fig, light golden brown in color, and the Black Mission fig may also be marketed dried, in boxes similar to prunes and raisins. The Kadota fig, somewhat smaller than the Calimyrna, is usually found in the market as a whole preserved fruit packed in light syrup in 17-ounce cans or jars.

EQUIVALENTS
Mission figlets (dried) 6 ounces = 1 cup
1 fresh fig = 1 to 1½ ounces

STORAGE
↭ AND PREPARATION ↭

Fresh figs may have the thin skin removed but it is not necessary. They should be eaten within a day of purchase, since fresh figs do not keep well. Dried figs may be stored for about six months in the refrigerator if securely wrapped to retain moisture. Some important tips on storage have come to us from the California Fig Advisory Board. First, do not store figs near grain products or other food items that may harbor storage insects, since the sweet aroma of the figs will attract these creatures. Second, if figs are stored for a long time, the natural fruit sugar may crystallize on the surface. A light wash with warm water will dissolve the sugar, but a more interesting idea is to place them in a warm oven at a low temperature for a few minutes, which will cause the sugar to dissolve and turn to a glaze. This would be attractive if serving them as an after-dinner snack.

↭   ↭

Fresh figs should be served at room temperature to enjoy the full flavor. Split them in half to show the pretty interior when serving them with a creamy cheese for either a first course or as a dessert. You might also team them with paper-thin slices of any smoked or spicy ham. Dried figs, always available, can be added to sauces for duck or game as well as desserts. Use figs for cake and cookie fillings and paired with ginger in ice cream or jam.

Fresh Figs and Prosciutto

Serves 4

A classic presentation for ripe figs.

> *Oakleaf lettuce, or other loose-head lettuce leaves for lining plates*
> 4 *fresh large figs*
> 8 *thin slices prosciutto*
> 4 *lime wedges*

Line 4 individual serving plates with cut-up curly or oakleaf lettuce. Cut each fig in half lengthwise and place on top of the lettuce. Fold each slice of prosciutto and arrange decoratively with the figs on the plate. Serve with a wedge of lime.

Grilled Figs and Smoked Sausage Kebabs

Serves 4

An unusual combination of flavors to start a meal.

> 12 *Mission figlets*
> 1 *cup dry red wine*
> 6 *ounces kielbasa smoked sausage, cut into 12 pieces*

Place the figs in a small saucepan with the wine. Cover and soak for at least 6 hours, or preferably overnight, then drain.

Preheat the broiler.

Thread the figs and sausage slices alternately on 2 skewers and place over a shallow baking dish lined with foil. Broil about 4 inches from the heat source for 7 to 8 minutes, turning occasionally to cook evenly. Remove from the heat, carefully prod from the skewers, and divide among 4 individual plates. Serve immediately.

Mission Figlets with Shrimp

Serves 4

An exotic-tasting first course. Serve on a bed of curly lettuce, or with a small timbale of rice.

 8 *Mission figlets*
 ¼ *cup orange juice*
 ¼ *cup medium-dry sherry*
 2 *tablespoons (¼ stick) unsalted butter*
12 *medium–large uncooked shrimp, deveined, tails left intact*
 1 *teaspoon Dijon mustard*
    Mixed greens to line the plates

Slice each figlet into thirds lengthwise, and place in a bowl. In a small saucepan, heat the orange juice and sherry, then pour over the figs. Soak for several hours to allow the figs to soften and plump up.

In a large skillet, melt 1 tablespoon of the butter and heat the shrimp over medium-high heat until they change color. Add the remaining butter, mustard, figs, and juices. Swirl the figs and shrimp around briefly for 3 to 4 minutes or until heated through and the sauce from the juices has reduced and somewhat thickened. Serve immediately on individual plates lined with the greens.

Fresh Fig and Grape Salad with Toasted Chopped Pecans

Serves 4

The combination of fresh ripe figs and grapes with a sprinkling of toasted pecans on a bed of loose-head lettuce make the beginnings of any meal sweet. For a main course on a hot day add cold sliced chicken or ham, or a piece of broiled chicken.

    Loose-head lettuce for lining plates
 8 *fresh large figs*
 8 *ounces red seedless grapes*
 1 *tablespoon red wine vinegar*
 2 *tablespoons orange juice*
 ½ *teaspoon Dijon mustard*
 3 *tablespoons olive oil*
    Salt and freshly ground pepper to taste
 ¼ *cup chopped pecans, lightly toasted*

Wash the lettuce, pat dry, and tear into bite-size pieces. Divide among and line 4 individual serving plates. Wash the figs and carefully dry with paper towels. Slice each fig in half lengthwise, and place on top of the lettuce. Rinse and halve the grapes, then arrange on the plates with the lettuce and figs. Combine the vinegar, orange juice, and mustard and blend in the oil. Mix well, then season with salt and pepper to taste. Pour some of the dressing over each portion and sprinkle the nuts over the top.

Fresh Figs with Mascarpone

Serves 4

Mascarpone is a delicately flavored, very rich Italian cream cheese, particularly well suited to fruit.

12 *fresh, fully ripe medium figs, or 8 large*
 6 *tablespoons mascarpone cheese*
1½ *tablespoons Frangelica (hazelnut liqueur)*
12 *or more hazelnuts*

Remove stems and cut the figs in half. Blend the mascarpone and liqueur. Place 1½ tablespoons of mascarpone in the center of each of 4 dessert plates. Surround with the fig halves and 3 or more hazelnuts in an attractive pattern.

NOTE: For a different flavor, use 1 tablespoon Cointreau for the liqueur and for the nuts try walnuts or pecans. For an appetizer course, blend a few grains of crushed black pepper with the cheese and place a sprig of watercress on the plate.

Fig and Ginger Ice Cream

Yields 1 pint

The small pieces of fig add crunch, and the ginger zest to this smooth and rich custard base. A second helping is inevitable.

 1 *cup dried Mission figs*
 2 *large egg yolks*
¼ *cup half-and-half*
⅜ *cup sugar*
 1 *cup whipping cream*
    Sprinkling of salt
 1 *teaspoon peeled and minced fresh ginger*
⅓ *cup chopped crystallized ginger*

Place the figs in a strainer set over a saucepan containing hot water and cover. Bring the water to a simmer and steam the figs for about 10 minutes. This is done to soften the skin. Remove from heat, put the figs on a board, and chop into small pieces.

In a bowl over a saucepan of simmering water, combine the egg yolks, half-and-half, and sugar. Using a hand-held electric beater, beat the mixture for about 5 to 7 minutes, or until thickened and increased in volume. Immediately remove the bowl from the heat and place in another bowl containing ice and cold water. Beat the mixture until cool. This should take no longer than 3 to 4 minutes.

Transfer the contents to an electric mixer, add the cream and salt, and beat until very thick. Stir in the figs, and fresh and crystallized ginger. At this stage, the mixture will have the appearance of a thick, creamy dessert. Immediately place in a pan, cover with plastic wrap, and put in the freezer to set.

After about 4 hours, remove from the freezer, break the mixture up with a spoon or a knife, and beat again to make the ice cream lighter and smooth. Place in a container and return to the freezer. If you have an ice cream maker, follow the directions from the manufacturer for freezing.

Dried Calimyrna Fig Sauce

Yields 2 cups

You will find many uses for this simple fig sauce. It combines well with game such as duck, quail, squab, or game hens. The flavor is equally pleasing with a pork roast or slices of pork tenderloin. When available, fresh figs may be used to make this sauce.

1 *cup dried Calimyrna figs*
1 *cup Port wine*
2 *tablespoons unsalted butter*
2 *tablespoons all-purpose flour*
1 *cup chicken stock (homemade if possible)*
½ *cup fresh orange juice*
1 *tablespoon balsamic vinegar*
  Salt and freshly ground pepper to taste

Put the figs in a small bowl, add the Port, and soak for at least 2 hours or overnight. Place the figs and Port in a small saucepan, bring to a boil, then lower the heat and simmer for 10 minutes. Remove from heat, drain the figs, and reserve the liquid. Slice each fig in half horizontally.

Melt the butter in a heavy saucepan over medium-high heat, then, still over heat, rapidly beat in the flour with a whisk until well combined, about 1 minute. Add the reserved Port, chicken stock, orange juice, and vinegar, and bring to a boil. Lower the heat to medium and cook, stirring with the whisk until the sauce has thickened, about 7 minutes. Season with salt and pepper, stir in the sliced figs, and cook just until heated through, about 3 minutes.

NOTE: If you use fresh figs, allow 1 large or 2 small figs per serving. Soak the figs in the Port as described, but do not cook them in the Port. Continue with the remainder of the recipe as directed.

❧ ❧

Fresh Figs with Ricotta Cream

Serves 4

The combination of orange with chocolate and ricotta cheese is similar to the fillings for Italian dessert pastries. Because there is no pastry in this dessert, crisp cookies or macaroons add a nice touch.

1 *cup ricotta cheese*
2 *tablespoons candied orange peel, chopped*
1½ *tablespoons orange-flavored liqueur*
1 *ounce bittersweet chocolate, coarsely chopped*
12 *fresh medium figs, or 8 large*

Place ricotta cheese, orange peel, and liqueur in blender or food processor and process until smooth and creamy. Add the chocolate and process just enough to mix thoroughly. Refrigerate for 2 or more hours before serving. Cut the figs in half and arrange them attractively on individual plates. Divide and pour the cream equally over the figs.

G·R·A·P·E·F·R·U·I·T

Broiled Grapefruit

Grapefruit Consommé

Citrus and Fennel Salad

Scallops and Grapefruit

Grapefruit Sorbet

Although a member of the citrus family, the grapefruit has a missing link in its not-very-ancient ancestry. The closest relative appears to be the pummelo, *Citrus grandis*, a native of Malaysia, which is still grown in its original form throughout the Orient. However, the first description of the grapefruit in this hemisphere appears in John Lunan's *Hortus Jamaicensis* in 1814. How it came to Jamaica is unknown. By 1840 botanists agreed that the grapefruit was a distinct species and it received the name *C. × paradisi*.

A nobleman from France, the count Odet Phillipe, planted the first grapefruit grove in the United States, near Tampa, Florida, in 1823. As early as 1890 it had gained the status of a major commercial venture in Florida, but it wasn't until after World War I that grapefruit became a breakfast fruit, and only after the Second World War that it gained

recognition in Europe. By the late 1950s, 90 percent of world production was in the United States. While Florida is still the country's major producer, grapefruit is now grown in California, Arizona, and the southern Rio Grande Valley of Texas.

Certain characteristics of the grapefruit make it attractive as a commercial crop. It is more tolerant of cold than other citrus, the trees start to produce salable harvests as soon as four to six years after planting, and they give incredibly heavy yields—1,300 to 1,500 pounds per tree annually. This has encouraged expansion of growing areas and the development of fruit in different seasons for year-round availability.

❧ HOME CULTIVATION ❧

Grapefruit trees can be grown in all frost-free areas. However, the grapefruit is a large tree, making it the least desirable of the citrus fruits for a small plot, and unsuitable for sunny window pot culture.

❧ NUTRITION ❧

The grapefruit is an excellent source of vitamin C, but only the pink variety provides vitamin A. Grapefruit also contains potassium and small amounts of other minerals and vitamins. Half of a five-inch grapefruit has 50 calories.

❧ SELECTION ❧

When selecting grapefruit, look for smooth, thin skins (rough skin will be thicker) on fruit that feels plump and heavy. Grapefruit is ripe when picked, and will not ripen further off the tree. Fresh segments in jars and fresh bottled juice are sold in the dairy sections of supermarkets. Grapefruit sections are also available in cans.

Grapefruit varieties fall into two groups: white and red or pink. Today we rarely find seeded grapefruit in the markets. (To be called seedless a fruit must have eleven seeds or less.) The flesh of white fruit is usually a pale yellow, but the red or pink can be a deep blood red, light red, or blush pink. The skin of the colored grapefruit usually shows a faint to marked blush on the yellow. Some people think the red or pink are sweeter, but professional testers claim that the color has no effect on the taste.

Varieties, flavor, and degree of sweetness will vary with weather conditions:

From the West (California and Arizona)

Golden—November to June. It is yellow, seedless, and very juicy.
Ruby—October to May. It is seedless with deep red flesh and the skin has a red blush.

From Texas

Ruby Sweet—October to May. It is one of the newer very dark red and seedless types.
Rio Star—October to May. This is yet another of the "Super Red" varieties.

From Florida

Marsh Red—October to June. It is seedless and has blush-colored segments.
White Seedless—October to July. It has a smooth yellow peel with white to amber flesh that is easy to section.
Duncan—October to July. It is large with a thin yellow peel and has a cluster of seeds in the center. It is considered to have the most juice of any Florida variety.

Pummelo—also known as the Chinese grapefruit or shaddock. A native of Malaysia, the pummelo has long been a popular fruit in all the oriental countries, but is relatively new to the California citrus industry and is rarely seen in the East. It is larger than a large grapefruit but with less juice. It has a round to pear shape, a thick rind, and white to deep pink, very sweet flesh. It is eaten in segments with all membrane removed.

Ugli—a cross with the tangerine but with the appearance of a not very attractive grapefruit. The skin is a russeted yellow that fits loosely on a fruit about the size of a grapefruit that seems a bit lopsided. The pulp separates easily into sections, is moderately sweet, but does not justify the high price of this novelty. Jamaica is the principal source.

EQUIVALENTS
1 medium fruit = 10 to 12 sections
= ⅔ cup juice
= 3 to 4 tablespoons grated peel

STORAGE ✤ AND PREPARATION ✤

Grapefruit can be kept at room temperature for five to six days. For longer periods it should be stored in the refrigerator, where it will keep for several weeks. Do not wrap tightly in plastic; lack of air promotes mold.

To prepare a grapefruit half, cut crosswise across the segments, then using a curved grapefruit knife, cut around each segment within the membrane. Cut halves may be served with special pointed grapefruit spoons, eliminating the need to cut individual sections.

For whole sections, first peel the grapefruit. With a sharp knife cut a slice from the top, then cut off the peel in strips from top to bottom, cutting deeply enough to remove the thick white pith which is bitter, or cut off the peel around the fruit in a spiral. Remove any remaining pith and the thin membrane, then slide your knife blade alongside the segment on each side and remove the section membrane-free. Hold over a bowl to catch the juice. When grated peel is wanted, using a small-holed grater, grate the zest only, which is the thin colored portion of the rind. Citrus peels grate best when thoroughly dry. When measuring grated peel, pack lightly in the spoon.

For julienned strips of rind, use a vegetable peeler to remove a long strip of the zest only, then lay flat on a cutting board and slice into very thin strips of the desired length.

✤ ✤

Grapefruit isn't just for breakfast anymore. This fact owes something to the development of fruit with both fewer seeds and a sweeter, more mellow flavor. Still, grapefruit remains tart enough to contrast with other citrus in salads, and this makes it an excellent companion to the avocado with a vinaigrette dressing. Use the seedless types for broiled halves with a spoon of sherry or Port wine added, and top with brown sugar for the beginning or end of a meal. The candied peel can top a grapefruit or other citrus sorbet or be added to an after-dinner tray of sweets. For a refreshing summertime drink, try pouring the juice over ice, then add a splash of grenadine and a sprig of mint.

Broiled Grapefruit

Serves 4

Easy and refreshing; serve it either to begin a meal or as a dessert.

2 *large pink grapefruit*
4 *teaspoons dark brown sugar*
4 *teaspoons brandy or sherry*

With a sharp knife, section each grapefruit half carefully and remove some of the pith and seeds. Sprinkle each portion with the sugar and brandy. Place on a baking or cookie tray about 4 or 5 inches under the broiling element and cook until well heated and the sugar has almost caramelized. Serve immediately.

Grapefruit Consommé

Serves 4

A simple but elegant way to start a meal.

2   *cups fresh grapefruit juice*
1½ *cups beef bouillon*
2   *teaspoons good dry sherry*
4   *thin slices lemon, unpeeled*
4   *sprigs parsley or cilantro (fresh coriander)*

Heat the grapefruit juice and bouillon just to simmer, add sherry, and heat about 2 minutes to blend flavors. Float a slice of lemon with sprig of parsley in center of each bowl of soup.

NOTE: If fresh grapefruit are unavailable, unsweetened bottled, or frozen concentrate may be substituted.

⊷   ⊷

Citrus and Fennel Salad

Serves 4–6

Because of its lighter flavor and texture, we prefer canola oil to olive oil for the dressing.

1   *grapefruit*
1   *large navel orange*
1   *fennel bulb (about 1 pound)*
     Loose-head lettuce for lining the serving platter
2   *tablespoons white wine vinegar*
¼   *teaspoon Dijon mustard*
½   *teaspoon sugar*
4   *tablespoons canola or other vegetable oil*
     Salt and freshly ground pepper to taste

Peel the grapefruit and section. Peel the orange and slice into eighths. Set aside.

Wash, trim, and quarter the fennel bulb, then cut into ⅛-inch-thick slices. Place the citrus and fennel in a bowl and toss.

Line a shallow bowl or serving dish with lettuce and arrange the salad attractively on top. In a small bowl combine vinegar, mustard, sugar, and oil. Whisk until well blended, then season with salt and pepper. Serve the vinaigrette sauce separately, since this salad is also extremely good without any dressing.

❧ ❧

Scallops and Grapefruit

Serves 4

We have eliminated any sauce except for the pan juices to make this a simple, nutritious dish. Serve with snow peas and rice with toasted almonds for a pretty, quick meal.

> 2 *medium grapefruit*
> 4 *tablespoons (½ stick) lightly salted butter*
> 1½ *pounds sea scallops, cut into pieces, or whole bay scallops*
>   *Freshly ground pepper (optional)*

Peel and section the grapefruit, removing all white membrane. Arrange on individual plates or around the perimeter of a large serving dish. Melt 2 tablespoons of the butter in a skillet large enough to hold the scallops in a single layer. Add scallops and sauté until opaque. Remove to a bowl with a slotted spoon. Reduce pan juices over high heat, then lower heat and add the remaining 2 tablespoons butter, a bit at a time, stirring to incorporate and thicken the sauce. Return scallops to reheat gently. Check for seasoning, add pepper if desired, but scallops usually need no extra salt. Remove to plates and pour any pan juices over scallops and grapefruit.

❧ ❧

Grapefruit Sorbet

Yields 1 pint

Serve this sorbet as a first course or between courses, plain or with a mint or cilantro sprig. For dessert add a few shreds of candied grapefruit peel. The sorbet can be made with bottled juice but the flavor is markedly better with freshly squeezed.

> ½ *cup sugar*
> ⅔ *cup water*
> 1½ *teaspoons grated grapefruit rind*
> 1 *cup fresh grapefruit juice*
> 1½ *teaspoons lemon juice*

Combine the sugar and water in a nonreactive saucepan. Bring to a boil, add grapefruit rind, and stir until sugar dissolves. Simmer for 10 minutes. Remove from heat, cool slightly, then add the grapefruit and lemon juices. Allow to cool, then freeze in an ice cream maker according to manufacturer's instructions and pack lightly in a freezer carton. Or pour into a flat pan (the wider the pan the faster mixture will freeze) and place in freezer. When mixture is frozen, place in a chilled bowl and beat with electric or hand rotary beater until light and smooth. Spoon lightly into freezer carton and return to freezer.

G·R·A·P·E·S

Salad of Grapes with Chèvre Cheese

Fruited Rice

Brussels Sprouts and Red Grapes

Fillets of Sole with Green Grapes

Roast Chicken with Grape Stuffing

Chicken Salad with Grapes

Cornish Hens with Grapes in Red Wine

Grapes with Yogurt and Brown Sugar

Concord Grape Pie

Grapes are a fruit of ancient lineage, uniquely valued since earliest times. Grape seeds have been found in prehistoric caves, suggesting that they are older than recorded history, but it is their ability to ferment into wine that figures prominently in most grape-related stories. In Egypt, vineyards were planted for funerary wines in 3000 B.C., and instructions for grape and wine production have been found in Egyptian hieroglyphics of 2400 B.C. Early Greek pottery was adorned with grape-inspired designs, and references to grapes and wine appear frequently in the Old Testament. By the first

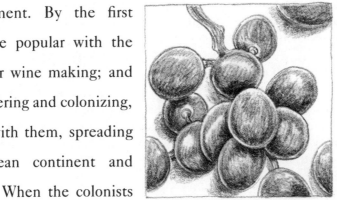

century B.C. grapes had become popular with the Romans, as an edible fruit and for wine making; and where the Romans went, conquering and colonizing, they took the culture of the vine with them, spreading this knowledge over the European continent and England.

When the colonists arrived in America, they attempted to transplant the European grapevines that they carried with them to the new continent. However, the climate and soil proved unsuitable, and they soon turned to the cultivation of the hardier wild grapes found growing in abundance. Among these grapes, the Concord (developed in Concord, Massachusetts) is the most widely planted variety. Used to make sweet kosher wine, it is considered too "foxy" in flavor for fine wines. However, the Concord grape's robust flavor and bright color make it the perfect choice for juice, jam, and jelly. Another American species, *Vitis rotundifolia*, known as muscadine, is native to the Southeast, where it flourishes in the warm, humid climate. The Scuppernong was the early native variety, and is still popular as a fresh fruit, for preserves, and for wine.

American grape varieties are sometimes eaten out of hand in the areas where they are grown, but most of the grapes we eat today are the European species *V. vinifera*. Although they did not survive the climate of the East Coast, they flourished in California, where they were first introduced by the Franciscans in 1769. California's climate so suited this species that by 1860 commercial grape growing was well established with countless varieties for wine production, table use, and raisins. California, which leads the world in table grape production, currently ships thirteen major grape varieties to markets throughout the United States and Canada, as well as to Japan, the South Pacific, Europe, and Central America.

California's San Joaquin Valley, one of the most fertile valleys in the world, is ideal for growing and air drying of raisins. It has ample sunshine, long, hot growing seasons, and a plentiful water supply from the nearby Sierra Nevada mountains. The Thompson, a green seedless variety and a principal table grape, is also the choice for raisin production. When ripe, the grapes are hand picked and laid on paper trays between the rows of vines, where they dry in the hot desert sun. It takes two to three weeks to reduce the moisture from 78 percent to about 15 percent, the perfect level of dryness. Four pounds of grapes yield just one pound of raisins. All of the United States raisin crop is produced here, most within a 100-mile radius of Fresno.

The dried fruit we know as currants is, in fact, dried Black Corinth grapes—not a currant but a miniature raisin. On box labels they are called Zante Currants, a name that probably originated in Greece where they were spoken of as *corinths*, likely corrupted to *currant*, and Zante was the name of the island near Greece where these grapes were originally grown.

❧ HOME CULTIVATION ❧

There are many hardy varieties from which to choose, but climate will be the deciding factor in the variety you select. Which ones suit your site can best be determined by your local nursery or agricultural field station advisor. Basic growing requirements are full exposure to sun, some type of trellis or arbor, and well-drained soil. Although grapes are not difficult to grow, for good production regular pruning is a must, since the fruit is produced on new shoots. In the North, both the blue and white Concords are hardy, and popular for eating fresh and, especially, for jelly and preserves. The Muscadine varieties are restricted to their native South, where they are popular for all uses, including wine making. All varieties of *V. vinifera* can be grown only in the areas of the West Coast, which meet their exacting climatic conditions.

❧ NUTRITION ❧

Grapes provide vitamin C and are a source of potassium. One cup of seedless grapes has 107 calories; 1 cup of seeded has 102 calories. One cup of raisins has 430 calories.

❧ SELECTION ❧

Grapes, though a seasonal fruit, appear nearly year round in our markets because of the many varieties with different harvesting times. This season has been further lengthened with importation from South America. When selecting, look for clusters with plump, well-colored berries attached to pliable, green stems. Soft or wrinkled grapes, or those with browned areas around the stem, are past their prime. You may find canned seedless grapes in specialty food sections. Although they have the appearance of grapes, the flavor is missing.

The following California varieties are all table grapes. They are listed in the order that they come into season.

Seedless Varieties

Perlette—A short but early season from May to July. The name is French for "little pearl." They are round and about the size of marbles, frosty green, with a mild sweet taste, and a crisp, firm texture.

Thompson Seedless—Available June through November. They are light green, verging on yellow when ripe. The jewel of California's grape industry, Thompsons account for 50 percent of the grape crop, 90 percent of U.S. raisins, and 25 percent of the grapes crushed for California wines and brandies. Originally from Iran, they came to California by way of England. Horticulturist William Thompson brought them to Los Angeles in 1872, and twenty years later, over 2 million cuttings had been shipped throughout Northern California—the beginning of the Thompson grape's success story.

Flame—From June through October. This is a California hybrid, second only to Thompson in popularity. They are large, round red berries with a slightly tart flavor.

Ruby—Appear in late summer, August through January. They are dark red, thin-skinned, have an oval shape, and are very sweet. The clusters are long and loose.

Table Grape Varieties with Seeds

Exotic—From June through August. These black, seeded grapes, a cross between the red Flame Tokays and the black Ribiers, are large beautiful berries with an excellent sweet flavor.

Ribier—From August through January. From Orleans, France, they crossed to England, where they were grown as a hothouse grape known as Alphonse Lavallees. Because of their history, Ribiers have a reputation for being an expensive luxury prized by Europeans. Twenty-five percent of all Ribier grapes in the United States are consumed by the European-influenced population of New York City. They are a handsome, very large, round, deep black berry, a dramatic addition to a fruit bowl. And, they usually command a premium price.

Emperor—From September through February. It is a sweet, light red berry that keeps well. This has been the Thanksgiving and Christmas grape, but it is losing popularity as more seedless types have come onto the market.

Tokay—Lasts for just two months, September through October. The Tokay is a large red berry that originated in North Africa and came to California in 1859 by way of Spain. It ranks third in California grape production. Only about 10 to 15 percent of the crop is harvested for the table; the rest is crushed for brandies and wines. The entire crop is grown around Lodi, 100 miles east of San Francisco.

Calmeria—From October through February. It is a distinctive grape with a long, oval shape, light green color, frosted with natural bloom, and a sweet flavor.

Eastern Grapes with Seeds

Concord—From late August to November. The rather thick skin of these grapes is readily slipped from the pulp when the fruit is gently squeezed, giving rise to the name "slip skins." The skin, dark blue with a silvery bloom, has an especially tart flavor, but the pale green pulp is quite sweet. These grapes make an excellent jelly. You will find them in local farm markets, and for a brief period in the supermarket.

> EQUIVALENTS
> 6 ounces stemmed grapes = 1 cup
> 1 cup = 35 to 45 average-size grapes,
> such as Thompson

Raisin Varieties

Natural Seedless—Account for 93 percent of total raisin crop. They are produced from the Thompson Seedless grapes, are naturally sun dried, with no chemicals used in their production, and are dark brown in color.

Golden Seedless—Also derived from the Thompson Seedless. They are mechanically dehydrated and treated with sulfur dioxide to preserve the golden color. They have a slightly different flavor from the brown raisin, a bit tart.

Muscat—From the Muscat grape. They are sun dried, with no chemical treatment. Seeds are mechanically removed. Muscats are a large, dark, extra-sweet raisin. They are sometimes available in clusters for eating out of hand. They are not as readily available as the seedless.

Zante Currants—From the Black Corinth grape. These are sun dried, with no chemical treatment. They are seedless, about one-fourth average raisin size, very dark brown, and have a tart, tangy flavor. They are chiefly used for baking.

Sultanas—From the Sultana grape. They are sun dried and no chemicals are used. The size and color is similar to regular raisins, with a somewhat tart flavor. Often designated in British recipes but not readily available in our markets.

> EQUIVALENTS
> 5½ ounces = 1 cup
> 1 pound = 3 cups

STORAGE AND ❧ PREPARATION ❧

To store grapes, place unwashed in plastic bags in the refrigerator. California table grapes can be stored for two to three days; Concord grapes up to a week. Just before serving, rinse thoroughly by spraying water to reach inside the clusters.

To keep raisins and currants soft, remove from cartons and store in glass jars, such as those used for canning, with snug-fitting lids. They can be stored this way on the pantry shelf indefinitely. If they should dry out, plump them with hot water, or if suitable for your use, soak them in wine or brandy.

❧   ❧

Because of their high sugar and water content combined with ease of handling, grapes are an ideal source of quick energy for athletes and hikers. Raisins have long served as a trail food for their nutritional qualities and packability. Small clusters of California grapes, red, green, or black, make great edible garnishes to place around a baked ham, on a platter of cold cuts, or with a molded salad. Seedless grapes tossed with a chicken salad or mixed with other cut-up fresh fruits add a pleasing difference in texture. Put them on skewers and take advantage of the different colors, alternating them with other fruits such as melon cubes, banana chunks, or whole small strawberries and serve as an hors d'oeuvre or with barbecued poultry or meat. To enjoy the sheer beauty of grapes, place great bunches as an edible decoration on the table or buffet.

Salad of Grapes with Chèvre Cheese

Serves 4–6

½ pound sweet seedless red grapes
2   tablespoons rice vinegar
4   tablespoons canola or other vegetable oil
*   Freshly ground pepper to taste*
1   head loose-head lettuce
3   ounces chèvre cheese
½ cup slivered almonds, toasted

Remove the grapes from the stems and halve. In a bowl, mix the rice vinegar, oil, and black pepper, add the grapes and carefully stir to blend. Tear the lettuce into bite-size pieces and place in a large salad bowl. Add the grape-dressing mixture to the lettuce. Crumble the cheese and blend into the salad. Sprinkle the almonds over the top. This salad may also be served on individual plates. Line the plates with the lettuce, then top with the grape-dressing mixture and the crumbled cheese.

NOTE: If desired, a little less of the dressing may be used. Add gradually to your own taste.

Fruited Rice

Serves 4–6

Served this way, the rice isn't just the necessary starch to balance a meal, but becomes a part of the dish it accompanies. It is particularly suited to foods prepared with Indian or North African spices.

1½ cups white rice, preferably long-grain
3   cups water
¼ cup golden raisins
¼ cup dried currants
2   tablespoons (¼ stick) lightly salted butter
½ teaspoon salt
½ cup pine nuts

Mix the rice and water in a deep, heavy-bottomed pot; bring to a boil, then put the raisins, currants, and butter on top. Turn down heat as low as possible and cook covered for about 20 minutes or until all the water is absorbed. Taste for seasoning, add pine nuts, and stir to distribute the fruit and nuts evenly. May be served hot or at room temperature.

Brussels Sprouts and Red Grapes

Serves 4–6

An unusual combination that goes especially well with grilled chicken.

1   *medium brussels sprouts*
2   *tablespoons (¼ stick) unsalted butter or margarine*
2   *cups seedless red grapes*
1   *tablespoon lemon juice*
    Salt and freshly ground pepper to taste

Remove any damaged outer leaves from the sprouts, trim the base, then cut a cross-hatch in the core to allow for even cooking. Soak in water for about 10 minutes. Boil the sprouts in a large pan of salted water for 6 to 8 minutes. Drain and immediately place in cold water to prevent discoloration. Drain again.

In a large nonreactive skillet, melt the butter and briskly sauté the grapes for only a minute or 2. Add the lemon juice and seasonings. Finally return the brussels sprouts and combine all the ingredients until thoroughly heated through.

NOTE: The sprouts may be prepared in a microwave oven following the directions of the manufacturer, then returned to the skillet along with the grapes.

Fillets of Sole with Green Grapes

Serves 4

The grapes liven up this dish.

4   *sole fillets, about 5 ounces each*
¼   *cup all-purpose flour, for dredging*
    Freshly ground pepper to taste
1   *tablespoon unsalted butter*
1   *tablespoon canola or other vegetable oil*
1   *teaspoon peeled and minced fresh ginger*
½   *cup dry white wine*
1   *cup seedless green grapes, halved*
1   *teaspoon sugar*
    Salt to taste
¼   *cup slivered almonds, toasted*

Dredge the fish in the flour seasoned with pepper. Melt butter and oil in a saucepan over medium-high heat. Add the ginger and sole fillets and sauté about 3 to 4 minutes on each side, just until the fillets begin to turn golden brown. Remove from pan to a plate, cover, and keep warm. Add the wine to the pan and cook briefly, scraping up the bits from the bottom and sides. Reduce the liquid slightly, then add the grapes and sugar and cook for 4 minutes, stirring constantly. Add salt and adjust the seasonings. To serve, spoon the sauce equally over the sole fillets and sprinkle with the toasted almonds.

Roast Chicken with Grape Stuffing

Serves 6

 2 *tablespoons margarine*
 ½ *cup chopped onion*
 1 *cup fresh white bread crumbs*
 2 *tablespoons chopped fresh parsley*
 1 *teaspoon dried thyme*
 1¾ *cups mixed seedless green grapes*
   Salt and freshly ground pepper to taste
 1 *chicken, 3 to 4 pounds*
 1 *tablespoon canola or other vegetable oil*
 ¾ *cup dry white wine*
 1 *chicken bouillon cube*

Preheat the oven to 475° F.

In a large skillet, heat the margarine, add the onion, and sauté over medium-high heat until soft but not brown, about 4 minutes. Stir in the bread crumbs, parsley, thyme, and 1 cup grapes, coarsely chopped, and mix until thoroughly blended. Season with salt and pepper.

Stuff the cavity of the chicken, then truss it. Season with pepper. Pour oil into a deep roasting pot, place the chicken in the pot, and turn until well coated with the oil. Place the chicken on its back and roast for 15 minutes. Reduce heat to 375° F. and continue roasting for another 15 minutes. Turn the chicken over and add the wine and bouillon cube. Baste the bird, scraping up the crusty bits from the bottom and sides of the pot. Bake for an additional 30 minutes. Baste and add the remaining ¾ cup grapes cut in half and cook for 15 minutes. Remove the chicken to a board or platter and cover to keep warm. Place the pot over medium heat on top of the stove, skim off as much fat as possible, stir well, and adjust the seasonings. Carve the chicken into individual serving portions, spoon some of the stuffing with each portion, and serve with the sauce.

Chicken Salad with Grapes

Serves 4

Chicken, grapes, celery, nuts, and a light sour-sweet dressing add up to a delectable summer salad for family and friends.

 1½ *pounds boneless and skinless chicken breasts, cooked and diced into bite-size pieces (2–2½ cups)*
 ½ *pound seedless red grapes*
 1 *celery stalk, sliced on the diagonal into ⅛-inch-thick slices*
 2 *tablespoons lemon juice*
 ½ *teaspoon Dijon mustard*
 2 *teaspoons honey*
 2 *tablespoons canola or other vegetable oil*
 ¼ *teaspoon paprika*
   Salt and freshly ground pepper to taste
   Mixed greens or loose-head lettuce for lining serving platter
 ½ *cup walnuts, slightly roasted and crushed*

In a large bowl, combine the chicken, grapes, and celery. In another bowl, mix the lemon juice, mustard, honey, oil, and paprika. Season to taste with salt and pepper. Pour the dressing over the chicken mixture and stir to blend. Line a large serving platter or individual serving plates with the lettuce leaves. Spoon the chicken salad on top of the lettuce and sprinkle the walnuts all over.

Cornish Hens with Grapes in Red Wine

Serves 4

The combination of grapes and red wine does wonders for Cornish game hens. It lends a colorful appearance and an interesting flavor to a bird that can be a bit bland.

2 *Cornish game hens, 1¼ pounds each*
   Freshly ground pepper to taste
3 *tablespoons canola or other vegetable oil*
½ *cup chopped onion*
½ *cup chopped carrots*
1 *cup coarsely chopped red grapes*
1 *teaspoon dried thyme*
1 *bay leaf*
1½ *cups red Rhone wine or Zinfandel*
1 *cup chicken stock*
1 *tablespoon unsalted butter*
1 *cup seedless red grapes, halved*
1 *cup seedless green grapes, halved*
2 *teaspoons Dijon mustard*
1 *teaspoon sugar*
1 *teaspoon fresh lemon juice*
   Salt to taste
1 *tablespoon cornstarch*
2 *tablespoons water*
   Extra red and green grapes, for garnish

Wash the hens and pat dry with paper towels. With a sharp knife or utility scissors, cut along each side of the backbone, and remove. With a spatula, flatten the hens, sprinkle with pepper, cover, and refrigerate.

In a large saucepan, heat 1 tablespoon of the oil, add the onion and carrots, and cook for about 4 minutes until softened. Add the chopped grapes, thyme, bay leaf, wine, and stock. Bring to a boil, lower the heat, and simmer until reduced to 2 cups, about 30 to 45 minutes. Transfer the mixture to a food processor or blender and puree. (This fruit stock may be prepared a day or two ahead and refrigerated or frozen. If frozen, thaw before using).

Preheat the oven to 400° F.

Place the hens in a shallow roasting pan, coat with the remaining 2 tablespoons oil, and arrange them skin side down. Bake for 20 minutes, then turn and continue cooking for 20 minutes. Baste occasionally. Remove the hens to a serving platter and cover to keep warm. Skim the fat from the pan and add the juices to the stock.

While the hens are cooking, complete the sauce. Melt butter in a saucepan, add the grape halves, and swirl around over medium-high heat, stirring, for 2 minutes. Stir in the mustard, sugar, and lemon juice. Add the fruit stock, bring to a boil, and reduce the sauce until 1½ cups remain. Adjust the seasonings adding salt to taste. Mix cornstarch with water and add to the sauce, stirring to thicken. To serve, uncover the hens, divide the sauce equally among the portions, and spoon over the birds. Garnish with the remaining whole red and green grapes.

Grapes with Yogurt and Brown Sugar

Serves 4

An old favorite that takes only a few minutes to prepare and that is used too infrequently. The original recipe was made with sour cream but we use a plain or vanilla low-fat yogurt.

1 pound green seedless grapes, removed
   from the stem and halved
½ cup plain low-fat yogurt
¼ cup light brown sugar
1 teaspoon ground cinnamon

In a large serving dish or in individual dishes, mix the grapes and yogurt well. Chill for 1 hour or more. In a small bowl, mix the brown sugar and cinnamon. Pass the sugar and cinnamon mixture separately when serving.

Concord Grape Pie

Yields one 9-inch pie

These New England grapes produce a beautiful rich purple filling that bubbles through the lattice topping of this pie. Because the pulp and the skin are so easily separated, this type of grape is referred to as a "slip skin." Just pinch the fruit between your thumb and forefinger and the pulp will pop out of the tiny hole at the stem end.

PASTRY

2¼ cups all-purpose flour
1⅛ teaspoons salt
¾ cup solid vegetable shortening
1½ teaspoons vinegar
6 tablespoons cold water, approximately

FILLING

4 cups purple Concord grapes
1 cup sugar
3 tablespoons flour
1 tablespoon lemon juice

Combine flour and salt in a large bowl. Cut in shortening with pastry blender or two knives until mixture resembles coarse meal. Add the vinegar to the water, then sprinkle half of it over the flour mixture and mix in with fingers or a fork, adding more water as needed, until all the flour is moistened. Gather into a ball, divide in halves, one half slightly larger than the other, and shape into flat disks. Roll out the larger disk on a floured board ⅛-inch thick and 10 inches in diameter. Line a 9-inch pie pan with pastry and place in freezer while making filling.

Preheat the oven to 425° F.

Separate the grape skins from the pulp, placing the skins in a bowl and the pulp in a medium saucepan. Over medium heat, bring pulp to a rolling boil (do not add water). Cook for 5 minutes, then remove from heat and while hot, rub through a sieve to remove seeds. Discard seeds, add the pulp to the skins, and stir in the sugar, flour, and lemon juice. Allow to cool, then pour filling into pastry-lined pan.

Roll out remaining pastry to make lattice strips. Cut 14 strips, ¾-inch wide, with knife or pastry wheel. Place 7 strips evenly spaced across filling, then place remaining strips diagonally across the first ones. Moisten edge and press strip ends into crust to seal. Fold overhang over strip ends, press together, and pinch into a high, decorative rim to contain the juices. Place the pie on the middle shelf of the oven and bake 40 to 45 minutes. When ready, crust will be golden and juices bubbling. Allow to stand an hour or more before cutting.

L·E·M·O·N·S
and
L·I·M·E·S

Seviche

Indian Lime Pickle

Salt-Preserved Lemons

Avgolemeno, or Greek Lemon Soup

Oaxaca Lime and Garlic Broth

Brown Rice with Spice and Lemon

Lemon Rice

Italian Bean, Tuna, and Preserved Lemon Casserole

Fish Tajine with Salt-Preserved Lemons

Shrimp with Lime Pickle

Lemon Chicken

Lemon Meringue Pie

Two-Crust Lemon Pie

Lemon Curd

Tropical Lime Pie

Lemon Sponge Pudding

Lemon Sherbet

Lemon Squares

Little has been told of the early history of lemons and limes. Generally those fruits most often the subject of art and poetry gained their popularity and recognition because their sweet succulent flesh made them suitable to eat out of hand. Although lemons and limes don't fit this description they did eventually travel the same westward trade routes from Asia to North Africa and the countries along the Mediterranean Sea. In the ideal climate of Spain and Italy they flourished, and by the eighth century were well established in that region. They arrived in the Americas with Columbus on the explorer's second voyage in 1494.

The lemon holds a unique place in cooking with fruit, acting as the flavor enhancer for nearly every other fruit. It can be subtle or bold, give balance to overly sweet foods, or stand alone. And it would be most difficult to find anyone who did not like its flavor. The lime fulfills a somewhat similar role, but it seems to work better with some fruit flavors than with others. However, this may be just a matter of parochial taste. In Central American countries where limes are used almost exclusively (and one term often specifies both fruits), one grows accustomed to having lime in hot tea, a wedge served with the fish, and a limeade when lemonade is requested. In our recipes, we always designate the one we prefer, but in many instances you can make the substitution of one for the other according to your preference or which you happen to have on hand.

Both trees grow in tropical climates, but the lime, *Citrus aurantifolia*, is not as adaptable to subtropical zones. The lemon, *C. limon*, though more frost resistant, tolerates less moisture in the form of heavy rains. Therefore commercial production of limes is confined chiefly to the warmer areas of southern Florida and the Keys, but the lemon, because it is susceptible to a variety of diseases if grown in a wet environment, is grown primarily in the drier climate of California.

You will see blossoms year round and fruit at all stages of growth on lemon trees. In commercial orchards the fruit is hand-picked, using small clippers to cut the stem close to the fruit when it is about two inches in diameter and still green. From the orchard it goes to controlled temperature holding rooms until the rind has turned to the familiar clear yellow, and it is ready to make its way to the produce counters. California provides nearly all of our domestic market and 30 percent of world production.

About half the lemon crop is shipped to be used fresh; the remainder is made into a wide array of juice products: lemonade, juice concentrates, and powdered flavoring (primarily for commercial baking). Other by-products are citric acid, used in beverages and any other food requiring a tart accent; lemon oil, an important ingredient in fine furniture polishes; and pectin, used with fruits lacking adequate amounts of their own, to make jams and jellies. The oil has been traditionally used in perfumes, soap, and flavoring extracts, but in recent years it has appeared in nearly every conceivable cleaning product from laundry detergents to window cleaners.

The lime tree, the smallest of the citrus group, is only eight to fifteen feet in height. The thin-skinned fruit can be dark or yellow green in color with a pale green pulp that is more acidic than the lemon. With overlapping periods of bloom, fruit ripens throughout the year, with the heaviest harvest in the summer months. Although Mexico leads in world production of limes, Florida is the principal provider to our domestic market. The distinctively flavored limes, grown on the Florida Keys, have gained justifiable recognition from the popularity of Key Lime Pie. Key lime fruit is not usually found outside of Florida, but you can purchase the bottled juice in supermarkets.

The citron is yet another citrus fruit, *C. medica,* which somewhat resembles the lemon but is larger with a coarser, very thick skin. In this country we do not find the fresh fruit, only the candied peel for use in baking. As with other fruit peels, it is now almost never sold in whole pieces, but is pre-cut into small dice and packaged in a plastic container. The flavor is far superior if the whole fruits can be had and the cook does her own chopping.

❦ HOME CULTIVATION ❦

The lime and the lemon are practical and attractive additions to the landscape in appropriate climates. Both have the virtue of being small trees and the lime can even be grown as a shrub. Lemons are particularly adaptable to being trained in patterns against a wall or fence. In colder climates fruit-producing trees can be satisfactorily grown in either a greenhouse or a sunny window.

❦ NUTRITION ❦

Lemons and limes are a superior source of vitamin C; in addition they also provide potassium, calcium, and vitamin A. One tablespoon of fresh lemon juice has 4 calories and 1 tablespoon of fresh lime juice has 3 calories.

❧ SELECTION ❧

When purchasing lemons, look for thin-skinned, plump-feeling fruit. Sometimes only those with coarse, thick skins are available, but these have the virtue of yielding larger quantities of rind for grating. Limes usually have thin skins and should have the same plump feel as other citrus. They may be dark green or pale yellow-green depending on variety, but they are not usually sold by varietal name.

EQUIVALENTS

6 medium lemons = 1 cup juice
1 medium lemon = 3 tablespoons juice
= 3 teaspoons grated rind

As a general rule limes will yield just a bit more than half the amounts given for the lemons. These amounts are simply guidelines since the amounts will vary with the size of the fruit and the thickness of the rind.

STORAGE AND
❧ PREPARATION ❧

Lemons and limes may be kept at room temperature for about a week, but if stored in the refrigerator they will keep for up to a month.

Rolling a lemon or lime on the counter before squeezing, or warming it either briefly in hot water or for about twenty seconds in the microwave, will make the juice more available.

Any type of juicer may be used. To obtain a spoonful of juice without cutting the lemon you can poke one end with a fork or skewer and squeeze for the amount needed, then return the lemon to the refrigerator. You can also buy a small cylindrical tool to insert in one end of the lemon for the same purpose. After juicing a lemon or lime, the leftover rind can be carefully plastic-wrapped and placed in the freezer. Once frozen, it is not only a ready source for grated rind but it is also easier to grate when frozen and hard.

For peeled lime or lemon slices, cut a slice of peel off one end, then with a sharp knife cut the rind, including the white pith, in a spiral. Always cut slices crosswise. For wedges, cut fruit lengthwise in half, then in quarters or eighths.

For grated zest (the thin colored part of the rind) use the small holes of a flat grater and rub the fruit back and forth. Use just the zest, not the underlying white pith. To measure, pack lightly in spoon.

For strips of peel use a vegetable peeler and remove thinly to desired size. To julienne, stack several pieces of desired length and cut as thinly as possible into strips.

❧　❧

If nature hadn't given us the lemon we would have had to invent it. It not only has the unique ability of bringing out the best flavor qualities of every other fruit, it can also assume this role with vegetables, fish, poultry, and even meat. So popular is it as a flavor enhancer that those on salt-free diets sprinkle lemon juice instead of salt. To save calories squeeze a lemon or lime wedge over green salads and vegetables instead of dressings with oil or butter. Lemons or limes can be used with equally good effect to drizzle over fruit salads for a piquant flavor while preventing pears, apples, and bananas from turning an unattractive brown. Lime juice has a special affinity for the tropical fruits such as papaya, banana, and mango. Although available and useful year round, these flavors are especially refreshing in summer drinks, ices, and desserts.

As a fruit cook's best friend the lemon has yet another virtue. When the preparation of fresh fruit or vegetables results in ugly stains on fingers and nails, just whip out a lemon and rub the areas with a bit of the juice and, voilà, lovely clean hands! It is equally effective for removal of fruit, and even wine, stains on most fabrics.

Seviche

Serves 4

Although this recipe calls for scallops, other fish may be used: shrimp, cleaned, sliced in half lengthwise and dipped in boiling water, just until they turn pink; firm fish such as mackerel or striped bass, boned, skinned, and cut into bite-size pieces and used raw; or use a mixture of fish, scallops, and shrimp. The lime juice "cooks" the fish—it will feel quite firm when done. We first tasted this dish on a tropical island picnic just off Cozumel in Mexico. On our way out to the island the crew dove for the fish.

✦ ✦

1 *pound scallops*
4 *tablespoons lime or lemon juice*
1 *small onion, diced*
2 *tablespoons chopped green pepper*
1 *medium tomato, seeded and chopped*
1 *tablespoon coarsely chopped cilantro*
   (fresh coriander)
6 *tablespoons olive oil*
   Salt and hot pepper sauce to taste
   Loose-headed lettuce for lining plates

Cut the sea scallops, into halves or quarters depending on their size, then place in a bowl and cover with lime juice, using more if necessary to cover. Marinate for at least 2 hours—until the scallops are opaque. Add onion, green pepper, tomato, cilantro, olive oil, salt, and hot pepper sauce. Mix well and allow to stand at least another hour in refrigerator. Drain and serve on lettuce-lined plates or large scallop shells.

Indian Lime Pickle

Yields 1 quart

These pickles are used in one of our favorite shrimp dishes (Shrimp with Lime Pickle, page 130) but they may be offered just as one would pass a chutney with meat, poultry, and other fish dishes. Add a teaspoon of the oil to French dressing for a unique touch to a tossed green salad.

    9   limes, cut in quarter-inch slices
    3   tablespoons coarse salt (kosher or
        sea salt)
 1²/₃   cups canola or other vegetable oil
    1   large garlic clove, mashed
    3   teaspoons red pepper flakes
    3   teaspoons peeled and grated fresh ginger
    1   teaspoon aniseed, crushed
 1¹/₄   teaspoons mustard seed
  ³/₄   teaspoon turmeric

Layer the lime slices with salt in a 1-quart preserving jar. In a small saucepan combine ¹/₃ cup of the oil, the garlic, red pepper, ginger, aniseed, mustard seed, and turmeric. Heat to a simmer and cook for 3 minutes being careful not to achieve a boil. Stir in the remaining oil and pour mixture over lime slices. Cover and let stand at room temperature for a week. Can then be kept in refrigerator indefinitely.

Salt-Preserved Lemons

Yields approximately 1 pint

Once you have enjoyed the special salty tart flavor of these lemons you will find an infinite number of dishes to which they can be added for a piquant lift. Try them added to noodles, pasta, or rice dishes. Since they keep for months in the refrigerator it is easy to always have some on hand.

    2   medium lemons
        Coarse salt (kosher or sea salt)
 ¹/₃–¹/₂ cup lemon juice
        Olive oil (optional)

Wash and dry the lemons. Cut each into eighths. Pour a layer of coarse salt in a shallow pan. Roll lemon sections in salt to coat well and pack into a pint canning jar. Pour the lemon juice over and close tightly. Allow to stand at room temperature for a week, turning the jar daily. The preserves will now be ready for use, but to keep longer pour olive oil just to cover and place in refrigerator where they can be kept for 6 months or more.

Avgolemeno, or Greek Lemon Soup

Serves 4

Our easy version of a traditional soup.

    4   cups chicken stock
    ¼   cup white rice
    2   large eggs
    4   tablespoons lemon juice
        Parsley clusters, for garnish

Bring the stock to a boil, add the rice, and cook until tender, about 20 minutes, then lower heat. Put the eggs and lemon juice in a blender or food processor and process for 1 minute; add 1 cup of the hot stock with the machine running and process just to blend. Remove pot from heat and stir blended mixture into stock. Heat the soup but do not boil as the eggs will curdle. Serve hot with parsley clusters as garnish.

Oaxaca Lime and Garlic Broth

Serves 4

This is an adaptation of a soup served in the delightful ambience of a restaurant balcony that overlooked the colorful night life of the *zocalo* (plaza) in Oaxaca, Mexico.

    6   cups chicken stock
    5   large garlic cloves, halved
    2   tablespoons lime juice
        Tortillas baked until crisp, or tortilla
        chips (unsalted)
        Cilantro leaves, for garnish

Heat stock to boiling, add garlic, and simmer for 20 minutes or more, covered. The garlic should be soft enough to mash with a fork; leave the garlic bits in the broth. Remove from heat and add lime juice. Place several pieces of crisp tortilla, or 4 or 5 chips, in each bowl and pour broth over. Garnish with few leaves of cilantro.

Brown Rice with Spice and Lemon

Serves 4

You can cook the rice ahead or use leftover rice for this dish. Because the flavor is so subtle it can accompany a wide variety of fish and poultry dishes without overwhelming or conflicting with other herbs and seasonings.

    ¼   cup (½ stick) lightly salted butter
    ½   teaspoon mustard seed
    ¾   teaspoon ground coriander
    ¼   teaspoon cayenne pepper
    ¾   cup cashew nuts, in coarse pieces
    2½ cups cooked brown rice
    ¼   cup lemon juice
    ½   teaspoon salt and freshly ground pepper
        to taste
    2   tablespoons chopped fresh parsley

In a skillet large enough to hold the rice, melt the butter and sauté the mustard seed for a few seconds before adding the coriander, cayenne, and nuts. Stir these ingredients over medium heat until nuts begin to change color. Stir in the cooked rice with lemon juice, salt, and pepper. Heat, taste, and adjust seasonings. Stir in the parsley just before serving.

Lemon Rice

Serves 6

Any white rice may be used; short-grain will be creamier than long-grain.

>   3 tablespoons lightly salted butter
> 1/2 medium onion, thinly sliced
> 1½ cups white rice
>   3 cups chicken stock
> 1/3 cup lemon juice
> 1/2 cup chopped chives
>   3 tablespoons thinly sliced lemon zest
> 1/4 teaspoon salt
>   Freshly ground pepper to taste

Melt the butter in a heavy-bottomed saucepan, add the onion, and cook until transparent. Add the rice, then stir to coat with butter. Add the stock and lemon juice, then bring to a boil. Reduce heat to very low and cover. (If using short-grain rice, stir after 10 minutes.) Cook until rice is tender, about 20 minutes. Add the chives and lemon zest, adjust seasonings, and stir well.

Italian Bean, Tuna, and Preserved Lemon Casserole

Serves 4–6

This makes a good vegetarian meal served with a green vegetable, a tossed salad, and crusty Italian bread, topped off with a bit of cheese and fresh fruit.

>   1 cup dried white beans
>   3 tablespoons olive oil
> 8–10 fresh sage leaves
>   3 garlic cloves
> 1/2 teaspoon salt
>   4 wedges Salt-Preserved Lemons (page 127), pulp removed and rind sliced
>   1 cup chicken or vegetable stock
>   2 tablespoons lemon juice
>   1 small (3½-ounce) can Italian tuna in olive oil
>   Freshly ground pepper to taste

Place the beans in a saucepan with cold water to cover by about 1 inch. Bring to a boil. Cover and allow to stand for 1 hour or more.

Drain the beans and place in a 1-quart casserole. Preheat the oven to 400° F. Stir the olive oil, sage, garlic, salt, lemon rind, and stock into the casserole. Cover tightly and bake on middle rack for 1½ hours, or until beans are tender. Stir once or twice during baking. When done, stir in the lemon juice, tuna, and pepper.

Fish Tajine with Salt-Preserved Lemons

Serves 4

Tajines are stews native to North Africa. Rice is a suitable accompaniment, either plain boiled or our Fruited Rice (page 117). Because there are so many vegetables in the casserole, a fresh salad and a crusty loaf are all that is needed for a very special meal.

   3 tablespoons cilantro (*fresh coriander*)
   2 garlic cloves
   2 teaspoons paprika
1½ teaspoons ground cumin
   1 teaspoon salt
 ¼ teaspoon cayenne pepper
   2 tablespoons lemon juice
   2 tablespoons olive oil
1½ pounds firm white fish such as cod or halibut, cut about 1 inch thick
 ½ cup hot water
   2 medium carrots, scraped and cut into thin slices
   1 pound tomatoes, cut into thin slices
   2 small green or red bell peppers, sliced into thin rings
   4 wedges Salt-Preserved Lemons (*page 127*)

Using a blender or food processor, chop cilantro and garlic with paprika, cumin, salt, and cayenne; add lemon juice and olive oil, then blend until smooth. Rub about half the sauce (reserve remaining sauce) over fish fillets, cover, and marinate no less than 1 hour in the refrigerator. If you have time, let them stay overnight.

Preheat the oven to 325° F.

Add hot water to the remaining marinade and spread enough just to coat bottom of a 2-quart baking dish. Make a layer of the carrots, then spread with half the tomatoes and half the pepper rings. Drizzle 2 tablespoons of sauce over vegetables and lay the fish pieces on top. Scrape the salt and pulp from the lemon sections and cut crosswise into ¼-inch pieces. Distribute the lemon pieces over the fish, then cover with a layer of tomatoes and lastly a layer of pepper rings. Heat the remaining sauce and pour evenly over all. Cover tightly and bake for 45 minutes.

Remove from oven and pour juices into a wide skillet (it doesn't matter that some juice will remain in bottom of the pan), set over high heat to reduce by half, about 10 minutes. Pour reduced juices over the fish and place under broiler for 5 minutes to lightly brown (some broilers may take a bit longer).

Shrimp with Lime Pickle

Serves 4

This makes a wonderful meal served with Fruited Rice (page 117). Pile the rice on a serving platter and heap the shrimp in the center with a border of the rice showing. Serve any kind of peas—shelled English peas, pea pods, or sugar snap peas—or a tossed mixed green salad to complete the meal.

1½ *pounds large raw shrimp, shelled and*
   deveined
2 *tablespoons lime juice*
1 *tablespoon olive oil*
1 *tablespoon lightly salted butter*
9 *slices Indian Lime Pickle (page 127),*
   cut into quarters, plus additional (op-
   tional) for garnish

Place the shrimp in a bowl with the lime juice, and toss to coat. Marinate for at least 1 hour in refrigerator. Heat the oil and butter in a very wide skillet, drain the shrimp and add them to the skillet. As they begin to turn pink add the lime pieces, stirring to distribute the limes evenly. Cook just until all shrimp are completely pink. Additional lime pickle may be used as a garnish or could be served as a condiment.

Lemon Chicken

Serves 6

This tangy chicken is equally good served piping hot or cold, even the day after it has been prepared. Remember this recipe for a picnic on a summer's day or when tailgating at a football or lacrosse game.

1½ *pounds boneless and skinless chicken*
   breasts
1½ *pounds boneless and skinless chicken*
   thighs

2 *teaspoons dried tarragon*
1 *garlic clove, minced*
1 *teaspoon salt*
1 *teaspoon sugar*
2 *tablespoons peeled and chopped shallots*
⅓ *cup fresh lemon juice*
1 *tablespoon grated lemon rind*
¼ *cup olive oil*
   Freshly ground pepper to taste
10 *thin lemon slices*
¼ *cup chopped fresh Italian parsley*

Remove any extra fat from the chicken pieces. Wash and pat dry. Cut the breasts and thighs into 2 or 3 serving portions depending on their size. Place in a large pan in a single layer. In a bowl, mix the tarragon, garlic, salt, sugar, shallots, lemon juice, lemon rind, oil, and pepper. Pour over the chicken pieces and place the lemon slices on top. Cover and refrigerate for at least 6 hours or overnight, turning once during this time and basting so that all the chicken has been well coated with the marinade.

Preheat the oven to 375° F.

Place the chicken thighs in a roasting pan with the lemon slices and some of the marinade and bake for 15 minutes. Add the breasts with the remaining marinade and cook for 15 minutes more. Baste with the marinade, pouring off liquid if there appears to be too much, and turn the pieces. Increase the temperature to 425° F. and bake for 5 minutes more. If desired, grill for a few minutes to crisp. Before serving, sprinkle with the fresh parsley.

NOTE: This chicken may be barbecued outdoors on a grill. Remember to allow less cooking time for the breasts. Turn frequently and baste with the marinade.

Lemon Meringue Pie

Yields one 9-inch pie

This old classic remains a favorite year-round dessert. Too often restaurant and bakery versions rely on powders and extracts for the lemon flavor, which makes this home-baked version with fresh lemon juice such a treat.

PASTRY (FOR 2 TART SHELLS)

1¾ cups all-purpose flour
¼ teaspoon salt
1 teaspoon sugar
½ cup (1 stick) unsalted butter, cut in bits
1 large egg yolk
4 tablespoons cold water, approximately

FILLING

1¼ cups sugar
⅓ cup cornstarch
1½ cups hot water
3 large egg yolks
3 tablespoons unsalted butter
5 tablespoons lemon juice
1⅓ tablespoons grated lemon rind

MERINGUE

3 large egg whites
¼ teaspoon cream of tartar
6 tablespoons sugar

Mix the flour, salt, and sugar in a medium bowl. Add the butter and blend with fingertips until the mixture resembles coarse meal. Make a well in the center, drop in the yolk and half the water, and mix with fingers just until dough comes together. If dough is slightly crumbly add just enough water to make dough form a ball. Form into 2 flattened disks, wrap in plastic, and place in refrigerator for 30 minutes (save one for another use).

Preheat the oven to 400° F.

Flour a board well, sprinkle flour on top of pastry disk, and flour rolling pin. Roll pastry to an 11-inch circle, fold in half, and transfer to 9-inch pie pan. Fit, without stretching, into the pan. Fold overhang under edge and press into upright rim. Use thumb and forefinger to press into decorative pattern. Prick with fork, line with foil, and fill with pie weights or beans and bake for 15 minutes; remove foil and weights and return to oven until golden brown, about 10 minutes. Let cool.

For filling, combine the sugar and cornstarch in a saucepan and gradually stir in the hot water. Place over moderate heat and, stirring constantly, cook until the mixture thickens and boils. Boil 1 minute, then beat about ½ cup of the mixture into the egg yolks. Beating constantly, turn the yolks back into the hot mixture and return to the heat. Stir and boil 1 minute longer. Remove from heat and blend in the butter, lemon juice, and lemon rind. Pour into the pie shell.

Make meringue. Beat egg whites until frothy, then add and beat in cream of tartar. As whites thicken, gradually add sugar, beating well to absorb each addition. Continue to beat until whites are stiff and glossy. Pile meringue onto filling, making sure the meringue meets the crust all the way around leaving no filling visible. This is important to keep it from pulling away as it cools. With a spoon or knife, make decorative pattern on top. Place on middle rack of oven and bake until lightly browned, 6 to 8 minutes.

Two-Crust Lemon Pie

Yields one 8-inch pie

The unusual filling made with fresh lemon gives this pie a wonderful zest.

PASTRY

1½ cups all-purpose flour
½ teaspoon salt
½ cup plus 1 tablespoon solid vegetable shortening
1 teaspoon vinegar
4 tablespoons cold water

FILLING

1¼ cups plus 1 tablespoon sugar
2 tablespoons flour
⅛ teaspoon salt
¼ cup (½ stick) lightly salted butter
3 large eggs, well beaten (reserve 1 tablespoon of white)
½ cup water
1 teaspoon grated lemon rind
1 medium lemon, peeled and thinly sliced

Preheat the oven to 400° F.

Combine flour and salt in a mixing bowl. Cut in shortening with a pastry blender until mixture resembles coarse meal. Sprinkle with the vinegar and water a tablespoon at a time, and mix with a fork until all the flour is moistened. Gather together with fingers until dough cleans the bowl. Press into a ball, then divide in half and roll out onto a well-floured board. Roll into circle 1 inch larger than pie pan and fit into 8-inch pan.

Mix 1¼ cups sugar with flour and salt in the bowl of an electric mixer. Add the butter and blend well. Add the eggs and beat until smooth. Stir in the water with the lemon rind and slices and mix well. Pour filling into pastry-lined pan. Roll out top crust, moisten edge of bottom pastry, and place pastry on top, pressing edges to seal. Turn top edge under bottom edge and flute. Brush top with reserved egg white, and sprinkle with about 1 tablespoon of sugar. Bake on middle rack for 30 to 35 minutes, or until top is golden brown.

Lemon Curd

Yields 1¼ cups

Lemon curd as it is known in England is actually a lemon cream. It is invaluable for filling many desserts. The time and patience spent in preparation is well worth the effort.

5 large egg yolks
½ cup sugar
   Juice and grated rind of 2 large lemons
4 tablespoons (½ stick) unsalted butter

In a heavy saucepan over medium-low heat, mix the yolks and sugar for about 3 minutes with a wooden spoon. Stirring constantly, add the lemon juice and grated rind. At this point, if you have a hand-held electric beater, use it, as the recipe will be completed more quickly. Add the butter in small amounts and keep stirring until the mixture becomes thick. When the mixture begins to take on a lighter yellow color, the bubbles on the surface disappear, and you can coat the back of spoon with the cream, it will be done. This should take about 20 minutes with an electric beater. Using a spoon will add an extra 10 minutes. Remove from heat and cool.

Tropical Lime Pie

Serves 6–8

Not as rich as the traditional Key Lime Pie, this has the same intense flavor. Use the dark green, thicker-skinned limes for grating since they give a better color and are easier to grate. If only the smaller, thin-skinned ones are available you will need more than one to give sufficient grated peel. This pie can be made with a conventional pastry crust or with chocolate wafers.

- ⅔ *cup sugar*
- 3 *tablespoons cornstarch*
- 2 *teaspoons grated lime rind*
- ⅓ *cup fresh lime juice*
- 1 *cup milk (do not substitute skim or low-fat)*
- 3 *tablespoons lightly salted butter or margarine, cut into pieces*
- 1 *cup sour cream*
- 1 *pre-baked 9-inch pie shell (see page 132)*
- 1 *cup whipping cream*
- 6–8 *thin slices of lime*

Mix sugar, cornstarch, and lime rind in a medium saucepan, blending well. Stir in lime juice, then milk, and add butter. Place over medium heat, stirring constantly, until mixture comes just to a boil and starts to thicken. It will take about 10 minutes. Remove from heat and cool to room temperature, stirring occasionally. Fold in the sour cream and turn into pie shell. Chill for 30 minutes or more before serving. Whip the cream and place a dollop on each serving; garnish with a thin slice of lime, twisted.

Lemon Sponge Pudding

Serves 4–6

There are countless versions of this dessert. This one comes to us from a friend, who by clever persuasion pried it from an innkeeper in Yorkshire, England.

- ½ *cup (1 stick) lightly salted butter*
- 1½ *cups sugar*
- ½ *cup all-purpose flour*
- ¼ *teaspoon salt*
- 6 *tablespoons lemon juice*
- 1½ *tablespoons grated lemon rind*
- 1½ *cups milk*
- 6 *large eggs, separated*

Preheat the oven to 300° F. Butter a 2-quart baking dish or pan.

Cream the butter and sugar together in a mixer bowl. Add the flour and salt to the sugar mixture, mix, then add the lemon juice, lemon rind, milk, and egg yolks, and beat thoroughly. Whip the egg whites until stiff, then fold into the batter, gently and completely. Bake 45 to 50 minutes on the middle oven rack. When done the top will be a light brown and the edges will begin to pull away from pan sides. The top will be a light baked sponge, the bottom will form a thick sauce. When serving, cut through from top to bottom, so each serving will receive both cake and sauce.

Lemon Sherbet

Serves 4

If the lemons are large enough, you can halve them, scoop out all the flesh, and fill the cavity with the sherbet. It looks really pretty if the lemon shell is served on a large green leaf, freshly picked from the garden and well washed.

 2 *large lemons*
 1 *cup milk*
 1 *cup light cream*
 1 *cup sugar*

Grate the rind from the lemons and then juice them. Stir together the grated rind and juice with the remaining ingredients and blend well. Transfer to an ice cream maker and process according to the manufacturer's instructions, or put in a container and place in freezer. When frozen, puree again until smooth and light in a blender or food processor, or beat with an electric or hand rotary beater. Pack in a container and return to freezer. Soften slightly to serve.

Lemon Squares

Yields sixteen 2-inch squares

These are good at any time with a cup of tea or coffee. Serve as a simple dessert or enhance with some sliced strawberries, a few raspberries, or blueberries. Best of all, they are easy to make.

BASE

 ½ *cup (1 stick) lightly salted butter*
 ¼ *cup confectioners' sugar*
 1 *cup all-purpose flour*

TOPPING

 1 *cup sugar*
 2 *large eggs, at room temperature*
 3 *tablespoons lemon juice*
 ¼ *teaspoon grated lemon rind*
 2 *tablespoons flour*
 ½ *teaspoon baking powder*
    Confectioners' sugar for dusting

Preheat the oven to 350° F. Butter an 8-inch baking pan, bottom and sides.

In a mixer, beat the butter and confectioners' sugar until smooth, then beat in the flour just until it comes together and pulls away from the sides of the bowl. (It may also be made in a processor with the steel blade: Cut butter into several pieces and place with sugar and flour in a work bowl. Process just until it comes together.) Pat dough evenly over the bottom of prepared pan and bake for 20 minutes. Set aside to cool. Maintain oven temperature.

Place sugar, eggs, lemon juice, lemon rind, flour, and baking powder in a food processor or mixer bowl and beat until well blended. Pour over cookie base and bake for 25 minutes. While warm run a spatula around the edges to prevent sticking, then place pan on rack and allow to cool completely before dusting with confectioners' sugar. Cut into squares of desired size.

M·A·N·G·O·S

Mango and Pepper Salad

Fresh Mango Relish

Mango Chutney

Baked Sole with Mangos

Stir-Fried Scallops with Mangos

Chicken and Mango Salad

Veal Scallops with Mango Sauce

Mango Refresher

Mango Sorbet

A few years ago, instead of having its own chapter, the mango would be found with Exotic Fruits. Despite its place as a fruit of first importance in the tropics, the mango has only recently become a familiar fruit to temperate-zone consumers. A native of Southeast Asia, the mango, *Mangifera indica*, has been cultivated in India for more than 4,000 years, but reached us only in the nineteenth century. In 1889 the U.S. Department of Agriculture sponsored a modest mango industry in Florida, the only mainland state with a climate suitable for its cultivation. In recent years Florida has grown from being a minor factor in the domestic mango market to supplying 50 percent of demand in the East. Mexico is still our largest supplier, with a smaller amount of an early season mango variety shipped from Haiti.

With its handsome evergreen foliage, enormous clusters of fragrant pink blossoms, and an impressive height of sixty feet, the mango is a favorite shade tree in the tropics. A charming legend tells of the presentation to Buddha of an extensive mango grove that he might meditate within its protective shade. The fruit can be round, oval, or kidney shaped, and vary in size from less than half a pound to two pounds or more. Depending on ripeness and variety, the brightly colored skin can be green, yellow, orange, red, or purple. This smooth, thin, leatherlike covering protects a bright orange, very juicy flesh that adheres tightly to a flat oval pit. The flesh can be velvety smooth in the best types; the less desirable ones contain woody fibers. The flavor, described as spicy, acid, and sweet, is unique and defies comparison with any other fruit.

⮞ HOME CULTIVATION ⮜

Outside of the tropics, the mango can be grown as an ornamental green plant from the seed. It should be kept above 50° F. and in moist potting soil. It should then germinate in about three weeks. However, it is unlikely to bloom or set fruit.

⮞ NUTRITION ⮜

Mangos are an excellent source of vitamin A and potassium, and a good source of vitamin C. One half-cup has 74 calories.

⮞ SELECTION ⮜

Select a mango that has fully developed color for its variety, that is firm, and free of blemishes. Cradled in the hand, it should yield to gentle pressure, but should not be very soft or shriveled. When fully ripe there is a pleasant fruity aroma. It is better to buy slightly firmer fruit and let it ripen at home for a few days at room temperature. A few markets, mainly catering to a Hispanic population, carry frozen mango, a convenient form that dispenses with pit removal and provides year-round availability.

In this country mangos are rarely identified in the markets as to variety, although the country of origin may be given. The following varieties are grown in Florida, Mexico, and Haiti. Unless otherwise stated, they average ten to sixteen ounces in weight.

Principal Types Presently Available

Haden—Late May and June, from Florida and Mexico. It is a medium, oval fruit, yellow with a crimson blush, has a good, sweet flavor, and contains some fiber.

Tommy Atkins—Late May to July, from Florida and Mexico. A medium to large fruit, it is oval with a broad rounded tip. There is a yellow-orange background with a red blush over most of the fruit. The flesh is somewhat stringy with fairly good flavor.

Francescae—May to June, from Haiti. This mango has an *S*-shape, is green overall, and turns yellow as it ripens. It contains a fair amount of fiber, but is the earliest in our markets.

Also Grown in Mexico and Florida, Not as Common

Van Dyke—June, July. It is small and oval, and has a yellow ground with red blush, and the flesh has little fiber.

Kent—From late June to August. This is a medium to large fruit with average weight eighteen to twenty ounces. It's round with a somewhat tapered end, and is yellow to apricot with dark red blush. The juicy, fiberless flesh is rich and sweet, considered of excellent quality.

Palmer—July, August. It can weigh up to thirty ounces, and has an elongated shape. The color is orange-yellow with a red blush; the flesh has a small amount of fiber and is of good quality.

Keitt—Late July to September. One of the largest, it can weigh up to 48 ounces, although the average size is just a little over half this weight. It has an oval shape with green ground, and is the only one with a yellow blush instead of red. It has a smooth, fiber-free flesh, with a small seed, and has a fairly sweet flavor.

```
┌─────────────────────────────────────────┐
│               EQUIVALENTS                 │
│  1 mango  =  approximately 1 cup of flesh │
└─────────────────────────────────────────┘
```

STORAGE
✤ AND PREPARATION ✤

Do not refrigerate until ripened at room temperature. Once ripe, mangos can be refrigerated for about a week. Removal of the pit is the real challenge in preparation, since the fiber clings to the pit with incredible tenacity (also between your teeth). Therefore, those varieties that have less fiber are definitely preferred. The flesh is very soft, and any cutting method that requires pressure will result in a messy puree and juice. The recommended method is to cut along each side of the pit, leaving a center rim of skin around the pit's length, and providing two cutaway sections. It is then possible to remove the fruit from the skin by slicing or with a spoon.

The center strip of flesh and skin can then be cut away from the seed with a knife. To do this, remove the pit, cut "spokes" into the ring, and then cut around the hole left by the pit to free the pieces.

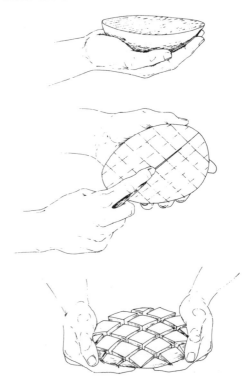

The two cutaway sections can be cubed by the so-called hedgehog technique. Hold each half, skin side down, in the palm of the hand, and make crosswise cuts through the flesh just to the skin. Turn the skin inside out, and you will have your hedgehog ready to slice from the skin into cubes.

In a third method, peel the skin and use a sharp knife to slice away from the pit in lengthwise slices.

Mangos need no special treatment to preserve the fresh color or flavor after they are cut.

⇝   ⇝

Mangos are usually eaten fresh, and despite the messiness of removing the peel are a popular fruit to eat out of hand in the tropical areas where they're grown. They are wonderful in salads and sauces sprinkled just with lime juice. Mangos take well to the Indian spices, turmeric, cumin, cardamom, and spicy peppers for both sweet and savory dishes. Add a bit of crystallized ginger to a serving of mango ice cream or beat up a cooling mango drink for a refreshing tropical conclusion to a summer meal. Chutneys and pickles made with ripe and green mangos are a traditional accompaniment to Eastern curries, but can serve equally well to accent American-style barbecued meat, fish, or poultry. Dried mangos added to hiker's trail food give a lift to the usual raisins and nuts. When mangos are plentiful and at their peak ripeness, freeze some of the pulp for future use.

Mango and Pepper Salad

Serves 4

If you're not careful, this salad may over-shadow the main dish. The contrast of the clear orange of the mango and the green of the peppers is striking and colorful and only the smallest amount of dressing is required to bring out the flavors.

- *1 small sweet Italian green pepper*
- *2 tablespoons cider vinegar*
- *2 mangos (12–14 ounces each)*
- *½ red bell pepper, seeded and coarsely diced*
- *½ green bell pepper, seeded and coarsely diced*
- *2 tablespoons canola or other vegetable oil*
   Salt and freshly ground pepper to taste
   Loose-headed lettuce for lining plates

Seed the Italian pepper, cut into julienne strips, and place in a small bowl. Pour the vinegar over and marinate for about 3 hours. Peel the mangos and dice the flesh into 1-inch cubes. Set aside in a separate bowl. Finely dice the red and green peppers and add to the mangos.

Shortly before serving, remove the Italian pepper from the vinegar and add it to the mango mixture. Combine the oil with the vinegar and stir vigorously to blend. Stir into the mangos and peppers and mix well. Season with salt and pepper. To serve, line individual plates with lettuce and spoon the salad on top of the lettuce leaves.

Fresh Mango Relish

Yields 1 cup

This relish may be used almost like a sauce and spread over grilled or baked chicken, or a grilled piece of steak or fish. As it is spicy, it is more suitable for hearty fish like tuna or swordfish.

- *1 teaspoon canola or other vegetable oil*
- *¼ cup finely chopped red onion*
- *1 teaspoon minced jalapeño pepper*
- *1 ripe mango (12–14 ounces)*
- *1 tablespoon dark brown sugar*
- *1 teaspoon peeled and minced fresh ginger*
   Juice of 1 lime
- *1 tablespoon cider vinegar*
   Salt and freshly ground black pepper to taste
- *2 teaspoons chopped cilantro (fresh coriander)*

(continued on next page)

In a saucepan heat the oil, add the onion and jalapeño pepper, and cook over medium heat, stirring occasionally, until the onion is soft, about 5 minutes.

Peel the mango and cut the flesh into ½-inch cubes. Add to saucepan. Add the brown sugar, ginger, lime juice, and vinegar. Cook over low heat for about 10 minutes, stirring occasionally. Season to taste, remove from heat, and mix in the cilantro. Cool, cover, and place in the refrigerator until ready to serve.

Mango Chutney

Yields 2½ cups

Most of the chutneys in India are made from fresh ingredients and served uncooked. This chutney is cooked, but still retains all of the richly complex flavor. Needless to say, it goes well with Indian food but will also enliven any number of other dishes.

    4 underripe mangos (10–12 ounces each)
    ½ teaspoon salt
    1 cup cider vinegar
    2 large garlic cloves, minced
       Cayenne pepper to taste
    1 teaspoon peeled and chopped fresh ginger
    1 teaspoon garam masala (see Note)
    ¾ cup sugar
    ½ cup dark or golden raisins

Peel the mangos and slice into thick pieces. Discard the pits. Place in a large bowl and sprinkle with salt.

Put the vinegar, garlic, spices, and sugar into a saucepan and bring to a boil. Lower the heat and simmer for about 15 minutes. Add the mangos and raisins and simmer until thick and syrupy, about 20 to 25 minutes.

Remove from the heat, cool, then put into airtight jars and store in the refrigerator.

NOTE: Garam masala is a mixture of fragrant ground spices, usually including coriander, cinnamon, black pepper, cloves, cumin, and nutmeg. There are many variations and strengths. Rather than make the mixture yourself, visit an Indian or oriental market and purchase a small amount that has already been prepared.

Baked Sole with Mangos

Serves 4

You can use either fresh or frozen mangos (thawed) and any mild white fish, preferably not too thick.

    1½ teaspoons soy sauce
     1 garlic clove, finely minced
    1½ pounds sole fillets
    1½ cups mango pieces
     1 teaspoon peeled and grated fresh ginger
     2 tablespoons lime juice
     ½ teaspoon salt
     ⅛ teaspoon cayenne pepper, or to taste

Preheat the oven to 375° F.

Mix 1 teaspoon of the soy sauce with the minced garlic. Place fish in a shallow baking dish just large enough to fit it in one layer, and spread with soy and garlic mixture. Allow to stand for 30 minutes or more.

Combine the mango, ginger, remaining ½ teaspoon soy sauce, lime juice, salt, and cayenne and spread over the fish. Place on the top rack of the oven and bake about 10 minutes depending on thickness of the fish. Fish is done when it flakes easily and is opaque.

Stir-Fried Scallops with Mangos

Serves 4

This recipe is an adaptation of a dish that Dorrit's son enjoyed in Hong Kong and related to her. Once the ingredients are organized, the meal can be prepared within 10 minutes.

1¼ pounds scallops
½ teaspoon sesame oil
1 tablespoon rice wine
¼ teaspoon salt
1 teaspoon sugar
2½ teaspoons cornstarch
2 ripe, firm mangos (about 12 ounces each)
3 ounces snow peas
1 medium carrot
1 tablespoon canola or other vegetable oil
1 teaspoon peeled and thinly sliced fresh ginger
½ teaspoon water
¼ cup concentrated chicken stock

Wash and pat dry the scallops with paper towels. If they are too large, cut them in half. In a shallow pie plate or flat serving plate, combine the sesame oil, rice wine, salt, sugar, and 2 teaspoons of the cornstarch. Place the scallops in the marinade, coat well, cover, and refrigerate for 45 minutes. Drain and pat dry with paper towels.

Peel the mangos, remove the flesh, and dice into pieces about the same size as the scallops. Cut the stems and string the snow peas, place in a small saucepan of water, bring to a boil, blanch for 10 seconds, and immediately drain under cold water. Put in paper towels to dry. Scrape and cut the carrot

into thin slices on the diagonal. Set all aside.

In a wok or large skillet, heat the oil, add the scallops, and cook over medium-high heat for 3 to 5 minutes, stirring. Remove, place on a plate, and set aside. Add the ginger and carrot to the wok and cook for 2 to 3 minutes over medium-high heat, stirring. Mix the remaining ½ teaspoon cornstarch and the water and add to the wok together with the chicken stock. Cook until the liquid has thickened slightly, about a minute. Return the scallops to the wok, add the mangos and snow peas, and cook, stirring until heated through, about 30 seconds. Serve immediately with rice.

Chicken and Mango Salad

Serves 4

1½ pounds skinned and boneless chicken breasts
    Freshly ground pepper to taste
1 tablespoon unsalted butter
2 teaspoons canola or other vegetable oil
2 mangos (about 12 ounces each)
4 ounces snow peas
1 (8-ounce) can whole water chestnuts
½ cup low-fat mayonnaise
½ cup plain low-fat yogurt
    Juice of 1 lime
1 teaspoon tomato paste
    Salt
    Pinch of cayenne pepper
8 leaves of loose-head green lettuce
½ red bell pepper, cut into fine julienne strips

(continued on next page)

Wash the chicken and pat dry. Season with pepper. In a large skillet, heat the butter and oil, add the chicken, and cook over medium heat for about 5 minutes. Turn and cook for a further 5 minutes or until the juices run clear when pricked with a knife and the chicken springs back to the touch. Remove from the heat and cool. Cut into bite-size pieces, about ¾ inches. If not using immediately, wrap in plastic wrap, unsliced, and refrigerate for up to 2 days.

Peel the mangos and cut the flesh from the pits. Cube into ¾-inch pieces. Set aside. Remove the stems and strings from the snow peas. Put a small amount of water in a saucepan, bring to a boil, add the snow peas, return the water to a boil, and blanch for 10 seconds. Immediately drain and rinse with cold water to retain their crispness. Place on paper towels and pat dry. Drain the water chestnuts and cut each into thirds. Set aside.

In a small bowl, combine the mayonnaise, yogurt, lime juice, and tomato paste. Mix well, season with salt and pepper, and sprinkle with just a touch of cayenne pepper.

Line a large serving platter or individual serving plates with lettuce. Mix the chicken, mangos, snow peas, and water chestnuts. Carefully stir in the dressing and blend well. Spoon onto the platter or individual plates and arrange the red pepper in a decorative pattern on the salad.

Veal Scallops with Mango Sauce

Serves 4

The pureed mango that is the basis for this sauce has a wonderful peachy golden color and a texture that is smooth and light. Serve this with small new potatoes and asparagus. For a change, you can substitute sautéed shrimp for the veal.

- *2 ripe mangos (12–14 ounces each)*
- *2 tablespoons sugar*
- *2 tablespoons water*
- *¼ cup red wine vinegar*
- *½ cup plain low-fat yogurt*
- *1 teaspoon cornstarch*
- *2 cups chicken stock*
- *Salt and freshly ground pepper to taste*
- *1 tablespoon lemon juice*
- *4 veal scallops (about 4 ounces each)*
- *Flour, for dredging*
- *1 tablespoon unsalted butter*
- *1 tablespoon canola or other vegetable oil*

Peel 1 of the mangos, remove the flesh, and cut into chunks. In a food processor or blender, puree until smooth and set aside; you will have approximately ¾ cup puree. Peel and slice the remaining mango into neat pieces and set aside.

In medium saucepan, combine the sugar and water, bring to a boil, and cook over high heat, swirling the pan until the sugar is dissolved and begins to caramelize. (Check that the sugar does not burn.) Lower the heat to medium, add the vinegar, and stir vigorously until well blended. Combine the yogurt with the cornstarch; this prevents separation on contact with heat. Add it to the sugar mixture, along with the chicken stock and pureed mango. Increase the heat to medium-high and reduce, stirring at intervals, until 1 cup remains. Season to taste and stir in the tablespoon of lemon juice. Keep hot.

Dredge the veal scallops with flour, shaking off the excess. In a large frying pan, melt the butter and oil, add the meat, and sauté over medium-high heat for about 4 minutes on each side. Remove and set aside. Spoon the sauce equally on 4 individual serving plates. Place a piece of veal on top of the sauce, and arrange 3 slices of mango in a fan shape.

⁋ ⁋

Mango Refresher

Serves 2

Throughout the tropics, the sidewalks and markets are studded with fresh-fruit-drink bars. We so enjoyed a mango drink at one such fruit bar in Jakarta that we created our own.

- ½ cup fresh orange juice
- 2 cups fresh mango, peeled, seeded, and chopped
- 1 teaspoon sugar, or to taste
- 1 tablespoon fresh lime juice
- 8 ice cubes
  Fresh mint for garnish

Combine all the ingredients in a blender or food processor and process until the mixture is smooth. Garnish with sprigs of fresh mint.

Mango Sorbet

Yields 3 cups

An intense mango flavor, cool and invigorating. Good alone, or served as a scoop over fruit salad, or with vanilla ice cream. As an extra treat, serve with grated chocolate.

- 1¼ cups water
- ¾ cup sugar
- 2–3 mangos (*about 2 pounds total*)
- 6 tablespoons fresh lime juice
- 2 tablespoons lemon juice

In a small saucepan, combine the water and sugar, bring to a boil, and cook over medium heat for 5 minutes, or until sugar is dissolved. Remove from heat, pour into a container, and chill for 1½ hours.

Peel the mangos, remove flesh from pits, and cut into large chunks. Place in the bowl of a blender or food processor and process until smooth. Transfer to a container and chill for 1 hour.

Combine the sugar syrup, mango puree, and lime and lemon juice in a blender or food processor and process until well mixed. Transfer to an ice cream maker and process according to the manufacturer's directions. Or pour into a wide container and place in freezer. When frozen, puree again until smooth and light in a blender or food processor or beat with an electric or hand rotary beater. Pack in a container and return to freezer. Soften slightly to serve.

M·E·L·O·N·S

Watermelon Hors d'Oeuvre

Honeydew and Cantaloupe with Capicola

Lime and Honeydew Melon Soup

Three Melon Summer Soup

Veal Curry with Honeydew Melon

Chilled Watermelon with Blueberry Sauce

Spiced Cantaloupe Pickle

Watermelon Sorbet

Watermelon, Strawberries, and Kiwis with Banana Sauce

Early writings and art place the origin of melons in the Middle East, although there is some possibility that they appeared in northern India at about the same period. Egyptian paintings dated at 2400 B.C. show fruit that has been identified as the melon, and we read in the Bible, Numbers 11:5, "We remember the fish, which we did eat in Egypt freely; the cucumbers, and the melons. . . ." At a later period the melon is referred to as the chief food of the poorer Egyptians. This reference may well have been to the watermelon, *Citrullus lanatus*, as it is believed to have been found growing along the banks of the Nile in the time of the pharoahs.

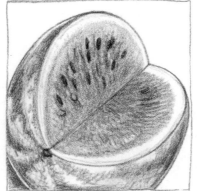

A second melon group, *Cucumis melo*, of Persian origin includes our familiar cantaloupe, also known as the muskmelon because of its fragrance when ripe. It was known to the Romans in the early Christian era and carried to the New World by Colum-bus on his second voyage in 1494. *C. melo* encompasses two broad categories. First, there is the netted melon (which includes the cantaloupe) with a raised network, generally lighter in color than the background green or yellow. Some of these are smooth; others have deep vertical grooves. These melons do best in a warm sunny climate, but they can be grown in nearly all regions of the United States. California, Arizona, Texas, and Colorado produce nearly two-thirds of the total amount marketed. The second category, referred to as not netted or smooth, are also called winter melons. Their skin may be smooth, corrugated, or ridged, and the flesh varies from palest green to deep orange. Among these are the Casaba, Crenshaw, Persian, and honeydew melons, which are principally grown in hot climates around the Mediter-ranean, Africa, the Caribbean, and Central and South America.

The watermelon most of us know best is the huge, dark green one served throughout the country at Fourth of July picnics and celebrations. The familiar oblong melon has a thick rind covering a rosy red, succulent flesh patterned with dark brown seeds. Many new varieties have been developed that allow us the choice of small and round, yellow flesh instead of red, and now, the popular seedless. Watermelons have traditionally come from our southern states and Texas, but with new smaller varieties, even in New England they are being grown on a local commercial scale.

❧ HOME CULTIVATION ❧

Southern gardeners can grow cantaloupe and watermelon with little problem other than space, since the vines will spread six or more feet in all directions from the base of the plant. In colder climates you're better off with varieties developed for short maturation periods, generally 68 to 80 days. In the television series, "The Victory Garden," cantaloupes were grown on a fence to conserve space and hasten ripening. When they were about grapefruit size each melon was placed in a netting bag attached to the fence, since the vine alone would not be able to hold the full weight of the mature fruit.

❧ NUTRITION ❧

Melons are about 94 percent water and about 6 percent sugar, making them a good diet food. They also contain vitamins C and A. Half of a five-inch cantaloupe has 60 calories, an eight-ounce slice of honeydew melon 55 calories, and a two-pound slice of watermelon 110 calories.

❧ SELECTION ❧

When fully ripe a cantaloupe will lift easily away from the stem, leaving a clean indentation behind. This condition, known as full slip, is an important indication of mature fruit. A good melon should be symmetrical, and the blossom end (this is the end opposite the stem) should give with slight pressure. These two signs are more important than color alone, although as a cantaloupe ripens it will develop more yellow. Avoid melons that look lumpy with pronounced soft spots, since they are overripe. With winter melon varieties, the color should be good for the type and there should be the same sort of give with pressure at the blossom end, however these melons do not separate from the stem; when harvested the stems are cut from the vine. If a winter melon is rock hard, don't buy it! It will become softer as it stands but it will not become sweeter.

There is no certain way to judge a whole watermelon. Cut sections, though more expensive on a per pound basis, make choosing far easier. Select a piece with mostly dark seeds and a deep rosy red flesh that has a crisp, compact look. If it is very pale with white seeds, it is immature; if it has a dark, purple cast, it is past its prime.

Varieties

Cantaloupe or Muskmelon—May be round or slightly oval with light netting over a background of green to orange. The flesh is salmon color, juicy, sweet, and when fully ripe, cuts easily with a spoon. A new Mini-loupe is being developed—a melon small enough to sell in food dispensing machines! The California and Arizona melons harvested June through November are rated best for flavor.

Casaba—Large, somewhat flattened at the stem end and pointed at the blossom end. The coarse skin is dark green to yellow; the flesh is pale green, with little flavor. Canary melon is a variant with a brilliant canary yellow and roughly corrugated skin. Santa Claus, yet another type, is slightly smaller, with a smooth, mottled, dark green and yellow skin.

Crenshaw—A cross of the Casaba and Cantaloupe, is rounded at the stem end and pointed at the blossom end. It has dark green skin that becomes yellow as it ripens. The succulent flesh is light coral, with an excellent full flavor.

Honeydew—Large, palest green to light yellow skin when ripe. The flesh is light green to white with a very sweet but mild flavor. If the blossom end does not give with slight pressure, and the melon is more green than yellow, it is not ripe. The orange-flesh honeydew is generally a bit smaller, but doesn't differ much in flavor.

Persian—Large, nearly round, gray-green, smooth skin under a light gray netting. The flesh is a deep salmon with a good full flavor. The Sharlyn is a variant with similar characteristics.

Watermelon—Rind is hard, may be dark or light green depending on variety, has pronounced stripes, is a large (up to thirty pounds) oblong melon. The flesh is rosy red with many seeds, which may be brown or near black with some immature white ones.

The smaller round Sugar Baby variety, sometimes called "ice-box" referring to its size, is one of the types found in the northern farm markets. The seedless red, another small type, has a somewhat smoother flesh with a sweet and reliably good flavor. The new yellow-flesh type has a flavor very much like the red, and has no advantage except for its novelty.

EQUIVALENTS	
1⅛ pounds	= fifty ⅞-inch melon balls
1½ pounds watermelon with rind	= 3 cups ½-inch dice
1¼ pounds honeydew melon	= 2½ cups ½-inch dice
1 average size cantaloupe	= 2 pounds
	= 3½ cups ½-inch dice

These weights are approximate and will vary with the amount of rind discarded. They are given as guidelines for purchasing melons.

STORAGE AND PREPARATION

A ripe cantaloupe that is slightly green and firm can be kept at room temperature until it softens and becomes golden yellow. It may be slightly chilled for serving, but overly cold melon will not be as flavorsome. Winter melons can be held at room temperature in the same way until there is an overall springy feel (not mushy), then chill to serve.

To serve cantaloupe in halves or slices simply cut in half, usually lengthwise, and remove seeds. For wedges or slices, cut until desired size is obtained.

For cubes, use a long sharp knife and cut under the flesh to loosen it from the skin, then cut across into slices of the desired width.

To make melon balls, push a melon baller directly into the melon, give a slight twist and scoop out. These look attractive, but there is more waste than with cubes.

You can make melon containers from small melons by removing the seeds and using the resulting cavity, or scoop out the flesh, make a decorative scalloped or serrated edge, and refill with the scooped-out fruit mixed with berries or other cut fruit.

Watermelon is best served well chilled, usually in wedges, but can be cubed and seeded, or shaped into balls.

To make a watermelon bowl or basket, use a long sharp knife and cut off the top, horizontally, three fourths of the way up from the bottom. For a bowl, cut completely across; for a basket, cut to center from each side leaving a band two inches wide to form the handle. Once you have removed the flesh you can scallop the edges, and even carve designs in the rind. To use a round melon you will need to cut a slice of the rind from the bottom to make it sit upright. Fill it with a colorful mixture of cut fruit and berries as a gorgeous edible centerpiece for a summer buffet.

‎❧   ❧

All varieties of melon can be chilled and cut into wedges, cubes, or balls to be served at breakfast, lunch, or dinner. You can mix them with each other or very nearly any other fruit for a cocktail mix with a simple lemon or lime juice dressing as the beginning or end of your meal. Pureed, they make excellent chilled summer soups with the addition of a dry white wine, citrus juice, and a bit of mint. A wedge of watermelon or cantaloupe makes a colorful and refreshing garnish to a dinner plate. Melons make excellent preserves and pickles, but they are really at their very best when served in peak season—fully ripe and succulent.

Watermelon Hors d'Oeuvre

Serves 6

In the South a chilled watermelon might be cut and served at nearly any time of day, always with a shaker of salt handy. Here we borrow a taste tip from our neighbors south of the border and add lime juice, tequila, and a touch of hot pepper sauce for an appetizer that is refreshing and fun. This is a good outdoor food for a casual party.

1 cup lime juice
1 teaspoon tequila
½ teaspoon salt
¼ teaspoon hot pepper sauce (see Note)
5 pounds ripe seedless watermelon, cut into 1-inch cubes

Mix lime juice, tequila, salt, and hot pepper sauce in a small bowl suitable for dipping cubes. Taste for seasoning. Pile the cubed watermelon on a platter with skewers for each person to use to dip into the lime juice mixture.

NOTE: You might wish to serve 2 bowls of juice—one medium and one very hot to suit individual tastes.

Honeydew and Cantaloupe with Capicola

Serves 4

1 honeydew melon
1 cantaloupe
8 thin slices capicola
Parsley sprigs
4 lime wedges

Halve each melon, then cut each half into 3 slices lengthwise, totaling 12 slices in all. Place 3 slices of melon, mixing the colors, along one side of each of 4 individual serving plates. Arrange 2 slices of capicola on the other side of each plate to make an attractive presentation. Garnish with a few sprigs of parsley clustered together. Serve with lime wedges.

Lime and Honeydew Melon Soup

Serves 4

A nice prelude to a hot spicy meal. If you can't find ginger marmalade use candied ginger.

> 3 cups cubed honeydew melon
> 6 tablespoons fresh lime juice
> 3 tablespoons ginger marmalade
> ¼ cup chicken stock
> 3 tablespoons plain yogurt
> 4 thin slices of lime, for garnish
>   Sweet paprika

In a medium bowl combine the melon and lime juice and chill, covered, for 1 hour. In a blender or food processor puree the melon mixture for about 1 minute, add the marmalade, stock, and yogurt and blend just until smooth. Chill for at least 30 minutes. Stir before serving and garnish with thin slices of lime sprinkled with the paprika.

Three Melon Summer Soup

Serves 4

A perfect hot-weather soup served refreshingly cold with a touch of mint. Make when melons are at their peak of flavor.

> 1 cup orange juice
> 1½ cups cubed cantaloupe
> 1½ cups cubed honeydew melon
> ⅓ cup lime juice
> ¼ cup honey
> 2 tablespoons sugar
> 2 teaspoons fresh mint finely chopped, by hand
> 1 cup cubed watermelon, in ¼-inch pieces
> 2 cups chilled sparkling wine

In a blender or food processor, puree the orange juice, cantaloupe, honeydew, lime juice, honey, and sugar. Pour into a bowl and stir in the mint, watermelon, and wine. Cover and chill for at least 2 hours before serving.

Veal Curry with Honeydew Melon

Serves 6

This recipe acquired on a trip to Bhutan three years ago is an adaptation of an Indian dish. It was served with a simply prepared rice and green bean casserole.

    1 tablespoon canola or other vegetable oil
    1 tablespoon unsalted butter
    2 large onions, finely chopped
    2 pounds lean veal cut from the shoulder,
       cut into 3/4-inch pieces
    1 teaspoon ground ginger
    1 teaspoon ground cumin
    1 teaspoon sugar
    1 teaspoon salt
    1 tablespoon ground coriander
    1/2 teaspoon ground cinnamon
    1/2 teaspoon turmeric
    1/2 teaspoon dried mint
       Dash of cayenne pepper
       Freshly ground pepper to taste
    1 cup beef stock
    1/4 cup fresh lime juice
    1/4 cup light cream, or low-fat yogurt mixed
       with 1 teaspoon cornstarch
    3 cups honeydew melon, peeled, seeded,
       and cut into 3/4-inch cubes

In a large saucepan, heat the oil and butter, add the onions, and cook over medium-high heat until softened, about 8 to 10 minutes. Add the veal, mixing with the onions but do not brown the meat. Add all the spices and the beef stock. Cover, lower the heat, and simmer for 1 hour, or until the meat

is tender, stirring occasionally to prevent any meat from sticking to the bottom of the pan. Add the lime juice and the cream and stir until completely blended. Add the melon cubes, stir to mix, remove from the heat, and serve immediately.

Chilled Watermelon with Blueberry Sauce

Serves 4

    1 pint fresh blueberries
    1/4 cup sugar
    1 tablespoon orange juice
    3 tablespoons fresh lime juice
    2-pound watermelon

Wash and pick over the blueberries. Combine the sugar, orange juice, and 1 tablespoon of the lime juice in a saucepan. Bring to a boil over medium-high heat and cook for 2 minutes, stirring occasionally until the sugar has dissolved. Add the berries and continue cooking until the liquid returns to a boil. Remove from the heat and cool to room temperature. This sauce is wonderful served at room temperature and does not have to be chilled ahead of time.

Remove the rind and seeds from the watermelon and cut into bite-size pieces. Place in a serving bowl and toss with the remaining 2 tablespoons of the lime juice. Cover with plastic wrap and chill. Serve individual portions and spoon the blueberry sauce over the watermelon.

Spiced Cantaloupe Pickle

Yields 2½ pints

Although this type of pickle is usually served as a condiment with poultry and meats such as roast pork or ham, it makes a delicious and unusual dessert sauce when cut into small dice and poured over vanilla or ginger ice cream with some of the syrup.

5–6   *pounds slightly underipe cantaloupe*
 ⅓   *cup salt*
 1   *quart water*
3½   *cups sugar*
1½   *cups vinegar*
 2   *cinnamon sticks*
12   *whole cloves*
2½   *cups water*

Cut the cantaloupe in half, then remove the seeds and rind. Cut flesh into 1-inch cubes. Dissolve the salt in the quart of water and pour over cubed melon. Allow to stand for 3 hours, then drain. Place the sugar, vinegar, cinnamon sticks, and cloves with the 2½ cups of water in a large non-reactive kettle and bring to a boil. Stir until the sugar is dissolved. Add the drained fruit and return to a boil. Boil gently for 10 minutes, remove from heat, and allow to cool. Cover and let stand at room temperature overnight.

The next day, remove the cantaloupe from the syrup, set aside, and bring the syrup to a boil for ten minutes, then add the cantaloupe and return to a boil. Lower the heat and simmer gently for 45 minutes or more. When done, the melon will be completely translucent. Pour into jars and seal. May be kept refrigerated indefinitely.

Watermelon Sorbet

Yields 1½ pints

This sorbet is a lovely shade of pink with a true watermelon flavor that is refreshing at any point in the meal. It's a spectacular dessert served over chilled watermelon cubes— the sorbet absolutely sparkles.

 ½   *cup water*
 ⅓   *cup sugar*
 1   *teaspoon grated lemon rind*
 2   *cups cubed watermelon*
 2   *teaspoons lemon juice*
 1   *teaspoon lime juice*

Combine water and sugar in a small saucepan, bring to a boil, and add the lemon rind. Simmer for 5 minutes, then set aside to cool. Puree the watermelon in a blender or food processor, then add with the lemon and lime juice to the cooled syrup. Freeze in an ice cream maker, following manufacturer's directions, and pack in a freezer carton, or pour into a flat pan (the wider the pan the faster mixture will freeze) and place in freezer. When mixture is frozen, spoon into a chilled bowl and beat with an electric or hand rotary beater until light and smooth. Pack lightly in a freezer carton and return to freezer.

Watermelon, Strawberries, and Kiwis with Banana Sauce

Serves 4–6

The simplest of preparations for a colorful refreshing dessert. The banana sauce provides a soft velvety cloak for the salad.

1¼ pounds watermelon
1 pint fresh strawberries
2 tablespoons fresh lime juice
3 kiwi fruits
   Banana Sauce (*recipe follows*)

Remove the rind and seeds from the watermelon and cut into bite-size pieces. Hull and clean the strawberries. Combine the fruit in a serving dish and toss with the lime juice. Cover with plastic wrap and chill for at least 2 hours, or until ready to serve. Just before serving, peel and slice the kiwis and add to the salad. Serve individually and spoon the Banana Sauce separately over each serving.

Banana Sauce

4 ripe, firm bananas
1 tablespoon fresh lime or lemon juice
3 tablespoons Grand Marnier or Kahlua

Peel and cut the bananas in half lengthwise. Coat with the lime juice, wrap individually in wax paper or plastic wrap, and place in freezer for 3 hours or more. Remove, unwrap, and puree in a food processor until a thick creamy consistency is obtained. Remove to a small serving bowl and blend in the Grand Marnier. This sauce will remain unchanged in color in the refrigerator for 3 hours. After this time, it will assume a light coffee color, but the taste will be unaffected. It should be made only shortly before serving.

O·R·A·N·G·E·S
and
K·U·M·Q·U·A·T·S

Gravlax in Citrus Juices

Gingered Orange and Tomato Soup

Jicama, Lettuce, and Orange Salad

Orange with Mixed Greens Salad

Tangerine Salad

Carrots à l'Orange

Chinese Cabbage with Orange Juice

Mexican Black Beans with Oranges

Parsnips Baked with Oranges

Salad of Smoked Salmon and Orange Slices

Scallops with Orange Sauce

Sole with Oranges

Duck à l'Orange

Roast Chicken with Kumquats

Oxtails with Oranges

Orange Veal

Kumquat Marmalade

Clementines with a Chocolate Dip

Orange Cake

Orange Slices in Grand Marnier

Oranges in Red Wine

The orange and the kumquat had their beginnings in ancient China, possibly as early as 2400 B.C. The orange followed the trade routes from India to Africa and eventually crossed the Mediterranean Sea, first to Spain and then to Italy. Well suited to the area's warm sunny climate, it flourished and was well established in Italy and southern France by the eleventh century. The orange's westward journey was continued by Columbus, who brought the orange to the New World when, on his second voyage in 1494, he carried seed, and possibly saplings, to the island of Hispaniola. Entrance to the United States followed into the subtropical area of St. Augustine, Florida, in the mid-sixteenth century. However, it wasn't until the early eighteenth century that the mission fathers of Mexico set out the first orange trees in the warm climates of Arizona and California.

Meanwhile, in Europe, French royalty had become fascinated with the orange, and in the fifteenth century, Charles VIII had an elaborate building constructed solely to grow the precious golden fruit. Thus was born the Orangerie. This led to something of a royal competition among the princes and kings of various countries, who built ever larger and more ornate buildings with great vaulted galleries and huge walls of south-facing glass. In those days of unlimited servants the trees were planted in tubs that could be rolled outdoors on warm, sunny days and returned to shelter in the case of a chill wind. You can still visit one of the most fabulous of all, the one built for Louis XIV at Versailles. The orange craze traveled northward, and even the English were to leave a heritage of architecturally clever conservatories as a monument to the orange.

In the nineteenth century oranges were still a special treat during the winter months, and depictions of Victorian Christmas frequently show this prized fruit in the bounty of children's Christmas stockings. The orange's blossoms became as much a nuptial symbol as wedding bells. The lovely creamy, virginal white blossoms might grace the bridal brow in the form of a circlet holding her veil in place, cascade from the bouquet she carried, or appear as the groom's boutonniere. Possibly the custom derives from Roman mythology where it is said that when Jupiter married Juno, he presented her with a golden orange on their wedding day.

There are three species of oranges grown commercially: the sweet orange, *Citrus sinensis;* the mandarin, *C. reticulata;* and the sour orange, *C. aurantium.* The sour, or Seville, orange is generally too acidic and bitter for use as a fresh fruit, but it is highly prized for making the finest English marmalades. Grown principally in Spain, it is also commercially important as a flavoring agent for candies and liqueurs such as Curaçao, Grand Marnier, and Cointreau.

Mandarin oranges include tangerines, which are, in this country, grown chiefly in Florida. The group is characterized by the loose skin that readily pulls away from the pulp, and by the segments that are easily separated from each other. The tangelo, a tangerine-grapefruit hybrid, and the temple orange, another hybrid, exhibit the same loose-skin character. Rather than the round shape of the orange, tangerines have a flattened top and bottom.

Of all these types, the sweet orange is the major commercial crop. Arizona and California are able to provide us with fresh oranges throughout the year with two varieties: the Navel orange, originally from Brazil, which is in season November through May, and the Valencia, with a season that starts in February, peaks in May, June, and July, and lasts through October. Florida grows four varieties with overlapping harvesting periods in addition to the tangerines and temple hybrids. Florida produces such notably good juice oranges that 90 percent of the crop is used for that purpose. Oranges provide the base for numerous products, some quite unexpected from such a lovely fruit. A partial list includes marmalade, syrup, wine, candy, a base for perfume, soap, insecticides, and food flavoring. Oil from the seeds can be used for cooking and as a salad oil, and even the leftover pulp can be used, when dried, as feed for cattle.

Orange trees have thick, dark green foliage, clusters of fragrant, waxy white blossoms, and both orange and green fruit year round. The average tree can be expected to yield 1,500 oranges a year, and individual trees have been known to yield as many as 12,000. Oranges do not continue to ripen once they are picked. Those such as Valencias, which ripen in the warmer months, can go through a process known as "regreening." The oranges turn golden before they are fully ripe, and if the weather gets warmer as they hang on the tree to ripen, they actually begin to turn green again, starting at the stem end. This in no way affects either flavor or quality.

The kumquat, also a native of eastern Asia, was brought to Europe in 1846 by Robert Fortune, a plant collector for the London Horticultural Society. Formerly known as *Citrus japonica,* the genus name was changed to *Fortunella* in his honor. It is a small tree with dark green, pointed leaves, often grown as a shrub. The small white blossoms resemble those of the orange in miniature. The fruit's rind is very aromatic and sweet, with a pulp that is very tart. Therefore, when eaten fresh, both the rind and the pulp are consumed together. Because of this tartness, most of the crop is used for preserved whole fruits and marmalade.

❧ HOME CULTIVATION ❧

In tropical and subtropical climates, orange trees are a fragrant and practical addition to the garden. Orange trees will grow from seeds and eventually produce fruit, but it takes twice as long for a seedling tree to bear fruit as it does a grafted one purchased from a nursery. In colder climates oranges are a handsome addition to the greenhouse or conservatory grown in pots or tubs, requiring pruning just to keep them to a manageable size.

❧ NUTRITION ❧

Oranges are a superior source of vitamin C. Tangerines provide a lesser amount, but both yield potassium, calcium, and vitamin A, with smaller amounts of phosphorus and the B vitamins. A three-inch orange contains about 70 calories depending on variety. Six ounces of fresh orange juice has 90 calories.

❧ SELECTION ❧

When selecting oranges, look for thin, unblemished skins on fruit that feels plump and heavy. Navel oranges have naturally thick skins, which makes selection of juicy fruits more difficult, but do not buy fruit with skin that is wrinkled or feels loose. Tangerines with thin skins will have the same plump feel as other citrus fruits but some varieties have a slightly thicker peel that has a loose feel.

These are less reliably juicy than those with thin skins. Juice comes in three forms: frozen concentrate, reconstituted from concentrate, and freshly squeezed. A type of small mandarin orange is the only variety regularly found canned.

Varieties

(Any difference in flavor among varieties is quite subjective since all within a grouping have a similar flavor. Sweetness depends somewhat on the weather conditions as the fruit matures.)

ORANGES

Navel—Known as the Washington Navel, originated in Brazil. It is large, slightly oval, with a "navel" at one end. The peel is thick and a deep orange and is easily removed. Considered primarily an eating orange it is seedless with a sweet flavor. The juice tends to become bitter if squeezed and allowed to sit for a prolonged period, even in the refrigerator. It is one of the principal varieties of Arizona and California, with lesser amounts shipped from Florida.

Valencia—A thinner skinned orange, nearly seedless. It is an important variety in California and Arizona as well as in Florida. It is an excellent juice orange, and the juice may be kept refrigerated overnight without loss of flavor or vitamin C. A tinge of green on the skin does not adversely affect the fruit in any way.

Pineapple Orange—A seeded juice orange. A Florida variety, it is available December through February. It is medium to large size with a pebbly peel.

Hamlin Orange—Also a Florida juice variety, nearly seedless. It has a smooth, thin peel and is available October through December.

Blood Orange—Usually imported from the Mediterranean area. They are now being grown in California. They are small, peel easily, have a somewhat sharp, tangy flavor, and the juice and pulp are a startling blood red.

MANDARINS

Mineola Tangelo—A tangerine-grapefruit hybrid. It looks like an orange, with a deep red-orange color and somewhat pebbly feel. It is somewhat bell shaped, usually with a distinctive bump at the top, has few seeds, and is easy to peel; it is grown in both California and Florida.

Temple Orange—Another hybrid with few seeds and an easy-to-peel skin. It is considered an eating orange with a tangy flavor.

Dancy Tangerine—Small to medium size, with an easy peeling, dark orange skin. It comes from Florida.

Honey Tangerine—Sometimes called Murcott. It is of medium size, has a characteristic flattened shape and a smooth, yellow-orange skin that can be russeted or tinged with green. The skin, as with all tangerines, is easy to peel, and it is thin, making it easy to feel the plumpness of a juicy fruit. Although not the prettiest fruit for a display it is the most reliably sweet and juicy.

Clementine—A cross between the mandarin and Seville orange. It is a small fruit with intense flavor that is grown along the Mediterranean. In New England, they come primarily from Morocco.

KUMQUATS

Kumquats are not sold by varietal name.

Equivalents	
2 to 4 medium oranges	= 1 cup juice
2 medium oranges	= 1 cup bite-size pieces
1 medium orange	= 10 to 12 sections
	= 4 teaspoons grated peel

STORAGE ❧ AND PREPARATION ❧

Oranges may be stored in a cool place for a week or more, but for longer periods should be stored in the refrigerator.

For peeled orange slices, cut a slice of peel off one end, then with a sharp knife cut the peel, including the white pith, in a spiral.

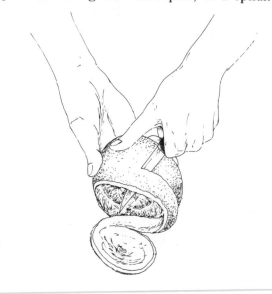

Always cut slices crosswise.

For whole sections, remove peel and any remaining pith or membrane, then slide your knife blade alongside the segment on each side and remove the section, membrane free. Hold over a bowl to catch the juice.

For grated zest (the thin colored part of the peel), make certain that the orange is dry, then use the small holes of a flat grater and rub the fruit back and forth. Use just the zest, not the underlying white pith. To measure, pack lightly in spoon.

For strips of peel use a vegetable peeler to remove thinly to desired size. To julienne, stack several pieces of desired length and cut as thinly as possible into strips.

❧　❧

Oranges have long been noted as an exceptional provider of quickly assimilated energy. Hikers and backpackers have prized them for their refreshing, self-contained juice, and marathon runners gratefully accept orange sections from race route bystanders. Despite these practical considerations, oranges take a prominent place in haute cuisine whether in a delicate soufflé or as a base for a sauce or salad dressing. The sweet-tart flavor can be assertive and assume a dominant role or blend admirably with a host of vegetables as well as other fruits in dishes from soup to dessert. Other citrus fruits and juices combine well with oranges, as do the spices and herbs of various ethnic cuisines such as the North African and Indian foods using cumin, turmeric, cinnamon, aniseed, and cardamom, or the spicy peppers and cilantro of Mexico. Greece, Italy, France, and Spain have for centuries enjoyed the refreshment of fresh oranges simply served over ice, in chilled juice drinks, and in various tarts, custards, and ices.

While thin slices of fresh kumquats are sometimes found in a salad, their tangy sharpness works best when whole fruits are preserved in syrup or made into pickles to be served as a condiment for meats and poultry. Anyone who enjoys marmalade with toast for breakfast will find the distinctive tangy flavor of kumquat marmalade an unusual treat.

Gravlax in Citrus Juices

Serves 18 for cocktails or 10 for a first course

Originally from Scandinavia and made with fresh salmon, gravlax now takes many variations. Even though salmon is still most frequently used, both bluefish and mahi-mahi are excellent. What is most important is to use an oily fish. Serve with lemon wedges, a horseradish, or a Danish mustard sauce, crackers or black bread and butter.

3½–4 *pounds bluefish fillet, center cut, skin left on*
  2½ *tablespoons salt*
  1½ *tablespoons sugar*
   2 *very large bunches fresh dill*
      Juice of 1 medium orange
      Juice of 1 lime
  3–4 *bricks or any other heavy weight that will fit easily over the fish in the dish*

Make certain that the fish is completely free of bones. If need be, use a pair of fishing or other long-armed tweezers to remove them. Combine the salt and sugar. Arrange one-third of the dill in a rectangular glass or enamel dish approximately 10 × 8 × 2 inches. Rub the flesh side of each fillet with

the salt and sugar mixture. Lay one fillet, skin side down, on top of the dill and sprinkle with half the orange and lime juices. Cover with another third of the dill and then the remaining fillet, but reversing the thin side to have the total bulk of fairly even thickness. Finally, pour over the remaining juice and place the last third of dill over the fish. Cover with plastic, place the weights evenly over the surface, and refrigerate.

After 2 days, uncover, turn the fillets, and baste with the juices. Cover and weight again for another 2 days. When ready to serve, remove fish from the marinade, scrape off the dill, and place fish on a suitable carving board. Slice diagonally, detaching the skin, with the knife parallel to the board. Gravlax prepared in this way will keep in the refrigerator for up to 7 days.

❧ ❧

Gingered Orange and Tomato Soup

Serves 6

A light soup with a complex flavor. For winter meals, it is a nice introduction to a roast pork dinner. In summer it can be the one hot food in a primarily cold supper.

3   tablespoons crystallized ginger, cut into
     fine julienne strips
5   cups chicken stock
¾   cup orange juice
     Zest of 1 large orange, preferably not
     navel, in julienne strips
1   tablespoon tomato paste
1¾ pounds tomatoes, seeded, and cut into
     ¼-inch strips
     Salt to taste
     Parsley sprigs for garnish, preferably
     curly type

Soak the ginger in warm water to remove excess sugar. Meanwhile, mix the stock, orange juice, orange zest, and tomato paste in a stainless steel pot. Cut the ginger into narrow strips, add to the broth, and simmer for a few minutes. Add the tomatoes, bring just to a boil, season with salt, remove from heat, and float sprigs of parsley on each serving.

❧ ❧

Jicama, Lettuce, and Orange Salad

Serves 4

The combination of sweet oranges and crunchy jicama with the lettuce makes a colorful and fresh tasting salad.

1   pound jicama
2   navel oranges
¼   cup orange juice
1   teaspoon Dijon mustard
2   tablespoons canola or other vegetable oil
     Salt and freshly ground pepper to taste
1   small head Boston or red-leaf lettuce

Peel and julienne the jicama to make 2 cups. Peel and thinly slice the oranges. In a large bowl, combine the remaining ingredients except lettuce, add the jicama, and mix well. To serve, place the lettuce on the bottom of a large platter and arrange the jicama and oranges over it.

❧ ❧

Orange with Mixed Greens Salad

Serves 6

The salad greens can be any variety available, but it is important to use a very mild onion such as the Vidalia.

1   small head Boston lettuce
6   large leaves red-leaf lettuce
6   inner leaves romaine lettuce
1   large orange, peeled, pith removed, sliced
½   small Vidalia or similar sweet onion,
     sliced into thin rings
2   tablespoons balsamic vinegar
6   tablespoons olive oil
½   teaspoon salt
     Freshly ground pepper to taste
12 pitted black olives (optional)

Wash the lettuces, tear into pieces, and spin dry; cut orange slices into quarters, slice onion and set aside. In a large salad bowl blend the vinegar, olive oil, salt, and pepper. Add the onion, orange, olives, and lettuces and toss just before serving.

Tangerine Salad

Serves 4

For those not familiar with Pickapeppa Sauce, it is a spicy condiment made in Jamaica. Although somewhat peppery, compared to most hot pepper sauces this one is mild but with a unique blending of spices.

- 3 *tablespoons lemon juice*
- 3 *tablespoons canola or other vegetable oil*
- 1½ *teaspoons Pickapeppa Sauce*
- ¾ *teaspoon honey*
  Salt to taste
- 8 *large leaves lettuce such as salad bowl or red-leaf or both*
- 2 *tangerines, sectioned and seeded*
- 2 *tablespoons slivered almonds*

Blend the lemon juice, oil, Pickapeppa Sauce, honey, and salt until thoroughly emulsified. Tear the lettuce into bite-size pieces and place in a salad bowl with the tangerine sections. Pour dressing over, sprinkle with almonds, and toss just before serving.

NOTE: To seed tangerine sections use pointed kitchen scissors to snip out edge of membrane covering seeds and they will pop out.

Carrots à l'Orange

Serves 4

The flavor of carrots is enriched and made more complex by the addition of orange juice and ginger. This vegetable goes equally well with meat or fish.

- 7 *thick carrots, each about 6–7 inches long*
- 2 *tablespoons (¼ stick) unsalted butter or margarine*
- ½ *cup orange juice*
- 2 *tablespoons sugar*
- 1 *teaspoon peeled and minced fresh ginger*
  Salt and freshly ground pepper to taste
- 1 *teaspoon lemon juice*
- 1 *tablespoon chopped fresh parsley*

Clean, scrape, and slice carrots into julienne strips. Place in a saucepan, cover with water, and bring to a boil. Cook for 3 minutes. Drain. In the same saucepan, melt the butter, add the orange juice, sugar, and ginger and return the carrots. Cook over medium-high heat, stirring until most of the liquid has evaporated and the carrots are glazed. Season to taste, sprinkle with lemon juice, and serve with chopped parsley.

Alternatively, use microwave oven. Cut the orange juice to ¼ cup and the lemon juice to ½ teaspoon. Place all the ingredients except the carrots and parsley in a microwave-safe shallow dish and microwave on high for 1 minute, uncovered, just until the butter has melted. Add the carrots, stir, then cover tightly with plastic wrap and cook for about 6 minutes. Cut a slit for air release and let stand for 1 minute. Adjust seasoning and add parsley before serving.

Chinese Cabbage with Orange Juice

Serves 4

Chinese cabbage has a clean, delicate flavor and produces no odor while cooking. The addition of orange juice and a few strips of orange rind rounds off the flavor. The recipe is quick and simple to prepare and it is an especially fine accompaniment to poultry.

- 2 pounds Chinese cabbage
- 1 navel orange
- 1 tablespoon canola or other vegetable oil
- 2 tablespoons finely sliced scallions, including 2 inches of green
- 1 tablespoon peeled and minced fresh ginger
  Salt and freshly ground pepper to taste

Wash the cabbage, cut crosswise into 1-inch pieces, and set aside. Juice the orange, then from the peel cut 12 julienne strips, getting as little pith as possible. Place in a small saucepan, cover with water, bring to a boil, and cook for 2 minutes. Drain and pat dry with paper towels. Set aside.

In a large skillet or wok heat the oil, add the scallions and ginger, and stir for 1 minute. Add the cabbage, stirring vigorously to mix really well, then add the orange juice, cover, and cook for 2 minutes. The cabbage should be hot but crisp and not overcooked. Season with salt and pepper, sprinkle with the julienned orange rind, and serve immediately.

Mexican Black Beans with Oranges

Serves 4

An excellent dish for a cold summer lunch or supper with smoked fish or with grilled or barbecued fish, poultry, or meat. For those who like their food peppery hot, add ¼ teaspoon cayenne pepper.

- 1 large orange, sectioned
- 1 can (16-ounce) black turtle beans, drained and rinsed
- ¾ cup frozen corn kernels, thawed
- 4 scallions, including 1 inch of green, sliced thin
- ½ teaspoon ground cumin
- 2 tablespoons coarsely chopped cilantro (fresh coriander)
- 1 tablespoon balsamic vinegar
- 3 tablespoons olive oil
- ½ teaspoon salt or to taste
- ⅛ teaspoon freshly ground pepper

Cut each orange section into 3 pieces. In a medium serving bowl, combine with the beans, corn, scallions, cumin, cilantro, vinegar, oil, salt, and pepper. Mix thoroughly, taking care not to mash beans. Chill before serving.

Parsnips Baked with Oranges

Serves 4

Serve these parsnips as an unusual side dish. To cut down on the sweetness, use less sugar. The flavor will still be great but they won't be as glazed.

- 1 *pound parsnips*
- 1 *orange, navel or Valencia*
- 1½ *tablespoons dark brown sugar*
- 4 *tablespoons (½ stick) lightly salted butter, melted*
- 5 *tablespoons orange juice*

Preheat the oven to 325° F.

Peel the parsnips and cut into 2-inch lengths, ½ inch thick. Cut the unpeeled orange into ¼-inch slices, then cut into quarters. Stir the brown sugar into the melted butter, heat until dissolved, then stir in the orange juice. Place parsnips and orange slices in a well-buttered shallow baking dish and coat with mixture. Cover tightly and place on the middle rack of the oven. Bake for 30 minutes, basting once or twice, then uncover and move to the top shelf. Bake about 15 minutes longer or until parsnips are tender and slightly glazed.

Salad of Smoked Salmon and Orange Slices

Serves 4–6

A last-minute preparation that makes a delicious and attractive luncheon course.

- 1 *Boston lettuce, or any loose-head lettuce*
- ¾ *pound sliced smoked salmon*
- 2 *navel oranges, peeled and cut into ⅛-inch slices*
- ¼ *cup capers*
- ⅓ *cup low-fat mayonnaise*
- ⅓ *cup plain low-fat yogurt*
- 1 *teaspoon Dijon mustard*
- 2 *tablespoons orange juice*
  Salt and freshly ground pepper to taste

Arrange the lettuce leaves in the bottom of a shallow serving platter or bowl. Place salmon and orange slices, one overlapping the other in an attractive pattern on top of the lettuce. Sprinkle the capers over all. In a small bowl, blend together the mayonnaise, yogurt, mustard, orange juice, salt, and pepper. Serve the sauce separately.

Scallops with Orange Sauce

Serves 4

This recipe is easy and quick to prepare. The scallops are steamed or cooked in the microwave oven but they could also be broiled or grilled. Whichever method you use, you'll find the orange sauce blends beautifully with the seafood.

1¼ *pounds sea scallops*
1 *tablespoon unsalted butter or margarine*
1 *large garlic clove, minced*
⅓ *cup finely chopped scallions*
¾ *cup orange juice*
½ *cup dry white wine*
 Salt and freshly ground pepper to taste

If too large, slice the scallops in half. Cook briefly, until white and opaque. Set aside.

In a saucepan, melt the butter, add the garlic and scallions, and cook over medium-high heat until soft, about 4 minutes. Add the orange juice and wine and continue cooking until the sauce begins to thicken. Add the scallops to the saucepan and stir until heated through. Season with salt and pepper. Serve immediately.

Sole with Oranges

Serves 6

This fish may be served with any type of rice, but is especially suited to our Brown Rice with Spice and Lemon (page 128). Add a simple green vegetable such as spinach for a meal of beautiful flavors and color.

6 *sole fillets (about 6 ounces each)*
¼ *cup milk*
2 *tablespoons flour*
 Salt and freshly ground pepper to taste
5 *tablespoons lightly salted butter*
1 *tablespoon finely chopped onion*
1 *cup orange juice*
1 *teaspoon grated orange rind*
½ *cup dry white wine*
3 *large oranges, peeled, pith removed, cut into half-inch slices and halved*

Dip the fillets in milk, then coat lightly with flour, seasoned with a bit of salt and pepper. Sauté in 2 tablespoons of the butter until well browned on each side and they flake easily with a fork. Transfer to a heated serving dish and keep warm.

Add another 2 tablespoons butter to the pan along with the chopped onion and cook until soft. Stir in orange juice, orange rind, and wine, season with salt and pepper, and simmer about 5 minutes, until slightly thickened. Blend in the remaining 1 tablespoon butter, then add orange segments and heat through. Arrange orange segments with the fish on a platter and pour sauce over.

Duck à l'Orange

Serves 4

This duck is crisp and without any fatty aftertaste. It will hold in a warm oven for up to two or three hours and still be as fresh as if just prepared. It is also an elegant course served cold with rice and a sour-sweet cold cucumber salad.

- 1 *duck, about 4–5 pounds*
  Freshly ground black pepper to taste
- 1/2 *teaspoon ground ginger*
- 1/3 *cup plus 2 tablespoons red wine vinegar*
- 1/2 *cup sugar*
- 3 *tablespoons water*
- 1 *cup orange juice*
- 1 *tablespoon lemon juice*
- 3/4 *cup consommé or Duck Stock (recipe follows)*
- 1 *tablespoon Triple Sec*
- 1 *tablespoon cognac*
  Salt to taste
- 2 *teaspoons cornstarch*
- 1 *orange, unpeeled, sliced thinly*

Preheat the oven to 425° F.

Wash the duck, remove any extra loose fat from the cavity areas, and prick the skin all over with a fork. Season with pepper and ginger, then pour 1/3 cup of the vinegar over the entire surface and inside the cavity. Place the duck breast side up on a rack in a roasting pan containing about 1 inch of water. This will prevent smoking from the dripping fat and also ensures the meat remaining moist while the skin becomes crisp during the roasting process. Roast for 45 minutes. Reduce the oven temperature to 375° F., turn the duck, and continue cooking for a further 45 minutes or until tender. Turn the duck twice during this period and prick the skin several more times. Remove from the oven and place on brown paper to drain. Cover lightly and keep in a warm oven.

While the duck is roasting, make the sauce. Melt the sugar and 1 tablespoon water in a heavy saucepan over medium-high heat and cook until it begins to color and caramelize, for about 8 to 10 minutes. Add the remaining 2 tablespoons vinegar, stirring vigorously until well mixed in with the sugar. Add the orange and lemon juices and the consommé. Bring to a boil and cook for 5 minutes or until the sauce is slightly reduced. Add the Triple Sec, cognac, and salt, and adjust the seasonings. Blend the cornstarch with the remaining 2 tablespoons water, stir into the sauce, and cook over low heat for about 2 minutes or until thickened. Keep hot.

Cut the duck into serving portions and place on one large platter or on individual plates. Arrange the orange slices around the duck pieces and pour over some of the sauce. Pour the remainder in a bowl and serve separately.

Duck Stock

- 1/2 *medium onion, sliced*
- 1 *carrot, about 6 inches long, scraped and sliced into 2-inch pieces*
- 1 *celery stalk, trimmed and sliced into 2-inch pieces*
- 1 *bay leaf*
- 4 *black peppercorns*
  Several sprigs fresh parsley
  Giblets and neck from the duck
  Salt to taste
- 1 *chicken bouillon cube (optional)*

Combine all the ingredients in a saucepan, cover with water, and bring to a boil. Lower the heat and simmer for 45 minutes. If the flavor is insufficiently strong, add a chicken bouillon cube and cook for 5 minutes until dissolved. Strain and set the stock aside to be added to the sauce. Either eat or discard the vegetables and giblets.

Roast Chicken with Kumquats

Serves 6

Even though the chicken is cut into portions and baked with the kumquats to complete the dish, roasting it first ensures that the breast meat is wonderfully moist and the legs and thighs are cooked to perfection. We also prefer roasting in a pot with high sides; the bird roasts just as well and the oven remains far cleaner.

CHICKEN

1 *roasting chicken, about 3–4 pounds*
Salt and freshly ground pepper to taste
1/2 *teaspoon ground ginger*

SAUCE

2 *cups orange juice*
2 *tablespoons dark brown sugar*
2 *teaspoons light soy sauce*
1 *teaspoon cornstarch*
1 *tablespoon water*
8 *ounces fresh kumquats, washed and left whole*
Salt and freshly ground pepper to taste

Preheat the oven to 375° F.

Remove the fat and giblets from inside the bird, and sprinkle with salt and pepper. Rub the outside with salt, pepper, and ginger and place in an oiled roasting pot. Roast in the oven, basting occasionally with the juices from the bird, until golden brown, for about 1 hour.

Remove, carve into serving-size pieces (do not slice), and place in casserole. Set aside and cover with foil to keep warm. Reserve 2 tablespoons juice from the roasting pot.

In a medium saucepan, add the reserved roasting juices, orange juice, brown sugar, and soy sauce. Bring to a boil, lower the heat, and simmer for 3 minutes. Dissolve the cornstarch in the water and add to the saucepan. Blend in and stir until the sauce is thickened. Add the kumquats and cook, stirring until thoroughly heated through. Season with salt and pepper.

Lower the heat to 300° F. Pour the sauce over the chicken pieces, return to the oven, and bake for 30 to 45 minutes, or until the chicken is tender and the sauce a little syrupy and slightly glazed. If desired, place under the grill to crisp for 2 or 3 minutes.

Oxtails with Oranges

Serves 4–6

This dish takes a long time to prepare, but the end result is so fragrant and delectable that your effort will be well appreciated. A favorite with our families and friends.

  4   *pounds oxtails, cut into 2½-inch pieces*
  ⅓   *cup all-purpose flour*
  ¼   *cup canola or other vegetable oil*
  2   *tablespoons (¼ stick) unsalted butter*
  2   *medium onions, thinly sliced*
  2   *garlic cloves, minced*
  2   *celery stalks, well washed, trimmed, and sliced*
  2   *medium carrots, scraped and sliced into rounds ⅛-inch thick*
  1   *cup dry white wine*
  1   *cup beef bouillon*
  1   *beef bouillon cube*
  2   *cups fresh orange juice*
  1   *(28-ounce) can Italian plum tomatoes, with juice*
1½   *teaspoons dried thyme*
1½   *teaspoons chopped fresh parsley*
      Orange rind from 1 orange, cut into thin julienne strips
  1   *cup water*
  3   *tablespoons red wine vinegar*
  1   *tablespoon sugar*
      Freshly ground pepper to taste

Trim the fat from the oxtails, then dredge with flour, shaking off the excess. Place the oil in a large casserole and brown the oxtails over medium-high heat. With a slotted spoon remove to a plate when browned. Pour the fat from the casserole and discard. Scrape the bottom and sides to free up any particles. In the same casserole, melt the butter, add the onions, garlic, celery, and carrots. Cook the vegetables over medium heat, stirring occasionally until the onions are soft but not brown. Increase the heat to high, add the wine, and cook for 4 minutes.

Return the oxtails to the casserole and add the bouillon, bouillon cube, orange juice, tomatoes, thyme, and parsley. Bring to a boil, cover, lower heat, and simmer for about 2 hours.

In a small saucepan combine the strips of orange rind in the water. Bring to a boil and then lower heat and simmer for 5 minutes. Drain, rinse with cold water, and set aside.

With a slotted spoon transfer the oxtails to a holding bowl, cover, and refrigerate. Cover and refrigerate the vegetables and cooking liquid either in the casserole or, if more convenient, in another bowl. (Refrigeration will cause any excess fat to solidify, making its removal much easier.) Some hours before serving remove the fat, while still solidified, from both containers. At this stage the ingredients may be left refrigerated for up to 2 days.

Preheat the oven to 350° F.

Puree the vegetables in a food processor and return to the casserole. Bring to a boil, add the vinegar and sugar, and cook, stirring, over medium-high heat for 5 minutes. Add the oxtails and the orange rind, season to taste with pepper, and bake uncovered in the oven for 30 to 35 minutes or until heated through. Serve with plain white rice and a salad of mixed greens.

Orange Veal

Serves 6

The orange flavor in this dish intensifies if made a day ahead. It also freezes well for up to six weeks. Serve simply, with rice or new potatoes, a green vegetable, and a salad.

 2 *navel oranges*
 2 *tablespoons (¼ stick) unsalted butter*
 2 *tablespoons canola or other vegetable oil*
 1 *large garlic clove, minced*
 2 *leeks, white portion only, thinly sliced*
 2 *carrots about 6–7 inches long, scraped and finely diced*
 2 *celery stalks each about 7–8 inches long, trimmed and finely diced*
 3 *pounds veal, cut from the shoulder into ¾-inch cubes*
 ¼ *cup all-purpose flour*
 ¼ *cup Triple Sec*
 2 *cups orange juice*
 2 *cups dry white wine*
 2 *bay leaves*
    Salt and freshly ground pepper to taste

Peel the oranges and remove the pith. Using only the orange part, cut the peel into very thin julienne strips. Place the strips in a small saucepan of boiling water, cook for 5 minutes, drain, and reserve.

In a large ovenproof saucepan, heat 1 tablespoon each of the butter and oil, add the garlic, leeks, carrots, and celery and cook over medium-high heat for 10 minutes or until the vegetables are soft and transparent. Transfer to a plate.

Preheat the oven to 350° F.

Dredge the veal with flour, shaking off the excess. Using the same pan, add the remaining butter and oil and brown the veal in

batches. With a slotted spoon, remove the meat to a plate as it is sautéed. Add the Triple Sec to the pan and deglaze, scraping up the loose bits from the bottom and sides. Add the orange juice, wine, bay leaves, and 6 of the julienned orange strips. Return the vegetables and meat, bring to a boil, and stir well to mix all the ingredients. Cover, place in oven, and bake for 1 hour, checking occasionally and stirring so that no meat sticks to the bottom.

After an hour, return the veal to the stovetop, season to taste, add the remaining julienned orange strips, and simmer for about 5 minutes over low heat, stirring gently to allow the sauce to thicken slightly before serving.

NOTE: Frequently when a dish is thawed out after having been frozen, it appears somewhat dry. Should this be the case here, mix 1 cup each of chicken stock (or a chicken bouillon cube dissolved in 1 cup of water) and orange juice in a small saucepan over medium heat. Cook for about 5 minutes, then add to the heated meat mixture and stir well.

Kumquat Marmalade

Yields 1½ pints

This recipe was the result of an unusually bountiful crop of fruit from a small tree grown indoors. The flavor is really quite different from that of any orange marmalade.

 1½ *pounds kumquats, sliced very fine, seeds discarded*
  1 *medium lemon, finely sliced with peel*
 8¼ *cups cold water*
  7 *cups sugar*

(continued on next page)

Cover the kumquats and lemon with the cold water and let stand for 24 hours. Place in a nonreactive saucepan, bring to a boil, add the sugar, then remove from the heat and stir until the sugar is dissolved. Cover and let stand again for 24 hours. Bring the mixture to a boil and simmer gently for 2 hours. The peel should be soft and transparent. Once more, bring to a boil and cook rapidly for 30 minutes or until 2 drops will run off the edge of a metal spoon simultaneously. If there is any foam on the surface, skim off before pouring into hot sterile jars. Seal tightly and store in refrigerator.

Clementines with a Chocolate Dip

Serves 4

Tangerines could also be served this way but the size and tanginess of the clementine makes it just perfect.

- 4 clementines, peeled with fibers removed but not membranes
- 6 ounces semisweet chocolate, in pieces
- 2 tablespoons orange liqueur
- 1 tablespoon whipping cream

Prepare the clementines and separate the sections, and place on individual dessert plates in an attractive circle, leaving center space for the chocolate. Place chocolate pieces with liqueur and cream in the top of a double boiler over hot water, stirring until melted. Do not let the upper pot touch the water. When the chocolate mixture is smooth and blended, spoon in a puddle in the center of the fruit.

Orange Cake

Serves 10

The addition of the orange zest adds intensity to the flavor, and the orange syrup ensures that it remains moist. Even after a day or two this large cake retains its wonderful taste.

CAKE

- 1 cup (2 sticks) unsalted butter, softened
- 1 cup sugar
- 3 large eggs
- 1 cup sour cream
- 1/3 cup orange juice
  Zest of 2 oranges
- 2 2/3 cups all-purpose flour
- 1 1/2 teaspoons baking powder
- 1/2 teaspoon baking soda
  Pinch of salt
- 1/3 cup miniature chocolate morsels (optional)

SYRUP

- 1/4 cup orange juice
- 1/4 cup plus 1 tablespoon sugar
- 2 tablespoons lemon juice

Preheat the oven to 350° F. Grease and flour a 9-inch tube or Bundt pan.

In the bowl of an electric mixer beat the butter and sugar on medium speed until light and fluffy, about 3 minutes. Scrape down the sides. Add the eggs one at a time and beat for 20 seconds after each addition. Scrape down the sides. Beat in the sour cream, orange juice, and orange zest and beat for another 30 seconds or until well integrated. Scrape down the sides.

In another bowl, combine the flour, baking powder, baking soda, and salt until well blended. Fold into the egg mixture, scraping down the sides at intervals until well mixed. Stir in the chocolate morsels if you're using them. Pour batter into prepared pan and smooth the top with a spatula. Bake for 50 minutes or until the cake springs back when pressed lightly in the center.

While the cake is baking, prepare the syrup. In a small saucepan heat the orange juice, sugar, and lemon juice until the sugar has dissolved. Keep hot.

Remove cake from oven and place on a rack over a plate. Poke holes over the top with a cake tester, brush with half the syrup, then invert it onto a lightly oiled rack, again over a plate. Poke more holes and brush both the top and sides with remaining syrup and cool completely. Cover and allow to stand for several hours before serving. This will allow the syrup to be fully absorbed into the cake.

Orange Slices in Grand Marnier

Serves 6

A refreshing dish that delights the eye as well as the palate.

  6 *large navel oranges*
  2 *tablespoons honey*
  1 *cup sugar*
 ½ *cup water*
 ¼ *cup orange juice*
 ¼ *cup Grand Marnier*

With a sharp paring knife or vegetable peeler remove the skin from the oranges. Cut the oranges into thin slices and place in a serving bowl. Using only the orange part of

the rind from 3 oranges, cut very fine julienne strips. Place the strips in a small saucepan, cover with water, and bring to a boil. Lower the heat and simmer for 10 minutes. Drain, rinse with cold water, and set aside.

Combine the honey, sugar, water, and orange juice in a saucepan. Bring to a boil, lower the heat, and simmer for 5 minutes. Add the Grand Marnier and cook for 5 more minutes. Strain the sauce over the oranges and add the rind. Cover and chill before serving.

Oranges in Red Wine

Serves 6

Our version of a classic recipe.

  8 *large navel oranges*
  1 *cup red Bordeaux wine*
  1 *cup water*
  2 *slices lemon*
 ½ *cup sugar*
  1 *3-inch cinnamon stick*
  6 *whole cloves*

With a sharp paring knife peel the oranges, making sure that all the pith is removed. Cut into thin slices. Reserve the skins of 4 of the oranges and using only the orange part of the rind cut into very fine julienne strips. Place the oranges in a bowl and sprinkle the rind over them.

In a medium nonreactive saucepan combine the wine, water, lemon, sugar, cinnamon, and cloves. Bring to a boil, lower the heat, and simmer for about 5 minutes or until the sugar is completely dissolved. Pour over the oranges while still warm. Cover with plastic wrap and chill until served. This dessert may be kept, refrigerated, for several days.

P·A·P·A·Y·A·S

Baked Papayas

Indonesian Fruit Salad

Salad of Broccoli, Snow Peas, and Papaya

Sautéed Shrimp with Papaya

Salad of Papaya, Grilled Red Peppers, and Smoked Turkey

Chicken Breasts with Papaya Puree

Beef-Stuffed Baked Papaya

Sautéed Papaya with Tia Maria and Vanilla Ice Cream

The papaya, a native of Mexico and Central America, is variously known as the pawpaw or papaw in the West Indies and South Africa, as *lechosa* in Puerto Rico, *melon zapote* in Mexico, and *fruta bomba* (fruit grenade) in Cuba. Although actually a herbaceous plant, it takes the form of a tree, growing to as much as twenty feet in height. The huge, deeply lobed leaves on their two-foot-long stalks sprout only from the top of the tree, giving it a palmlike appearance. The fruit forms in clusters just below this leaf crown, looking somewhat like a bunch of coconuts. Papayas can vary greatly in size; some are as large as melons while others are more nearly pear size. When the fruit is halved, it resembles a melon, with a thick band of pink to orange flesh surrounding a cavity filled with small black seeds. These seeds have a gelatinous coating inviting a comparison to black caviar. The papaya is known to have a somewhat irregular sex life with some plants male, some female, and others bisexual. Since males serve only to fertilize the females, growers discard most of the male plants. The bisexual plant is protected from this destruction by being self-fertilizing. In frost-free climates the plant grows readily from seed, and is now grown in all tropical parts of the world and warm parts of the subtropics. The two states with a favorable climate for large-scale production are Hawaii and Florida.

Long consumed as a fresh fruit for its sweet, succulent flesh, it also contains the enzyme papain, used in aids to digestion and as a meat tenderizer. In the tropics, it was a common practice to wrap chicken or other meat in the leaves and allow it to stand overnight before cooking to tenderize it. The same effect is obtained if the juice is sprinkled on meat before cooking, or if it is cooked with the leaves.

↪ HOME CULTIVATION ↪

These plants will grow readily from seed in a tropical climate. The development is rapid, with fruit production before the end of the first year, after which they continue to produce for about five years. The commercial growers replace plants every three to four years. Generally, fruit matures throughout the year.

↪ NUTRITION ↪

Papayas are an unusually good source of both vitamins A and C as well as potassium. Seven ounces, about half a papaya, is 78 calories.

↪ SELECTION ↪

The papayas usually found in our produce markets are those slightly larger than a pear with a plump, bulbous base and narrow neck (actually somewhat like a light bulb in contour), and have a longitudinally ridged skin. Select those with skin that is smooth and unblemished. They should yield to slight pressure, but be handled gently.

Since the degree of softness is not as accurate a determinant of ripeness as the color, follow these guidelines:

Green, with slight yellow tinge at larger end = ¼ ripe—keep at room temperature 5–7 days.

⅓ yellow, ⅔ green = ½ ripe—keep at room temperature 2–4 days.

½ green, ½ yellow = ¾ ripe—keep at room temperature 1–2 days.

Yellow-orange = completely ripe—will keep in refrigerator for up to a week.

EQUIVALENTS
Papayas in our markets average
12 to 16 ounces
5 ounces of pulp = 1 cup

↪ STORAGE AND PREPARATION ↪

Once ripe a papaya can be stored in the refrigerator for 1 or 2 days.

The thin skin can be removed with a vegetable peeler after the fruit is halved and the seeds scooped out with a spoon. It can then be sliced, diced, or cubed as desired. Fresh-cut papaya can be left standing at room temperature for several hours with no loss of color, flavor, or texture.

↪ ↪

In tropical countries papayas are as common as the apple is to us. The simplest preparation is to cut in half, remove the seeds, and serve with a wedge of lime, or sprinkle lime juice just as you might serve a wedge of melon. Sprinkle a lime-based dressing over a fresh fruit salad of papaya, bananas, and passion fruit. The pureed pulp can be made into fish and poultry sauces seasoned with Indian or hot Mexican spices, or with lime juice and sugar turned into sweet dessert sauces, puddings, and ices.

Baked Papayas

Serves 8

If you want to serve smaller portions the halves can be cut into quarters after baking, using a long, sharp knife. This could be the main course of a light meal, accompanied by freshly baked biscuits, or served as a side dish with broiled chicken.

3 cups small-curd cream-style cottage cheese
3 tablespoons hot Indian chutney
1 tablespoon medium curry powder, such as Madras
½ cup diced tart apple, such as Granny Smith
2 tablespoons golden raisins
4 medium papayas (each 12–16 ounces), fully ripe, halved and seeds removed
¼ cup (½ stick) lightly salted butter, melted

Preheat the oven to 450° F.

Blend the cottage cheese, chutney, and curry powder, then stir in the apple and raisins. Divide evenly into hollow centers of the papaya halves. Place in a baking dish and pour 1 tablespoon of melted butter over each. Bake on the middle rack of the oven for about 15 minutes.

Indonesian Fruit Salad

Serves 6 as an appetizer

When Rolce's daughter, Cymie, was on a photographic assignment in Indonesia, she became fascinated with the intriguing variety of exotic fruits and how they were served. This is our adaptation of one of the recipes she brought back. It may be served with skewers as an appetizer, in a Boston lettuce leaf as a first course, or as an accompaniment to a main course, such as grilled fish or poultry.

3 tablespoons tamarind paste (found in oriental markets)
½ cup water
½ cup dark brown sugar
½ teaspoon salt
¼ teaspoon red pepper flakes, or to taste
1 cup chopped partly ripe mango, in 1-inch cubes
1 cup chopped partly ripe papaya, in 1-inch cubes
1 cup chopped seeded cucumber, in 1-inch pieces
2 oranges, peeled, pith removed, sections cut into 3 pieces

Dissolve the tamarind paste in the water and strain, then mix the liquid with brown sugar, salt, and red pepper in a serving bowl. Blanch the mango and papaya in boiling water for 1 minute; drain well. Stir the papaya, mango, cucumber, and orange pieces into the sauce and coat well. May be chilled or served at room temperature.

Salad of Broccoli, Snow Peas, and Papaya

Serves 4

    3 tablespoons fresh lime juice
    3 tablespoons canola or other vegetable oil
 1½ teaspoons Pickapeppa Sauce
  ¾ teaspoons honey
 1½ pounds fresh broccoli, or frozen broccoli
       spears
    3 ounces fresh snow peas
    1 papaya (12–16 ounces)

Combine the lime juice, oil, Pickapeppa Sauce, and honey in a bowl or small jar, mix well, and chill for 1 hour or more.

If using fresh broccoli, separate the flowerets about 2½ inches down the stem, peel the stems, and cut into 2½-inch pieces. In a saucepan of boiling water, blanch for about 3 to 4 minutes. Immediately plunge into cold water, drain, place on paper towels to dry, and set aside. The frozen broccoli should be cooked in boiling water for about the same period of time, but sliced after it has been drained and dried. The broccoli should be crunchy.

Remove the stems and strings from the snow peas, place in a saucepan of boiling water, and blanch for 10 seconds. Immediately plunge into cold water, then drain and place on paper towels to dry. Cut the papaya in half, remove the seeds, and peel. Slice into sections about 2½ inches by ½ inch. If not using immediately, cover with plastic wrap and refrigerate.

In a large serving bowl, combine the broccoli and snow peas; add the papaya just be-fore serving, then carefully toss the salad with the dressing.

NOTE: It is advisable to prepare this salad shortly before serving because broccoli always has a tendency to discolor and lose some of its crunchiness, even if cooked for only a very short period in advance.

Sautéed Shrimp with Papaya

Serves 4

This colorful dish is especially good when served with a rice casserole and pureed or sautéed spinach.

    1 ripe papaya (12–16 ounces), halved,
       seeded, peeled, and cut into ½-inch
       strips
    2 scallions, thinly sliced, including 2 inches
       of green (about 3 tablespoons)
  ½ teaspoon peeled and grated ginger
       Juice of 1 lime
    3 tablespoons finely julienned sweet Italian
       green pepper
  ½ cup chicken stock
    2 teaspoons honey
    1 teaspoon cornstarch
    1 tablespoon unsalted butter
    1 tablespoon canola or other vegetable oil
  24 large shrimp (about 1 pound) peeled,
       deveined, with tails intact
  ½ teaspoon paprika

In a bowl, combine the papaya, scallions, ginger, lime juice, pepper, stock, and honey. Stir in the cornstarch and set aside. In a large skillet, melt the butter and oil, add the shrimp and sauté over medium-high heat until pink, about 4 minutes. Add the papaya mixture to the shrimp, then cook for about 3 minutes, stirring, until the sauce is heated through and has thickened slightly. Season with paprika. Serve immediately.

Salad of Papaya, Grilled Red Peppers, and Smoked Turkey

Serves 4–6

An unusual addition to this salad is a potato, cut into ¼-inch pieces. It combines beautifully with the other ingredients and counterbalances the somewhat spicy dressing. Smoked chicken, ham, or perhaps even grilled chicken breast may be substituted for the turkey.

- 3 tablespoons balsamic vinegar
- ½ cup canola or other vegetable oil
- 2 teaspoons finely chopped cilantro (fresh coriander)
- ¼ teaspoon minced jalapeño pepper
  Salt and freshly ground black pepper to taste
- 2 medium red bell peppers
- 4 small new potatoes
- 2 papayas (10–12 ounces each)
- 12 ounces smoked turkey, cut ¼ inch thick
- 8 loose-head lettuce leaves, or 3 cups mesclun

Prepare the dressing. In a small bowl, combine the vinegar, oil, cilantro, and jalapeño. Season with salt and pepper and stir vigorously with a whisk to mix well. Chill while completing the recipe.

Preheat the broiler.

Place the peppers on a foil-lined shallow baking pan and broil, turning them to char evenly until the skins are black and blistered. Immediately remove from the oven and place in either a plastic or brown paper bag. Close the bag and leave for about 15 minutes. Carefully remove, peel off the skin, and seed the peppers. Place on paper towels to dry, then slice into ¼-inch strips and set aside.

Bring some water to boil in a small saucepan, add the potatoes, and cook until soft but still firm. Remove, cool, then slice into ¼-inch rounds. Peeling the potato is not absolutely necessary.

Halve, seed, and peel the papayas. Slice each half into ¼-inch lengthwise strips. Slice the turkey into ¼-inch julienned strips.

Tear the lettuce into bite-size pieces, place in a large bowl, and toss with only a few teaspoons of the dressing to moisten. Arrange the bottom of a large serving platter with the lettuce, then decoratively place the papaya, peppers, turkey, and potatoes on top of the greens. Drizzle a small amount more of the dressing over the peppers and potatoes. Serve immediately, or wrap tightly with plastic wrap and refrigerate. Pass remaining dressing in a small bowl.

Chicken Breasts with Papaya Puree

Serves 4–6

Coconut crust on the chicken breasts adds a nutty flavor and the lovely orange color of the papaya makes this a particularly appealing plate.

1   *whole papaya (12–16 ounces)*
2   *tablespoons fresh lime juice*
2   *tablespoons (¼ stick) unsalted butter*
¼   *cup finely chopped shallots*
⅔   *cup chicken stock*
½   *teaspoon ground ginger*
¼   *teaspoon paprika*
1   *teaspoon cornstarch*
1   *tablespoon water*
1   *tablespoon Peach and Apricot Chutney (page 187), or Major Grey type (optional)*
    Salt and freshly ground pepper to taste
2   *whole chicken breasts (about 1 pound each), skinned and boned*
¾   *cup shredded, unsweetened coconut*
1   *tablespoon canola or other vegetable oil*

Halve, peel, and remove the seeds from the papaya. Cut into chunks about ¾ inch square and place in a bowl with the lime juice. Coat the fruit well. Set aside.

In a saucepan, melt 1 tablespoon of the butter, add the shallots, and cook over medium heat for about 3 minutes. Add the stock, ginger, and paprika and simmer for 5 minutes. Stir the cornstarch into the water, then add to the stock mixture and stir until slightly thickened, about 3 minutes. Add the papaya and lime juice and blend well. Blend in the chutney and transfer to a blender or food processor to process until pureed. Season to taste. Return to the saucepan, reheat, and keep hot.

Split the chicken breasts, rinse, pat dry, and coat with the coconut. In a large skillet, heat the remaining tablespoon of butter and the oil, add the chicken, and cook for about 2 minutes on each side over medium-high heat. Reduce the heat to medium and cook for another 3 minutes on each side, or until the juices run clear when pierced with a knife. Place on a serving platter, or on individual plates and spoon the hot papaya sauce over the chicken. Serve immediately.

Beef~Stuffed Baked Papaya

Serves 4

The sweetness of the papaya blends perfectly with the flavored beef. Serve with a baked potato and a mixed green salad.

2   *ripe, firm papayas (10–12 ounces each)*
1   *tablespoon canola or other vegetable oil*
¼   *cup chopped onion*
¼   *cup chopped green bell pepper*
1½ *pounds chopped lean beef*
¼   *cup tomato puree or plain tomato sauce*
½   *teaspoon dried thyme*
    Salt and freshly ground pepper to taste

Preheat the oven to 350° F.

Halve the papayas and remove the seeds. Set aside. In a large saucepan, heat the oil, add the onion and green pepper, and cook over medium heat, stirring occasionally for 5 to 7 minutes until softened. Add the beef and cook for 10 to 12 minutes until browned. Pour off as much fat as possible. Add the tomato puree, lower the heat, and simmer for 10 minutes more or until almost no liquid remains. Season to taste with the thyme, salt, and pepper.

Fill the papaya halves with the beef mixture. Carefully place in a baking pan containing about ½ inch of water and bake for 45 minutes or until the top of the meat is crisp. Remove and serve immediately.

Sautéed Papaya with Tia Maria and Vanilla Ice Cream

Serves 4

This dessert was originally sampled in Jamaica. Now that papayas are more readily available, we can regularly enjoy this simple-to-prepare tropical treat.

2   *ripe, firm papayas (10–12 ounces each)*
2   *tablespoons (¼ stick) unsalted butter*
2   *tablespoons dark brown sugar*
3   *tablespoons Tia Maria or other coffee-flavored liqueur*
    Vanilla ice cream

Cut the papayas in half, remove the seeds, and peel. Slice each half into thirds. In a skillet, melt the butter, add the brown sugar, and stir until blended. Add the papaya slices and stir until heated through and well coated with the butter-sugar mixture. Pour the liqueur into the pan and swirl the mixture around for 5 seconds. Immediately place in individual serving dishes and top with a scoop of vanilla ice cream.

P·E·A·C·H·E·S
and
N·E·C·T·A·R·I·N·E·S

Cold Peach Soup

Peach Salad Topped with Crisp Bacon

Fresh Peach Relish

Peach and Apricot Chutney

Fish Curry with Fresh Peaches

Pork Chops with Peaches

Sandwich of Sliced Turkey with Peach and Apricot Chutney

Chicken Thighs with Peach Chutney Sauce

Chicken and Peach Pie

Peach Pie

Nectarine Kuchen

Peach Duff

Peach Wine Sorbet

The peach's early history lies in ancient China, where it was considered a symbol of long life and immortality and is found in poetry, paintings, and the decoration of porcelain. Because of its association with longevity a piece of porcelain decorated with peach blossoms was a highly esteemed birthday gift. The Chinese peach traveled the caravan routes to the Near East and was cultivated in Persia long before it reached Europe. Early writers thought of Persia as the original home of the peach and gave the species the name *Prunus persica*. However, botanical and archeological evidence confirms China as its true place of origin.

The nectarine is often, quite mistakenly, thought to be a cross between a peach and a plum; rather, it is simply a variety of the peach. The "fuzzy" peach's botanical name is *P. persica*, and the nectarine is *P. persica* var. *nectarina*. The chief difference between the two is in the skin—fuzzy on the peach and sleek and smooth on the nectarine. It sometimes happens that a peach tree will produce a branch of nectarines, or that a nectarine tree will sport peaches. Peach and nectarine varieties fall into two groups: freestones, in which the flesh separates readily from the stone, and clingstones, in which the flesh adheres firmly to the stone. The flesh of either may be yellow or white, and although there are subtle differences in flavor between peaches and nectarines, you can use either in our recipes.

The first Spanish explorers brought the peach to the New World, and as early as 1600, peaches were found in Mexico. By the late 1700s the missionaries had established them in California. Today, the United States is the largest producer in the world, although they are widely grown in Europe, Asia, South Africa, Australia, and

South America. California supplies about 95 percent of the domestic market for nectarines and almost 50 percent of the peaches. Other important peach-growing states are South Carolina, Georgia, New Jersey, and Pennsylvania, in that order.

HOME CULTIVATION

Because of its small size, the peach tree is an attractive addition to the home garden, and can be grown outdoors in most of the United States. A dwarf or miniature variety will adapt especially well to pot culture for the patio, terrace, or roof garden, as well as in a glass house. In English gardens, where sun exposure is an important factor, peaches (as well as other fruits) are frequently espaliered against a south-facing wall that will absorb the heat and hasten ripening. This can be a most attractive garden feature if done in formal patterns. The trees are handsome with a profusion of pink or white blossoms in spring. Although trees can be grown from pits (the seed is enclosed in a hard outer casing), they will not necessarily develop true to the variety planted. For the best quality fruit, a nursery-grown tree of a variety suitable to your local climate is the best choice. The taste of a tree-ripened peach is well worth the effort to produce it.

NUTRITION

Peaches and nectarines are a good source of vitamin C, with the yellow-fleshed varieties especially rich in vitamin A. They are also a source of fiber and of potassium, phosphorus, and even some calcium. A medium peach or nectarine (five ounces) has about 40 calories.

SELECTION

The red blush on a peach does not indicate ripeness. The background color should be overall creamy or yellowish. A green ground suggests a fruit that was picked too early, and it will not ripen further. Peaches and nectarines will soften at home, but they do not gain sugar once they are picked. A peach should not feel hard to gentle pressure and should be free of blemishes with an unwrinkled skin. Unlike some other fruits, such as apples and pears, the varieties are usually not indicated in the markets. The season for domestically grown peaches and nectarines runs from May to December, with July and August as the peak months. From January through April we receive some peaches and nectarines from South America, which makes fresh fruit available year round.

EQUIVALENTS
1 large peach = 8 ounces
1 medium peach = 6 ounces
2 medium = 1 cup sliced
= ¾ cup mashed

STORAGE AND PREPARATION

When peaches are soft to the touch they may be kept, unwashed, in the refrigerator for up to two weeks but should be checked frequently for brown spots. Firmer ones should be left at room temperature for further ripening, stored in a single layer to minimize bruising. Supermarket peaches have been mechanically defuzzed, but if you have some that haven't been treated, simply wash and rub gently with a towel to eat fresh without peeling.

To peel, place the fruit in a pot of boiling water for one minute, then lift out with a slotted spoon, plunge in cold water for easier handling, then with a knife tip to start it, pull off the skin.

To halve, cut along the natural indentation and lift away from the pit. To prevent darkening of the fruit, sprinkle with lemon or lime juice. Because peaches take well to canning, freezing, and drying, they can be used year round. Many recipes can be adapted to frozen or canned peaches with only a slight difference in flavor.

Start your day with peaches—fresh with cream, sliced over a bowl of cereal, or made into a nourishing shake. The summer berries served with peaches are a delight to eye and palate. Toss whole blueberries with your bowl of peaches and cream or cereal, use them as the garnish for chilled peach soup, or crush them as a sauce for peach ice cream or sorbet. Raspberries and peaches are a classic combination, as in peach melba, consisting of a poached peach half, topped with vanilla ice cream and fresh raspberry sauce. Peach flavor needs little enhancement, but a touch of cinnamon, nutmeg, or lemon juice can give variety to cakes, pies, and cobblers. In chutneys and sauces for poultry and meats, the Indian and oriental spices are so harmonious as to give full credence to the peach's Far East birthplace.

Cold Peach Soup

Serves 6

The sour cream gives body and smoothness but retains the slightly tart flavor that makes this soup an ideal first course for a summer meal. A slightly sweet wine or a bit more sugar may be used for a sweeter taste.

  1½ *pounds peaches (3 large), peeled (reserve peelings) and chopped*
  ½ *cup water*
  1 *teaspoon sugar*
  ¾ *cup orange juice*
  1 *tablespoon lime juice*
  1 *cup sour cream*
  ½ *cup medium-dry sherry*
  ½ *cup dry white wine*

Combine reserved peelings with the water and sugar in a small saucepan. Simmer uncovered until reduced by about one-half; press all liquid from peelings, then discard solids and cool liquid. Meanwhile, place chopped peaches in a blender or food processor, add orange and lime juices, and puree just until pulverized but with some texture left. Add the sour cream, sherry, wine, and cooled peach liquid and mix, just to blend thoroughly. Chill 1 hour or more before serving. Garnish with additional chopped fresh peaches or a slice of lime.

Peach Salad Topped with Crisp Bacon

Serves 6

Make this amount to serve six as a first course or four as a lunch salad. For lunch, round out the meal with hot rolls or freshly baked fruit muffins. It is essential to have the bacon very crisp and well drained.

  ½ *teaspoon ground cumin*
  1 *teaspoon grated ginger*
  ¼ *teaspoon salt*
  ⅛ *teaspoon cayenne pepper, or to taste*
  3 *tablespoons lemon juice*
  2 *tablespoons canola or other vegetable oil*
  2 *tablespoons olive oil*
  1 *small head red-leaf lettuce*
  1 *bunch watercress*
  3 *fully ripe large peaches (1½ pounds total), peeled and sliced ½ inch thick*
  4 *slices bacon, fried until crisp and drained well*

Beat together the cumin, ginger, salt, cayenne, lemon juice, and oils. Place lettuce leaves on a serving platter or individual plates, distribute watercress sprigs over lettuce, then add peach slices and crumble bacon over peaches. Dressing may be drizzled over or passed separately.

Fresh Peach Relish

Yields 1½ cups

This is an uncooked relish that adds interest to a variety of dishes. Use it as a condiment for grilled fish, chicken, and even steak. It may be prepared several hours before serving and refrigerated.

2   ripe but firm medium peaches (*about 12 ounces*)
1   tablespoon canola or other vegetable oil
1   tablespoon fresh lime juice
¼   cup diced red bell pepper
¼   cup diced green pepper
¼   cup finely chopped red onion
1   tablespoon chopped cilantro (*fresh coriander*)
1   teaspoon minced jalapeño pepper
½   teaspoon salt
⅛   teaspoon crushed red pepper flakes
    Freshly ground pepper to taste

Wash the peaches. Leave unpeeled, cut into halves, and remove the pits. Cut into ½-inch cubes. In a large bowl mix the oil and lime juice. Add the diced peaches, red and green peppers, red onion, and cilantro. Mix well. Add the jalapeño, ½ teaspoon at a time, to make certain that the flavor is not too strong. Finally add the salt, red pepper flakes, and black pepper. Mix again, cover, and refrigerate until ready to serve. This relish may be kept for one extra day in the refrigerator. After this time it will lose some of its crispness, even though the flavors will still be pronounced.

Peach and Apricot Chutney

Yields 3¼ cups

A chutney that magically transforms the most mundane of dishes into epicurean delights.

2½   pounds fresh peaches (*6–7 large*)
1   cup coarsely diced dried apricots
1   small white onion, finely diced
1½   cups dark brown sugar
1½   cups cider vinegar
2   teaspoons peeled and minced fresh ginger
2   teaspoons ground ginger
2   teaspoons ground coriander
½   teaspoon ground cumin
1   teaspoon salt
½   cup raisins

Wash the peaches, halve, and remove the pits. Leave unpeeled and cut into 1-inch chunks. In a large saucepan, combine all the ingredients except the raisins, bring to a boil, then cook over medium-low heat for about 1¼ hours, stirring occasionally to prevent any sticking or burning on the bottom of the pan. Add the raisins and cook for 30 minutes more, or until the mixture takes on a jamlike consistency. Remove from the heat, cool, and store in airtight containers in the refrigerator. This chutney will keep for many months refrigerated.

Fish Curry with Fresh Peaches

Serves 6

This is an adaptation of a dish we were served in a small country restaurant in the town of Hall in Tirol, just outside of Innsbruck, Austria. Serve with plain rice.

- 1/2 cup dry white wine
- 1 1/4 cups fish stock
- 1 1/4 cups whipping cream
- 1 small onion, finely chopped
- 6 tablespoons (3/4 stick) lightly salted butter
- 1 2-inch piece fresh ginger, peeled and minced
- 2 1/2 teaspoons medium curry power
- 2 1/2 pounds monkfish or other firm white fish fillets, cut into 1-inch pieces and dredged in flour
- 1 1/2 tablespoons cold lightly salted butter
- 1 tablespoon lemon juice
  Salt and freshly ground pepper to taste
- 2 large or 3 small peaches (1 pound), peeled, pitted, and sliced

Combine the wine and fish stock in a saucepan over high heat and reduce by two-thirds. Add the cream and simmer for 5 minutes. Set aside. Sauté the onion in the butter until softened, then stir in the ginger and curry powder. Add the diced fish and cook until opaque and flakes easily with a fork, about 5 minutes. Return the wine sauce to the heat and whisk in the cold butter to thicken; stir in lemon juice. Season to taste with salt and pepper. Pour the sauce into the pan with the fish and combine gently. Place the fish mixture on a heated serving platter and place the sliced peaches over and around it. Serve hot.

❧ ❧

Pork Chops with Peaches

Serves 6

Peaches provide an interesting variation from the usual prunes and apples served with pork.

- 6 pork chops, cut 3/4 inch thick
- 2 teaspoons olive oil
- 1/2 teaspoon salt
  Freshly ground pepper to taste
- 1/2 cup orange juice
- 3 tablespoons lemon juice
- 1 tablespoon honey
- 1/2 teaspoon ground cinnamon
- 1/2 teaspoon ground ginger
- 2 cups peeled and sliced fresh peaches, 1/2 inch thick

In a heavy skillet sauté the pork chops in the olive oil until golden brown on both sides. Then season with salt and pepper to taste. Combine the orange and lemon juices with the honey, cinnamon, and ginger, and pour over the chops. Cover tightly and cook for approximately 20 minutes over medium heat. Add the peaches, cover again, and cook until heated through, about 10 minutes. Remove the chops and peaches to a warm serving platter, arranging the peaches attractively around the chops. Reduce the sauce until slightly thickened over high heat, about 5 minutes. Pour over the chops and peaches. Serve immediately.

Sandwich of Sliced Turkey with Peach and Apricot Chutney

Serves 4

Casual eating and sandwiches are synonymous with summer. Take a few slices of turkey, chicken, or ham, any variety of interesting breads, one or even a mixture of several chutneys, and see how wonderfully different a sandwich can taste.

> 1/4 *cup low-fat mayonnaise*
> 8 *slices mixed-grain bread*
> 8 *slices turkey breast*
> 1/3–1/2 *cup Peach and Apricot Chutney (page 187)*
> 1/2 *sweet onion, thinly sliced*
> 8 *whole lettuce leaves*

Spread mayonnaise evenly on one side of each slice of bread and layer half the bread slices with the turkey. Spread the chutney on top of the turkey and complete with a layer each of onion and lettuce. Top with the remaining bread and press firmly.

Chicken Thighs with Peach Chutney Sauce

Serves 6

This dish may be served hot or at room temperature. The chutney sauce was created especially to enrich the flavor of baked chicken or Cornish game hens. It may be brushed over the meat for a glaze during baking or used as a sauce or accompaniment. Use in a similar way for grilled or broiled birds.

> 1 *tablespoon olive oil*
> 6 *whole, boned and skinned chicken thigh cutlets*
> *Peach Chutney Sauce (recipe follows)*

Preheat the oven to 400° F.

Brush a large ovenproof dish with olive oil. Place the chicken thighs in one layer and spread chutney over the meat. Bake for 40 minutes, basting twice during cooking. Pour off juice into a small saucepan and reduce over high heat for about 5 minutes. Stir to avoid sticking. Remove chicken from oven and pour sauce over and serve.

Peach Chutney Sauce

> 1 *tablespoon olive oil*
> 1 *garlic clove, minced*
> 1 *shallot, minced*
> 1 *teaspoon peeled and minced fresh ginger*
> 2 *tablespoons cider vinegar*
> 1/4 *cup dark brown sugar*
> 2 *firm ripe peaches (3/4 pound total), peeled and thinly sliced*
> 1/4 *cup raisins, preferably golden*
> 1 *tablespoon Dijon mustard*
> *Pinch of cayenne pepper or to taste*

In a saucepan heat the oil and sauté the garlic, shallot, and ginger over low heat for about 3 minutes, or until shallot is soft and translucent but not brown. Add the remaining ingredients, cover the pan, and cook over medium to low heat for 10 minutes. Check and stir frequently to avoid sticking and burning. Remove from heat and use at once, or place in jar and refrigerate. May be kept in refrigerator or up to 2 weeks.

Chicken and Peach Pie

Serves 6

While in Cape Town some years ago, we were served this most unlikely yet delicious combination of meat and fruit. It turned out to be as interesting as our view of Table Mountain from the courtyard of a South African–style relais.

1   chicken (2–3 pounds)
    Salt and freshly ground pepper to taste
½   teaspoon ground ginger
2   tablespoons canola or other vegetable oil
1   medium onion, peeled and sliced
2   celery stalks, well washed, trimmed, and
    cut into 2-inch pieces
1   leek, including only a little of the green
    top, well washed and sliced into 2-inch
    pieces
1½ cups chicken stock
4   whole cloves
5   medium, fresh peaches (1½ pounds),
    ripe but firm
¼   cup dry white wine
1   garlic clove, chopped
1   teaspoon fresh ginger, peeled and minced

PASTRY

2   cups all-purpose flour
¼   teaspoon salt
¾   cup unsalted butter
4–6 tablespoons iced water
1   teaspoon fresh lemon juice

2   teaspoons cornstarch
1   tablespoon water
1   egg (optional)
1   tablespoon water (optional)

Remove any excess fat from the cavity of the chicken. Rinse with water and pat dry with paper towels. Rub the skin all over with the salt, pepper, and ground ginger. In a large pot, heat the oil, add the vegetables and chicken, and brown lightly for about 15 minutes over medium heat. Add the chicken stock and cloves, and bring to a boil. Cover, lower the heat, and cook for 1¼ hours. Remove the chicken, cool a little, and discard the skin and bones. Reserve the cooking liquid. Cut the chicken into bite-size pieces. Peel and slice the peaches into bite-size cubes and mix into the chicken with the wine, garlic, and ginger. Cover and set aside in the refrigerator.

Remove the whole cloves from the cooking liquid, then puree the mixture in a blender or food processor. (There will be about 2 cups of the puree.) Place this puree in the freezer for about 45 minutes, then remove the fat from the surface. Pour the puree into a saucepan and set aside.

Sift the flour and salt and place in a bowl. Cut butter into ½-inch cubes and, using a pastry blender or fork, cut it into the flour until the mixture resembles coarse cornmeal. Mix the water with the lemon juice and add enough to the flour to make a soft, but not sticky, dough. Form into a ball, wrap in wax paper and chill for 15 minutes.

On a lightly floured surface, roll out the pastry into a rectangular shape measuring approximately 6 × 18 inches. Fold into thirds, make a half-turn with the dough, and roll out again. Repeat the folding and rolling another three times, always rolling from the center out toward the edge. Divide the pastry into two halves, wrap each one separately, and chill again for about 30 minutes.

While the dough is chilling, heat the vegetable puree and thicken with the cornstarch mixed into the water. Add to the chicken-peach mixture and stir until well blended.

Preheat the oven to 400° F. Grease a 10 × 6½ × 2-inch casserole, or any baking dish with equivalent overall measurements, such as a 9 or 10 × 2-inch round Pyrex dish.

On a lightly floured board, roll out one half of the pastry about ⅛-inch thick and 1½-inches larger all around than the top of the dish. Place this in the greased dish. Spoon the chicken-peach filling into the pastry. Roll out the remaining pastry so that it will fit easily over the filling. Moisten the bottom pastry edge, then press the top and bottom edges together along the rim to seal. Fold the bottom overhang over the top edge and crimp decoratively. Pierce the top in several places and brush with a mixture of the egg beaten with water, if desired. Bake for 30 minutes at 400° F, then lower the temperature to 350° F and bake for another 20 minutes. The top of the dough should be somewhat flaky and golden brown. If it appears to be browning too quickly, over loosely with foil. Remove from oven, allow to cool for 10 minutes before serving.

NOTE: For those who prefer a lighter, thinner sauce in the pie, the cornstarch may be omitted. Also, if you wish, use about half of the pastry dough to make a 1-crust pie, covering only the top of the chicken-peach mixture. The remaining dough may be frozen and used at another time.

⋧   ⋧

Peach Pie

Yields one 9-inch pie

This one-crust pie is filled to the brim with unpeeled fully ripe fresh peaches. A touch of crystallized ginger rounds off the flavor. Serve it alone, or with a scoop of ice cream.

CRUST

1½ cups all-purpose flour
2 teaspoons sugar
¼ teaspoon salt
½ cup (1 stick) unsalted butter, in pieces
¼ cup solid vegetable shortening, in pieces
2–3 tablespoons ice water

FILLING

3 pounds peaches (6 large), unpeeled, pitted, and sliced into twelfths
2 teaspoons lemon juice
¼ cup coarsely chopped crystallized ginger
½ cup sugar
½ cup all-purpose flour
2 tablespoons (¼ stick) unsalted butter

In a large bowl, combine the flour, sugar, and salt and mix well. Either with a pastry cutter or with your fingers, cut in the butter, a tablespoon at a time, and the shortening until the mixture resembles coarse meal. Add 2 tablespoons of water, toss to blend, and work the dough with your fingers until it holds together. Add more water as needed. Press into a disk, wrap in plastic, and refrigerate for at least 1 hour.

While the dough is resting, place the peaches in a large bowl, add the lemon juice, and mix well. Add the chopped ginger. In another bowl, mix the sugar and flour. Set aside.

Preheat the oven to 425° F. Grease and flour a 9-inch pie plate, 3 inches deep. Shake out any surplus flour.

Roll out the dough on a lightly floured surface to a ⅛-inch thickness. Fit the dough into the pan, allowing 1 inch extra to fold back for an edge. Press the edge with a fork to make a neat finish. Line the shell with foil and fill with pie weights or rice. Bake for 7

(continued on next page)

minutes, remove from oven, and lift out foil with weights. Lower the temperature to 400° F.

Pile the peaches in the shell. Sprinkle the flour-sugar mixture over the peaches and dot with the butter. Bake for 45 to 50 minutes or until the peaches are bubbling and the top is crisp. Remove from the oven and cool to room temperature before serving.

NOTE: If you have a food processor, use it to mix the dough. This dough may be prepared 3 days ahead and refrigerated, or frozen for up to 1 month. Allow to come to room temperature before rolling out.

꽃   꽃

Nectarine Kuchen

Serves 6–8

This is not a kuchen in the strictest sense, since it contains no yeast, but the batter puffs up in the same way. The apricot glaze glistens on top of the nectarines and is bordered with a ground almond mixture.

  1   *cup all-purpose flour*
1½   *teaspoons baking powder*
  ¼   *teaspoon salt*
  4   *tablespoons (½ stick) unsalted butter*
  ⅓   *cup plus 2 teaspoons sugar*
  1   *large egg, lightly beaten*
  1   *teaspoon grated lemon rind*
  ⅓   *cup milk*
4–5   *large, ripe but firm nectarines (about 1½ pounds), unpeeled, pitted, and sliced into eighths*

TOPPING

  3   *tablespoons unsalted butter, softened*
  ¾   *cup ground almonds*
  ¼   *cup light brown sugar*
  ¼   *cup all-purpose flour*

GLAZE

  ¼   *cup apricot jam or preserves*
  1   *tablespoon kirsch, cognac, or water*

Preheat the oven to 375° F. Grease and flour a 9 × 2-inch deep baking pan or pie dish.

Sift together the flour, baking powder, and salt. Set aside. In a large bowl, or the bowl of an electric mixer, cream the butter and ⅓ cup sugar, and beat until light and fluffy. Add the egg, and beat until well blended. Add the grated lemon rind. Add the flour mixture and milk. Scrape the sides with a spatula and mix the last few turns by hand. Spoon the batter into the prepared pan and spread evenly. Arrange the nectarines, peel side up, on top of the batter in a circle beginning on the outer edge and working toward the middle. Sprinkle with the remaining 2 teaspoons of sugar and bake for 35 minutes.

Prepare the topping and glaze while the kuchen is baking. Blend the topping ingredients until thoroughly mixed. Set aside. In a small saucepan, bring the jam and liqueur to a boil and cook for 1 to 2 minutes. Remove from heat but keep hot.

After 35 minutes, remove the pan from the oven and increase the temperature to 400° F. Spread the topping around the outer edge of the kuchen in a band about 1 inch wide, return to the oven, and bake for 10 to 12 minutes more. Remove from oven and spread the glaze over the exposed nectarines. Cool for at least 30 minutes and serve.

Peach Duff

Serves 4–6

Because this recipe is simple, quick, and not too sweet, it is an excellent breakfast or brunch dessert.

¼	cup (½ stick) *lightly salted butter or margarine*
1	cup all-purpose flour
3	teaspoons baking powder
¼	teaspoon salt
½	cup sugar
⅔	cup milk
4 to 6	peaches (*about 1½ pounds*), *peeled and thickly sliced*

Preheat the oven to 375° F.

Melt the butter in an 8-inch square baking pan. Sift together the flour, baking powder, salt, and sugar. Gradually add the milk and stir just until the flour mixture is moistened. Spoon the batter evenly onto the melted butter. Arrange the peach slices in rows on top of the batter. Bake 35 minutes. Serve slightly warm.

NOTE: To make for two, halve the ingredients and bake in an 8-inch cake pan with the peach slices arranged in circles.

Peach Wine Sorbet

Yields 1 pint

Tart enough to be a pleasant palate cleanser between courses, this sorbet can also be a refreshing dessert. It is especially good (and pretty) served with a fresh blueberry sauce.

⅓	cup sugar
½	cup water
1½	cups peeled and coarsely chopped peaches
1	tablespoon lemon juice
½	cup medium-dry white wine

Place the sugar and water in a small saucepan and bring to a boil. Simmer for 5 minutes, then cool. Puree the peaches, lemon juice, and wine in a blender or food processor and add the cooled syrup. Blend thoroughly. (The peel from ¼ peach may be added with the peaches for a stronger peach flavor and color.) Freeze in an ice cream maker according to manufacturer's directions and pack in a freezer carton. Or pour into a flat pan (the wider the pan the faster mixture will freeze) and place in freezer. When mixture is frozen, spoon into a chilled bowl and beat with an electric or hand rotary beater until light and smooth. Pack lightly in a freezer carton and return to freezer.

P·E·A·R·S

Pear and Leek Soup

Pears and Endive with Honey-Lime Dressing

Pear Salad with Pecans

Curried Pear and Potato Salad

Casserole of Pears, Chinese Cabbage, Potatoes, and Onions

Chopped Pears with Spinach

Sole with Pears

Boned Chicken with Spinach and Pear Stuffing, Served with Pear Sauce

Cornish Game Hens with Pears and Fennel

Basic Recipe for Poaching Pears

Baked Caramel Pears

Pear Galette

Champagne Pear Sorbet

Pear-Topped Gingerbread

The pear is one of the ancient fruits, with a history that predates Christianity by 2,000 years. Some of the earliest writings place its origin in China, and there is evidence of pear orchards in Greece in Homer's time. Even in that pre-Christian era, grafting methods were used to develop improved varieties, in all probability stimulated by the fact that wild pears were too bitter to be eaten without prolonged cooking. Since then, about 5,000 varieties have been named in European publications, and some 1,000 in the United States. The species from which most cultivated pears have been developed is *Pyrus* 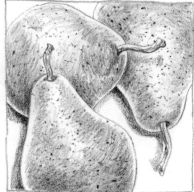 *communis*.

The pear traveled with the early colonists from England and France to North America. In 1640 pear trees were planted in the Massachusetts Bay Colony, and some sixty years later, about 1700, the French settlers introduced pears along the Detroit River. In California, the Spanish friars were, once again, responsible for the introduction of yet another species of fruit to that state with its near-perfect climate.

Because pears blossom earlier in the spring than apples, their climate range is more limited. The western states of California, Oregon, and Washington, with their ideal growing weather, raise nearly all the pears marketed in this country. In the East, a secondary but important orchard area is in the region of Lake Michigan and to the south of Lake Ontario, where these large bodies of water moderate the cold of winter and the frosts in spring.

Pears are grown in all the temperate-climate countries throughout Europe and Asia, as well as in Australia, New Zealand, South Africa, and South America. In the United States most of the commercially grown fruit is used fresh and canned, in contrast to Europe, where most of the crop is used in the production of alcoholic beverages.

Asiatic pears have been developed from the Chinese sand pear, *P. pyrifolia*, characterized by a gritty or sandy flesh. Crosses of this pear with more desirable varieties are grown in the eastern United States because they are more resistant to fire blight, a serious plant disease in that region. Asiatic pears found in our produce markets are sold under a variety of names such as Asian Pear, Chinese Pear, and Pear-Apple or Apple-Pear because of an apple-like roundness, but with the pale green or yellow of the pear. The flesh is very hard and crisp, juicy and somewhat gritty, with a mildly sweet, quite bland flavor.

⊷ HOME CULTIVATION ⊷

Although pears can be grown east of the Rocky Mountains, only the Pacific Northwest has an ideal climate for the production of high-quality fruit. For the home garden, dwarf trees are a good choice. Pears take particularly well to formal espalier training against a wall or fence. In England's Cotswolds the entire facade of one old inn is covered with one of these trees, and the famous partridge is often depicted in just such an espaliered pear tree.

⊷ NUTRITION ⊷

The 98 calories contained in a pear are made up of 98 percent carbohydrates. It is an excellent source of both dietary and crude fiber, and is rich in potassium and vitamin C.

⊷ SELECTION ⊷

When selecting pears, look for fruit without blemishes and with stems intact. Pears are picked green because they become mealy if left to ripen on the tree. It is best to buy pears that are slightly underripe and let them ripen at room temperature after purchase. You know the pear is ripe when it yields to gentle pressure at the stem end. Under the list of varieties you will see the appropriate color of ripe fruit for each type. Pears may be bought fresh, canned, and dried. The juice is sold as pear nectar.

Varieties

Varieties and dates given are for those domestically grown.

Bartlett—From August through December. That season is extended when the Chilean Bartletts come on the market in March, although these have not been of as good flavor as the domestic ones. The Bartlett has a typical bell shape, with a thin yellow skin, which may have a red blush when fully ripe. The flesh is smooth, white, and juicy, with an excellent sweet flavor, which makes it a superior fruit for eating fresh and for use in desserts and salads. This is the variety usually found canned. In England and Europe the Williams is another name for this same pear. The eau-de-vie Poire William, made from this variety, is delicious and costly.

Red Bartlett—The same as the yellow except the skin should turn from a dark green-red to a brilliant red when ripe. It is not worth the higher price unless you are using it decoratively.

Anjou—Long-keeping pear available from October through May. The skin is somewhat coarse, light green to yellow-green when ripe, and is somewhat egg shaped with almost no shoulder. The flesh is white, sweet, and juicy. This is a firmer fruit than the Bartlett, but less flavorsome.

Red Anjou—The same as the green but red.

Bosc—Available September through May. The color and shape of the Bosc is different from any of the others. It has a long tapering neck with a symmetrical body. The skin is deeply russeted with an underlying gold when ripe; to be absolutely certain of its ripeness, it should yield to gentle pressure at the stem end. The flesh is aromatic, not quite as juicy as other varieties, but holds its shape well for baking, broiling, and poaching.

Comice—Available October through February. It has a chubby shape, and can be medium to very large in size. It turns from green to yellow-green when ripe, with a moderately thin skin. This is a superior eating pear, with flesh that is smooth, extremely juicy, and with an especially fine, sweet flavor. It is the choice for very expensive holiday fruit packages. With increased demand has come increased production and, happily, some reduction in price.

Seckel—Although the producers claim the seckel is available from August through January, it appears very briefly in northeastern markets. The smallest of the pears, it is very firm, which makes it popular for canning and pickling.

Packham—A late-season pear with the overall size and shape of the Anjou, but with a bumpy surface. The green becomes lighter with a yellow undercast when it ripens. Once fully ripe this is a wonderful juicy sweet fruit

to eat fresh. It has an excellent flavor in cooked dishes, but should be used while still a bit firm.

Asian Pears—There are many varieties that appear somewhat sporadically in eastern markets. One is the Japanese Twentieth Century, which has pale yellow, coarse skin and a transparent crisp flesh that exudes a very sweet juice with little flavor. This lack of flavor may simply be the problem of all fruits that travel great distances from where they are grown.

EQUIVALENTS
1 pound = 2 average pears, Anjou or similar
= 2 cups sliced

STORAGE
⊷ AND PREPARATION ⊷

Pears may be ripened at room temperature, then should be stored in the refrigerator.

Pears may be peeled with any sharp paring knife but the swivel-bladed vegetable peeler removes a thinner peel. For easiest removal, peel vertically from stem to blossom end.

To remove core to bake or poach fruit whole, use a coring tool or melon baller from the blossom end. When using halves, remove the core with the small end of a melon baller, small knife, or teaspoon.

To keep cut pears from turning brown dip them into water to which lemon juice has been added. One restaurateur suggests using a bowl of lemonade for dipping the fruit.

⊷   ⊷

Pears are an excellent choice as one of the first fruits for young children, whether cooked into a lovely smooth pear sauce or eaten out of hand. Biting into the buttery flesh is easy even with missing teeth. Pears are a great foil for sharper-flavored fruits such as cranberries, can take the sometimes metallic edge from spinach, and work well to thicken and flavor hot or cold soups. When served fresh in salads, use a lemon vinaigrette to enhance the flavor and preserve their color. For a first course serve pears with one of the blue cheeses or conclude with a triple-crème dessert cheese and toasted walnuts. Preserved ginger is marvelous chopped over poached pears or the fresh fruit slices in a salad. To appreciate the delicate fruit flavor unadorned make a simple pastry tart of sliced pears, sugar, and a bit of butter. Poach pears in red wine and serve with a crème anglaise or poach in syrup and serve with chocolate sauce; a puree of strawberries, blueberries, or raspberries makes a delicious sauce for poached pears.

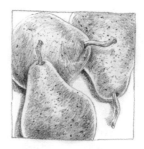

Pear and Leek Soup

Serves 6–8

This soup is also excellent when served at room temperature. We use either Anjou or Comice pears for this dish and, if at all possible, homemade stock.

    3   cups leeks, thinly sliced
    4   tablespoons (½ stick) unsalted butter or
        margarine
    4   pears (2 pounds), peeled and diced
    1   medium potato, peeled and diced
    6   cups chicken stock
    1   teaspoon chopped summer savory
    1   teaspoon lemon juice
        Salt and freshly ground pepper to taste
        Sprig of dill or parsley

In a saucepan, sauté the leeks in butter over moderate heat until softened. Add the pears and continue cooking for about 5 minutes, stirring constantly. Add potato, stock, savory, and lemon juice, then bring liquid to a boil, and simmer for 20 minutes. Puree the mixture in batches in blender or food processor. Transfer the soup back to the saucepan, add salt and pepper, and heat soup until hot. Garnish with dill or parsley sprig.

Pears and Endive with Honey-Lime Dressing

Serves 4

This unusual combination looks very attractive but tastes even better.

    ½   cup lime juice
    ½   teaspoon Dijon mustard
    ¼   cup honey or more to taste
    ¼   teaspoon salt
    ¼   teaspoon paprika
    ¼   teaspoon lemon rind
    ¼   cup canola or other vegetable oil
    4   ripe but firm Comice or Anjou pears
        (2 pounds)
    4   loose-head lettuce leaves
    2   Belgian endive

Put aside 2 tablespoons of the lime juice. Mix the remaining juice with the mustard, honey, salt, paprika, lemon rind, and oil. Set aside. Slice each pear into eighths, carefully removing the core and seeds. Leave unpeeled. Place on a plate and coat well with reserved lime juice to avoid discoloration.

Line a large serving dish or individual serving plates with lettuce. Arrange the pear slices and the endive to make an attractive display. Spoon the dressing over the fruit and serve immediately.

Pear Salad with Pecans

Serves 4

Marinating the pears allows them to absorb more flavor from the dressing but if you are pressed for time, just proceed without the marinating.

- 2 tablespoons lemon juice
- 1 tablespoon Dijon mustard
- ¼ teaspoon salt
  Freshly ground pepper to taste
- 3 tablespoons olive oil
- 1 tablespoon safflower oil
- 2 firm but fully ripe pears such as Bartlett, yellow or red (1 pound)
- ½ cup pecans
- 1 medium head Romaine or other crisp lettuce

In the bottom of a salad bowl, mix the lemon juice, mustard, salt, and pepper, then beat in the oils until well blended and somewhat thickened. Quarter and core the unpeeled pears, and cut into ½-inch or larger chunks. Stir gently into the dressing to coat. If time allows, let pears stand in dressing for 1 hour. Toast pecans briefly in a nonstick skillet and cool. Place torn lettuce over the pears and top with pecans. Toss to coat the lettuce just before serving.

Curried Pear and Potato Salad

Serves 8

Almost any fruit can be seasoned with curry to good advantage. Make this salad ahead and let it stand in the dressing for several hours for the flavors to blend.

- 2 pounds waxy potatoes such as Long Island or Florida (*not baking type*)
- ¼ cup cider vinegar
- ½ teaspoon sugar
- 1 teaspoon whole-grain mustard
- 1 tablespoon curry powder
- ½ teaspoon salt
- ¼ teaspoon freshly ground pepper
- ½ cup olive oil
- 2 scallions, finely sliced, including part of green
- ¼ cup chutney, large pieces chopped (use any spicy fruit chutney)
- 1½ pounds firm, ripe pears (3 medium), unpeeled
- ¼ cup chopped pistachio nuts

Boil the potatoes until barely tender, then set aside to cool. In a large bowl, mix the vinegar, sugar, mustard, curry powder, salt, and pepper. Beat in the oil until the dressing is smooth and thickened. Stir in the scallions and chutney. Quarter and core the pears, cut into ¼-inch thick crosswise slices, and add to the dressing in the bowl. Peel, quarter, and slice the potatoes; add to the bowl and stir to coat all with dressing. Taste for seasoning and sprinkle with pistachios just before serving.

Casserole of Pears, Chinese Cabbage, Potatoes, and Onions

Serves 4

1¼–1½   *pounds all-purpose potatoes*
2   *pounds Chinese cabbage*
2   *medium ripe but firm Bosc, Anjou, or Bartlett pears (1 pound)*
2   *tablespoons lemon juice*
1   *tablespoon unsalted butter*
1   *tablespoon canola or other vegetable oil*
3   *medium onions, thinly sliced*
½   *teaspoon dried sage*
    Salt and freshly ground pepper to taste
½   *cup chicken stock*

Preheat the oven to 400° F.

Peel and cut the potatoes into very thin slices. Wash the cabbage and cut into 1½-inch crosswise slices. Core and slice the pears into twelfths, but do not peel. Immediately coat with the lemon juice to avoid discoloration.

In a large ovenproof skillet, heat the butter and oil, and sauté the onions for about 4 minutes, or until soft but not brown. Add the cabbage, mix with the onions, and cook until wilted, about 3 minutes. Blend in the sliced pears, add sage, and season with salt and pepper. Add the potatoes and stock. Cover, place in oven, and bake for 25 minutes. Uncover, stir the mixture well, add the remaining ¼ cup stock, and continue cooking for 20 minutes more. Remove from oven and serve.

Chopped Pears with Spinach

Serves 4

The pears soften the sharpness of the spinach but should be fully ripe for best flavor. Makes a good broiled fish or poultry accompaniment.

2   *pounds fresh spinach, or 3 (10-ounce) packages frozen spinach*
5   *tablespoons lightly salted butter or margarine, or more if needed*
2   *ripe pears, preferably Bartlett (1 pound), peeled, cored, and chopped*
    Salt to taste
    Few gratings of nutmeg

Pick over spinach, removing any coarse stems, and rinse thoroughly. Place in a covered saucepan without adding water and cook over medium heat just until it is wilted (stir once with fork). Drain, refresh with cold water, and then press out as much water as possible by squeezing with paper towels.

In a skillet heat 2 tablespoons of the butter and cook the chopped pears, stirring until tender but still retaining their shape. Place the spinach in a food processor fitted with a steel blade, or in a blender, and chop—do not puree—then add to the pears with salt to taste, gratings of nutmeg, and remaining 3 tablespoons of butter. Before serving, stir over moderate heat until warm.

NOTE: If you make this recipe with frozen spinach, be careful not to overcook it.

Sole with Pears

Serves 4

It is best to serve this dish directly onto individual plates in the kitchen, rather than from a platter at the table, since the fish is quite delicate and may break up with too much handling. Serve with Lemon Rice (page 129), a green vegetable, or a colorful medley of mixed vegetables.

2   medium ripe but firm pears (*1 pound*), *peeled, halved, and cored*
2   cups Court Bouillon (*recipe follows*)
¾   cup dry white wine
4   fillets of sole (*1¼ pounds*), *not too thick* Salt to taste
½   cup whipping cream
2   teaspoons pear eau-de-vie Parsley sprigs, for garnish

Place pear halves in a wide skillet with Court Bouillon, and poach until just tender, about 5 minutes (easily pierced with a cake tester). Lift out the pears, set aside, and add the wine to the bouillon. Wrap each pear half with a fish fillet, securing with a toothpick. Salt lightly and poach gently in the bouillon until the fish is opaque—no longer. Lift out the fish and pears, and keep warm. Reduce liquid to about one-third, add the cream, and simmer for 10 minutes, or until the sauce is slightly thickened. Add the pear eau-de-vie, and adjust seasoning. Serve with a coating of sauce and a sprig of parsley for garnish.

Court Bouillon

1   bay leaf
½   onion, coarsely sliced
2   sprigs parsley Few celery leaves
¼   teaspoon salt
3   black peppercorns
2½   cups water
1   tablespoon dry vermouth

Place all ingredients in saucepan and simmer for 20 minutes.

Boned Chicken with Spinach and Pear Stuffing, Served with Pear Sauce

Serves 6–8

Once the chicken is deboned, this recipe is relatively simple to prepare. If you are unable to debone it yourself, ask your butcher to do it for you. The completed dish is both impressive to look at and elegant to serve. If any is left over, it is extremely good sliced cold, or with bread in a sandwich.

2 *(10-ounce) packages frozen chopped*
   spinach
3 *ripe Bartlett or Anjou pears (about 8*
   ounces each)
3 *tablespoons lemon juice*
1 *tablespoon unsalted butter*
1 *tablespon canola or other vegetable oil*
1 *medium onion, chopped*
½ *cup fresh unflavored bread crumbs*
½ *teaspoon ground nutmeg*
   Salt and freshly ground pepper to taste
1 *roasting or frying chicken (3–5 pounds),*
   deboned
   Pear Sauce (recipe follows)

Prepare the stuffing. Cook the spinach in boiling water for about 5 minutes, just until you can separate it easily with a fork. Remove from heat and drain well, pressing out as much water as possible. Set aside. Peel, core, and chop the pears until almost a puree. (This may be done in a blender or food processor.) Mix in the lemon juice to prevent discoloration.

In a large saucepan, heat the butter and oil, add the onion, and sauté over medium-high heat until soft but not brown, about 3 minutes. Add the chopped pears, bring to a boil, and continue cooking for another 3 minutes. Still over heat, blend in the spinach, bread crumbs, nutmeg, salt, and pepper. Remove from heat and set aside. (You should have 3 cups stuffing.)

Preheat the oven to 425°F. Put the chicken on a working board or tray, open it to lie flat, breast side up, and sprinkle with salt and pepper. Spread the stuffing on the chicken, then bring the two side sections back together over the stuffing. It should resemble its natural shape. Skewer through, tighten, and lace up with string, making sure that the

stuffing is packed well inside the folded chicken.

Place the chicken in a lightly oiled roasting pan, and bake for 35 to 40 minutes, occasionally basting with the pan juices. Remove from the oven onto a plate, cover, and keep warm while making the Pear Sauce. Reserve the pan juices, skimming off as much of the fat as possible.

To serve, cut each person a slice of the chicken about ¾ inch thick, and arrange on individual serving places, or on a serving platter. Spoon some of the Pear Sauce over each slice and serve immediately. Serve with small parsleyed new potatoes and a salad.

Pear Sauce

1 *ripe Bartlett or Anjou pear (8 ounces),*
   peeled, cored, and coarsely chopped
2½ *cups chicken stock*
½ *cup pan juices*
2 *teaspoons thyme*
⅛ *teaspoon nutmeg*
1 *teaspoon sugar*
   Salt and freshly ground pepper to taste
1 *teaspoon cornstarch*
1 *tablespoon water*
1 *tablespoon Poire William liqueur*
   (optional)

Combine the pear, chicken stock, pan juices, thyme, and nutmeg in a saucepan and bring to a boil. Reduce over medium-high heat for 8 to 10 minutes, or until the sauce begins to thicken. There should be 2 to 2½ cups remaining. Add the sugar, salt, and pepper. If the sauce is not sufficiently thick, dissolve the cornstarch in the water and stir into the sauce. Stir in the pear liqueur if desired. Keep hot.

Cornish Game Hens with Pears and Fennel

Serves 4

Make this special dish during the fall and winter when both pears and fennel are at their peak. The anise flavor of the fennel harmonizes with the sweetness of the ripe pear; the texture is a combination of crispness and velvet.

- 2 *Cornish game hens (about 1¼ pounds each), split, backbone and giblets reserved*
- 2 *sprigs parsley*
- 6 *black peppercorns*
- ½ *chicken bouillon cube*
- 1 *fennel bulb*
- 2 *large ripe but firm Anjou or Bosc pears (1 pound total)*
  Juice of 1 lemon
- 2 *tablespoons canola or other vegetable oil*
  Salt and freshly ground pepper to taste
- ½ *cup cognac*
- 2 *tablespoons finely chopped onion*
- 1 *cup dry white wine*

Place giblets, neck, and backbone in a small saucepan, cover with about ¾ cup water, and add parsley, peppercorns, and ½ a bouillon cube. Bring to a boil, cover, and cook over medium heat until tender, about 30 minutes. Strain and set aside.

Cut the stalks from the fennel bulb, but reserve about ¼ cup of the feathery leaves and chop them. Set aside. Trim and halve the bulb, cut away and discard the core, then slice into ½-inch-thick pieces. Bring a large pot of water to a boil, add the fennel, return the water to a boil, and cook for 3 minutes.

Remove from heat and immediately drain, rinse under cold water, and set aside. Cut the pears into quarters, remove the cores, but do not peel. Slice each quarter into 4 pieces and place on a flat plate or tray. Immediately coat with the lemon juice to prevent discoloration.

Preheat the oven to 400° F.

Brush the hens with 1 tablespoon of the oil, season with salt and pepper, and arrange skin side down in a roasting pan in a single layer. Pour over half of the cognac and roast for 20 minutes. Raise the temperature to 425° F. Turn the hens, baste the birds with the pan juices, and continue to roast for 20 minutes more.

While the hens are cooking, heat the remaining tablespoon of oil in a large saucepan, add the onion, and sauté until soft but not brown. Add the wine and the strained stock and cook over medium-high heat for about 10 minutes or until partly reduced. Add the fennel and pears, lower the heat, and cook, covered, for about 4 minutes. Add the remaining cognac and cook briefly to blend, about 1 to 2 minutes. Adjust seasonings. Remove from heat and keep warm.

When the hens are ready, remove from oven and arrange either on 1 large serving dish or on 4 individual plates. Spoon the sauce on top before serving. Top with a sprinkling of chopped fennel leaves.

Basic Recipe for Poaching Pears

Serves 4

Although pears should be firm for cooking, for best flavor they must be fully ripe. The syrup in this recipe is not overly sweet and has just enough lemon to bring out the pear flavor. Both sugar and lemon can be adjusted to suit personal preference.

4 *ripe medium pears (1½ pounds)*
4 *cups water*
1 *cup sugar*
4 *strips lemon zest, about 2 inches*
2 *teaspoons lemon juice*

Peel and core the pears. They may be left whole with stems intact (in which case you remove the core from the bottom), halved, or quartered. Bring water and sugar to a boil in a saucepan large enough to hold the pears in one layer. Add the lemon zest and boil gently for 3 minutes until the sugar is completely dissolved. Add the pears and lemon juice and simmer until the flesh is easily pierced with a fork and appears transparent. This will take about 15 minutes for quarters and longer for halves or whole pears. The variety will also make a difference in cooking time. If the syrup does not completely cover the fruit, heat more water with the same proportion of sugar, boil, and add to saucepan. When done, place pears in a bowl, pour syrup over, and chill when cooled.

VARIATION: Poach pears whole with stem intact. Place each pear upright in a crystal serving dish and drizzle chocolate sauce from the stem to coat upper part of the fruit.

Served with vanilla ice cream this becomes Poires Helene.

Baked Caramel Pears

Serves 6

Serve warm as a nice touch for a winter meal or to end an otherwise cold summer supper.

6 *ripe but firm pears, such as Anjou
    (3 pounds), peeled, halved, and cored*
½ *cup (1 stick) lightly salted butter*
6 *tablespoons sugar*
1 *cup whipping cream*

Preheat the oven to 400° F.

Arrange the pear halves close together in a shallow baking dish. Place 2 teaspoons of butter in the hollow pear centers and sprinkle half a tablespoon of sugar over each half. Bake in the center of the oven for about 20 minutes or until the sugar is caramelized. Remove the pears to serving dishes. Stir the cream into the pan juices and pour over the halves. May be served warm or at room temperature.

NOTE: If you want to make this dessert ahead of time and serve it warm, set aside the pan juices and keep the individual serving dishes covered and warm. Just before serving, rewarm the pan juices, add the cream, and serve as directed.

Pear Galette

Yields one 9-inch tart

A galette is a flat round pastry with a baked topping. Other fruits such as peaches, plums, or apricots could be prepared in this manner.

PASTRY

    1 cup all-purpose flour
    1 teaspoon sugar
   ¼ teaspoon salt
    5 tablespoons unsalted butter, cut into pieces
   ½ beaten egg
    4 tablespoons apricot preserves, sieved
   1½ teaspoons apricot liqueur

TOPPING

    2 firm, ripe pears (about 8 ounces each)
    2 tablespoons (¼ stick) lightly salted butter, melted
    1 teaspoon sugar

In a medium bowl, combine the flour, sugar, and salt. Cut in the butter with a pastry blender or tips of fingers until the mixture resembles coarse meal. Add the beaten egg and work into flour until dough comes together in a ball. Flatten into a disk and place in freezer for 10 minutes.

Roll the dough out on a floured board to a 9¾-inch circle (use a 9-inch cake pan as a pattern). Slide onto a baking sheet and turn up the edge ½ inch, making a raised, fluted rim. Melt the apricot preserves in a small saucepan with the apricot liqueur and brush some over the bottom of the tart shell. Reserve remainder.

Preheat the oven to 425° F.

Peel, quarter, and core the pears. Slice lengthwise into slices between ¼ and ½ inch thick, and arrange in overlapping circles, thin end toward center. Cut any leftover slices to fill the center. Brush the pears with melted butter and sprinkle with the sugar. Place on the center rack of the oven and bake for 10 minutes, then lower heat to 350° F. and bake 25 to 30 minutes longer or until pears and pastry are golden brown. Remove to a rack to cool. Add a teaspoon or so of water to reserved apricot glaze, reheat slightly to liquefy, and brush over the fruit.

Champagne Pear Sorbet

Yields 1 pint

Serve with sugar wafers or, even better, with freshly baked madeleines.

    1 (16-ounce) can pear halves in syrup
    2 teaspoons sugar
    1 teaspoon lemon juice
   ⅓ cup champagne

Drain pears; reserve ⅓ cup syrup. Puree the pears with the reserved syrup, sugar, and lemon juice in a food processor or blender. Stir in the champagne and chill. Freeze in an ice cream maker, following manfacturer's instructions, and pack in a freezer carton. Or pour into a flat pan (the wider the pan the faster mixture will freeze) and when an inch of the mixture is frozen, place in a chilled bowl and beat with an electric or hand rotary beater until light and smooth. Return to tray and refreeze. For even smoother sorbet, repeat procedure once more.

Pear-Topped Gingerbread

Yields one 8-inch square

It's important to use fresh, full-flavored ground ginger to give this cake the intense ginger taste that sets off the delicacy of the pears. If using Bartlett pears they should be just a little underripe.

- ½ cup (1 stick) plus 2 teaspoons lightly salted butter
- ½ cup firmly packed dark brown sugar
- 1½ cups all-purpose flour
- 1 teaspoon baking soda
- ¼ teaspoon salt
- 2 teaspoons ground ginger
- ½ teaspoon ground allspice
- ¼ teaspoon freshly grated nutmeg
- ¼ teaspoon ground cloves
- 2 large eggs, at room temperature
- ¼ cup unsulfured molasses
- ⅔ cup buttermilk or soured milk
- 2 ripe but firm pears, such as Anjou (1 pound), peeled, cored, and sliced about ¼ inch thick
- 2 tablespoons chopped crystallized ginger, in ¼-inch pieces

Preheat the oven to 325° F. Butter and flour an 8-inch square cake pan.

With an electric mixer or food processor, cream the ½ cup butter with the brown sugar until light. Meanwhile mix the flour, baking soda, salt, ginger, allspice, nutmeg, and cloves and set aside. Add the eggs to the butter one at a time, beating well after each addition, then add molasses; mix just to blend. Beat in half the dry ingredients, then beat in buttermilk. Add the remaining dry ingredients and blend well, but do not over-beat. Pour the batter into the baking pan and spread evenly with a spatula. Place the pear slices, close together, in 3 rows across top and sprinkle chopped ginger and remaining butter in tiny bits evenly over the pears. Bake for about 45 minutes or until a tester inserted in the center comes out clean. Place on a rack to cool. Cut into squares to serve.

P·I·N·E·A·P·P·L·E

Pineapple Relish

Pineapple, Cabbage, and Carrot Salad

Noodle Pudding with Pineapple

Grilled Halibut with Pineapple Sauce

Pineapple Stuffing for a Capon

Chicken with Pineapple and Lychees

Baked Spareribs with Pineapple

Pineapple, Lychee, and Kiwi Salad

Pineapple Upside-Down Cake

Pineapple Pavlova

Pineapple Cooler

Anyone who grows houseplants will quickly identify the pineapple as a relative of the countless variety of exotic plants known as bromeliads. One prominent characteristic is the succulent spiky leaves, often with sawlike edges. It is an interesting plant, with its rosette of closely spaced leaves on a thick stem from which the fruit develops. The fruit's shape and diamond pattern of the "eyes" gave rise to the association with a pine cone, certainly an oversized one. In common with other members of the family Bromeliaceae, it is indigenous to both tropical and subtropical America. Columbus dis-covered it growing in the West Indies in 1493. It gained ready acceptance by the Europeans, and during the fifteenth century was carried, perhaps by the Portuguese traders, to Africa, Madagascar, and India. Pineapple was a useful food shipboard, since it could be kept for relatively long periods and provided the sailors with much needed vitamin C. Since the plant grows readily from the discarded top, this might account for the plant's appearing wherever the sailors landed, so long as the climate was suitable.

The species from which all cultivated varieties have descended is *Ananas comosus*. There are relatively few varieties in commercial cultivation. The Smooth Cayenne is probably still the most important because it cans well. The Red Spanish traveled well and was grown in the Caribbean but is being supplanted by the larger Smooth Cayenne. Several others are grown in Central America and Puerto Rico but in smaller quantities.

If a dish is designated "Hawaiian Style," you can be fairly certain pineapple is a prominent ingredient. Until recently nearly all pineapple imported into mainland

United States came from Hawaii. Now, however, the market is shared with Central America and Puerto Rico. Hawaii still dominates in production worldwide, but does not hold the monopoly that it once did. Florida was the only mainland state to grow pineapples, but production there is now negligible owing to a variety of growing problems.

Pineapples are at peak flavor when field ripened, but do not travel well once fully ripe. This was of particular concern in Hawaii before the development of modern transportation and refrigeration. It was possible for a major industry to become established only after a canning operation was created by Dole's company in 1903. That year less than 2,000 cases were packed, two years later the cannery produced 25,000 cases. Today, pineapple is available in frozen products, as well as crushed fruit, whole slices, chunks, and juice in cans.

❧ HOME CULTIVATION ❧

The pineapple crown can be grown as follows: remove three or four leaves from the bottom, then place in a dry, shady place for a week to allow the end to harden, to prevent rot. Put drainage material in the bottom of an eight-inch pot and fill with a good, light potting soil, then set the crown in the soil. In cold climates keep indoors until all danger of frost is past; in warm climates it can be set out in the garden. In Hawaii, a crown takes twenty-four to twenty-six months to produce a ripe fruit, so expect your plant to take somewhat longer. It is an interesting project for a very patient gardener.

❧ NUTRITION ❧

Pineapple is an excellent source of vitamin C and a superior source of vitamin A. It is also high in potassium and dietary fiber. One cup of fresh pineapple has 80 calories. One half-cup of canned pineapple chunks in syrup has 95 calories.

❧ SELECTION ❧

It is important to select a pineapple that is ripe, since they do not ripen further after they are picked. When fully ripe, pineapples develop a reddish-gold color and should have a strong pineapple aroma. Being able to pull a leaf out easily does not denote ripeness. Examine for soft spots, since this is a sign of an overripe fruit. Those grown in Hawaii are superior in sweetness and flavor, possibly because they can be picked riper as they are shipped by air, whereas those from Central America are sent by truck and ship.

EQUIVALENTS		
1 medium pineapple	=	about 4 pounds
	=	5½ cups diced
1 pineapple purchased and cored	=	2½ cups diced

STORAGE ❧ AND PREPARATION ❧

Pineapple is best used soon after purchase. It can be refrigerated for a day or two, but wrap it in plastic to protect the flavor of other foods.

To peel, first remove the top by twisting it off, or using a sharp knife, cut just below the crown and remove a slice from the bottom, then stand in a shallow pan to catch the juice. Holding the pineapple upright, use a sharp knife and peel in vertical strips, removing the eyes with the knife tip.

If the fruit is to be served in slices or cubed, slice it crosswise, then cut the slices in half, remove the hard, woody core (the fruit's stem), and using your sharp knife, remove the outer rind.

For long spears, after removing the crown, cut a thin slice from the bottom, then halve lengthwise, cut in quarters, and remove core. It can then be cut to the desired size.

Fruit that is already peeled and cored can now be purchased in plastic bags. Certainly easier to use, but it is more expensive.

To use the shell for serving, cut in half lengthwise through the crown, and using a curved grapefruit knife, remove the fruit, leaving a ¾-inch shell. It may be filled with the removed fruit, which has been cubed and mixed with other fruits, or with a pineapple and chicken or seafood salad.

As fresh fruits have become more available, the market shelves of canned types have continued to shrink, but not so with pineapple. It is not only very much present but the only fruit that can be had in slices, spears, chunks, crushed, and as juice. Although the canned has excellent flavor when grilled, try fresh pineapple slices with a touch of butter and brown sugar the next time you barbecue poultry or meat. Remember, however, that for dishes containing gelatin, you cannot use fresh pineapple because it contains an enzyme that will inhibit jelling. Some traditional pineapple dishes are broiled or baked slices with baked ham, pineapple chunks in Chinese sweet-and-sour dishes, and pineapple upside-down cake. For a newer taste, mix fresh fruit with other tropical fruits such as mango, papaya, kiwi, and passion fruit in a dessert mélange with a bit of orange liqueur or in a meringue shell with whipped cream (Pavlova). But for the simplest preparation of a perfectly ripened pineapple, cut it into slices about ¾ inch thick, quarter the slice, remove core, and eat with knife and fork or—simplest of all—just pick up the wedge and eat out of hand.

Pineapple Relish

Yields 3 cups

Try this relish with poultry or fish, or use it to top off a sandwich filling. Since this relish is cooked, it will keep for several months in the refrigerator.

1 *fresh pineapple, peeled, cored, and cut into 1-inch cubes*
¼ *cup cider vinegar*
½ *cup sugar*
½ *teaspoon salt*
2 *tablespoons canola or other vegetable oil*
2 *teaspoons peeled and minced fresh ginger*
1 *teaspoon mustard seeds*
1 *teaspoon fennel seeds*
½ *teaspoon whole black peppercorns*
½ *teaspoon cumin seeds*
1 *teaspoon ground coriander*
½ *teaspoon turmeric*
   Dash of cayenne pepper

In a large saucepan, combine all the ingredients, bring to a boil, lower the heat to medium, and cook, uncovered, for about 35 to 50 minutes, or until the mixture has begun to take on a jamlike consistency. (It will take this amount of time because pineapple gives off a lot of juice as it cooks.) Stir frequently to prevent any sticking and burning on the bottom of the pan. Remove from heat, cool, then place in airtight containers and refrigerate.

Pineapple, Cabbage, and Carrot Salad

Serves 6

An inviting summer salad, especially on a buffet table or at an outdoor barbeque; equally good served with fish, poultry, or meat. You can even make it a day early since it holds exceptionally well.

1 *head savoy cabbage*
½ *fresh pineapple, peeled and diced; or 8 ounces canned pineapple chunks, drained*
2 *large carrots, each about 7 inches long, scraped*
6 *tablespoons red wine vinegar*
4 *tablespoons canola or other vegetable oil*
1 *tablespoon sugar*
   Salt and freshly ground pepper to taste

Slice the cabbage as finely as possible by hand, or shred it in a food processor. If the pineapple chunks are very large, dice. Shred the carrots. Place all in a bowl and mix well.

Combine the vinegar, oil, and sugar, and season to taste with salt and pepper. Mix all the ingredients thoroughly and blend into the salad. Chill for several hours before serving.

NOTE: If savoy cabbage is unavailable, use green cabbage.

Noodle Pudding with Pineapple

Serves 8–10

This variation on the traditional rich noodle kugel uses lower-calorie ingredients. It is usually served hot, but does well at room temperature. It can also be refrigerated for several days or frozen for up to three months, then brought to room temperature or reheated.

PUDDING

12 *ounces wide egg noodles*
 2 *large eggs, well beaten*
 1 *(16-ounce) container plain low-fat yogurt*
 1 *(16-ounce) container small-curd low-fat cottage cheese*
¾ *cup low-fat milk*
⅔ *cup sugar*
 1 *(8-ounce) can crushed pineapple in natural juices, drained*
½ *cup raisins*

TOPPING

¾ *cup crushed cornflakes*
 2 *teaspoons ground cinnamon*
 1 *teaspoon sugar*

Preheat the oven to 350° F. Grease a 13 × 9-inch glass baking dish or pan with 2-inch sides.

Cook the noodles according to package directions, and drain well. Combine eggs, yogurt, cottage cheese, milk, and sugar in a food processor until well blended. Add the crushed pineapple and raisins. Pour into prepared dish.

Blend ingredients for topping and sprinkle on top of pudding. Bake for 40 minutes or until golden brown and crisp on the top. Remove from the oven and allow to rest 30 minutes before serving.

Grilled Halibut with Pineapple Sauce

Serves 4

Pineapple and halibut merge happily. The fish broiled with the lower third immersed in water ensures a juicy and succulent result, and there is no need to turn it during the cooking.

 1 *fresh pineapple*
 1 *tablespoon canola or other vegetable oil*
 2 *tablespoons (¼ stick) unsalted butter*
 3 *tablespoons finely chopped onion*
 3 *tablespoons lime juice*
 1 *tablespoon light soy sauce*
 1 *teaspoon cornstarch*
 1 *tablespoon water*
    Salt and freshly ground pepper to taste
 4 *halibut steaks, about 6 ounces each*
⅓ *cup fresh bread crumbs*

Cut the skin from the pineapple, then slice it and cut the slices into ¾-inch cubes. Put the diced pineapple in a colander over a bowl, set aside, and leave for the juice to collect. Allow to stand for about 30 minutes.

Heat the oil and 1 tablespoon of the butter in a saucepan; add the onion and sauté for about 5 minutes over medium-high heat until softened. Add only the pineapple cubes

(continued on next page)

and continue cooking, stirring, for 4 to 5 minutes. Add the lime juice and soy sauce. With a slotted spoon remove the pineapple from the pan and place it back in the colander over the bowl and set aside. Add the juice that has collected from the pineapple to the sauce and cook for 5 minutes over medium-high heat until slightly reduced. Mix the cornstarch and water and stir into the sauce until thickened. Return the pineapple together with any additional juice and blend in. Keep hot and reheat thoroughly if necessary before serving.

Preheat the broiler. Season the fish steaks and place in a pan containing sufficient water to immerse the lower third of the fish. Dot with remaining tablespoon butter and broil for 5 minutes. Sprinkle with the bread crumbs and continue cooking for 5 minutes or until done and slightly brown. Remove from the oven and serve immediately with the pineapple sauce.

Pineapple Stuffing for a Capon

Yields 4 cups

This can also be served as a side dish for meats and poultry.

1 *tablespoon canola or other vegetable oil*
1 *tablespoon unsalted butter*
1/4 *cup finely chopped onion*
1 *cup finely chopped celery*
2 *tablespoons finely chopped fresh parsley*
3 *cups cooked wild rice*
1/4 *teaspoon paprika*
1/4 *teaspoon ground cloves*

1 *cup pineapple chunks, drained*
1 *cup crushed pineapple, drained*
1/2 *cup raisins*
Salt and freshly ground pepper to taste

In a large skillet heat the oil and butter, add the onion, and cook over medium heat until lightly browned, about 5 minutes. Add the celery and parsley, and cook, stirring, for 2 minutes. Mix in the wild rice, paprika, and cloves. Dice each pineapple chunk into 4 and add to the rice mixture with the remaining ingredients, stirring until well blended. Season to taste with salt and pepper.

NOTE: A combination of wild rice and long-grain white rice may also be used. Two cups of stuffing are needed to fill a 7-pound capon.

Chicken with Pineapple and Lychees

Serves 4

This recipe was inspired by a dish from Hong Kong.

2 *whole chicken breasts, skinned and boned*
1 *tablespoon plus 2 teaspoons cornstarch*
1/4 *teaspoon salt*
1/2 *teaspoon ground ginger*
2 *carrots, each about 7 inches long*
1 *(8-ounce) can pineapple chunks in natural juices*
1 *(20-ounce) can lychees in syrup*
2 *tablespoons medium-dry sherry*
2 *tablespoons canola or other vegetable oil*
1/4 *teaspoon peeled and minced fresh ginger*
2 *tablespoons finely chopped scallions, including 2 inches of green*
1/4 *cup salted cashew nuts*

Rinse, then pat the chicken breasts dry with paper towels. Cut into strips about 1½ inches by ½ inch. Mix the 1 tablespoon of cornstarch, salt, and ginger. Coat the chicken pieces with this mixture in a plastic bag and set aside for about 20 minutes.

Scrape the carrots and cut on the diagonal into slices ⅛ inch thick. Drain the pineapple and reserve ¼ cup of the juice. Cut the chunks in half. Drain the lychees and reserve ⅓ cup of the juice. Slice the lychees into halves, and set aside. In a small bowl, combine the sherry, fruit juices, and remaining 2 teaspoons of cornstarch. Set all aside.

Heat the oil in a wok or large skillet, add the chicken, and cook, stirring, over medium to medium-high heat for 3 minutes. Add the carrots and cook for a further 3 minutes. Stir the sherry mixture, then add to the wok. Stirring constantly, add the ginger and scallions, and cook for about 3 minutes. Lastly, stir in the pineapple, lychees, and cashew nuts and cook until heated through for another 3 minutes. Serve immediately with thin noodles or steamed white rice.

Baked Spareribs with Pineapple

Serves 4

The sweet taste of the pineapple with the added oriental flavor won't overpower the ribs.

1   (20-ounce) *can pineapple chunks in natural juices*
1   *tablespoon canola or other vegetable oil*
½   *medium onion, finely chopped*
2   *tablespoons light soy sauce*
2   *tablespoons lemon juice*
2   *tablespoons dry sherry*
2   *tablespoons honey*
1   *tablespoon Pickapeppa Sauce*
¼   *teaspoon minced fresh garlic*
½   *teaspoon peeled and minced fresh ginger*
1   *teaspoon salt*
2   *teaspoons cornstarch*
2   *tablespoons water*
     Tabasco to taste
2   *pounds pork baby back ribs*

Drain the pineapple and reserve the juice. Chop the chunks into smaller cubes but do not crush. In a large saucepan, heat the oil, add the onion, and cook over medium heat until lightly browned, about 10 to 12 minutes. Add the chopped pineapple and ½ cup of the pineapple juice and all the remaining ingredients except the ribs. Stir to mix well. Bring to a boil, then simmer for 20 minutes. Remove from heat.

Place the ribs in a pan, preferably in a single layer, add the marinade, cover, and refrigerate overnight. Turn once during this time.

Preheat the oven to 325° F.

Bake the ribs for 45 minutes, turn, and continue cooking for a further 45 minutes. If desired, broil to crisp before serving.

Pineapple, Lychee, and Kiwi Salad

Serves 4–6

This is surely one of the most exotic fruit salads you will ever eat. The lychees add a lightness and clean flavor that is unequaled.

    1 (20-ounce) can lychees in syrup
    1 fresh pineapple, peeled and cored
    3 kiwi fruits
    1 tablespoon lime juice
    3 tablespoons Triple Sec

Drain the lychees and cut in half. (The juice may be chilled and if desired used for a drink.) Cut the pineapple into ½-inch-thick slices, then dice into ¾-inch chunks. You will have 2 cups of pineapple chunks. Peel the kiwi fruits and slice crosswise ⅛ inch thick.

In an attractive serving bowl, combine all the fruit and stir gently to mix. Add the lime juice and Triple Sec, and stir again. Cover and chill for at least 3 hours before serving.

NOTE: If available, fresh lychees may be used. The flavor of the salad will be somewhat less sweet.

❧   ❧

Pineapple Upside-Down Cake

Serves 8–10

The rich caramel coating over the pineapple pattern is so attractive that, if you serve whipped cream, you will want to pass it rather than putting it on the cake itself.

    ⅓ cup lightly salted butter
    ½ cup dark brown sugar
    1 (1 pound) can sliced pineapple, unsweetened, drained
    1 cup all-purpose flour
    ¾ cup granulated sugar
    1½ teaspoons baking powder
    ½ teaspoon salt
    ¼ cup solid vegetable shortening
    ½ cup milk
    1 large egg
    ¾ teaspoon vanilla extract

Preheat the oven to 350° F.

Melt the butter in a heavy ovenproof, 10-inch skillet or baking dish, then turn pan to coat sides. Sprinkle the brown sugar evenly over the butter and arrange the pineapple slices in an attractive pattern. Use all slices—center one, and push the others to go up sides about 1 inch, if necessary, to make them fit. The last slice can be cut into wedges, and fitted in to fill the spaces.

Combine the flour, granulated sugar, baking powder, and salt in mixer bowl, add the shortening, pour in half of the milk, and beat to blend. Add remaining milk with egg and vanilla and beat for about 2 minutes. Pour the batter evenly over the pineapple. Place on the middle rack of the oven and bake for 45 to 60 minutes, or until a cake tester comes out clean.

Allow cake to rest for 3 or 4 minutes, then place a plate over the pan and invert onto the plate. Remove pan carefully, and if any pieces stick to the pan, replace onto the cake. (Make sure the plate is about 1 inch or more wider than the pan to allow room for the syrup to run down.) Serve plain or with whipped cream.

P i n e a p p l e   P a v l o v a

Serves 8

Although Dorrit was long familiar with this dessert of Australian origin (named in honor of the Russian ballerina, Anna Pavlova), Rolce first became acquainted with it when Pam Maclean, a former member of the Harvard Book Club, brought this to one of our meetings. Pam has long since returned to her medical practice in Dundee, Scotland, but her awe-inspiring recipe has been a pleasant and frequent reminder of her sojourn at Harvard. As with all meringues, it is best made on days with little humidity.

> 4   *large egg whites, at room temperature*
> 1/4   *teaspoon salt*
> 1   *cup sugar*
> 2   *teaspoons cornstarch*
> 1/2   *teaspoon vanilla extract*
> 1/2   *teaspoon distilled white vinegar*
> 1   *cup whipping cream, whipped*
> 2–3   *cups fresh fruit in bite-size pieces; pineapple, peaches, raspberries, bananas, blueberries, strawberries, kiwi, and passion fruit may all be used in different combinations*

Preheat the oven to 275° F.

With an electric beater or whisk, beat the egg whites until they are foamy; add the salt and continue to beat until the whites form soft peaks. Continue beating while adding the sugar a tablespoon at a time. Then beat in the cornstarch, vanilla, and vinegar until thoroughly incorporated.

Use parchment or wax paper to fit a cookie sheet, stick down at the corners with a dab of the meringue, and draw a 10-inch circle, tracing around a cake pan. Spoon about three-fourths of the mixture into the center of the circle. With a spatula spread the meringue to the edge of the circle, leaving a layer about 1 inch thick in the center and building up the sides 2 inches and about 1 inch wide. Or, using a pastry bag make continuous circles to fill in the base, then build up the outer edge. Bake for 1¼ hours, or until the outside is firm. It should have little or no color.

Remove meringue from oven and let cool. It may crack but that doesn't matter. Just before serving, spread whipped cream in the bottom, and arrange fruit in an attractive pattern over the cream. Additional whipped cream may be served with it. The meringue can be stored, loosely covered for a day, but the fruit and cream should be assembled shortly before serving.

NOTE: A 10-inch pie plate can be used instead of a cookie sheet. Cover the bottom with a round of buttered wax paper and dust with cornstarch. Remove from the pan when cool.

P i n e a p p l e   C o o l e r

Serves 2 generously

A thirst quencher that hits the spot on a hot sultry day.

> 1   *cup unsweetened pineapple juice*
> 1   *mango, peeled, seeded, and chopped*
> 1   *ripe banana, peeled and cut into 4 pieces*
> 4   *ice cubes*

Combine the pineapple juice, mango, and banana in the bowl of a blender or food processor. Process until pureed and smooth. Pour into 2 tall glasses and add the ice cubes.

P·L·U·M·S
and
P·R·U·N·E·S

Cabbage and Prune Salad
Prune and Chestnut Turkey Stuffing
Flaumen Tzimmes (Prune Tzimmes)
Karla's Curry
Pork Chops with Prunes
Plum Kuchen
Gingered Prune Cake
Plum Tart
Wine-Soaked Prunes
Cold Prune Soufflé
Armagnac Prune Ice Cream
Plum Sorbet
Matzo Fruit Pudding
Prune, Apple, and Nut Dessert

Plums, with more varieties than any other of the stone fruits, have their origins in three continents—Europe, Asia, and North America. Actually, cultivated plums are the result of multiple crosses between the different groups. The common European plum, *Prunus domestica,* comes from the area of the Caucasus and the area bordering the Caspian Sea, and includes the blue plums and prunes of Europe. These were brought to New England and Canada by the early English and French settlers. The Japanese or Oriental plum, *P. salicina,* is native to China, but was long cultivated in Japan and was intro-

duced to California by the Japanese. This type is yellow to red, never blue, is not as hardy as the ones from Europe, and grows best in the more felicitous environment of the West Coast. A third group, *P. americana,* is found over much of the eastern and central United States. Included in these native Americans is the small, shrubby beach plum, *P. maritima,* which grows along the East Coast. For many New Englanders, gathering beach plums and turning them into a delicious jam is a summer tradition. A variety of the domestica, the damson, from the Old World, is named for the general area of its origins, Damascus. It is in every way a smaller version of the domesticas—a small tree, with small leaves and blossoms and a small fruit that is much like a large olive in shape, and has a very tart taste. This quality of tartness makes it especially suitable for preserves and jams.

The plum, like the peach and cherry, is a stone or drupe fruit of the genus *Prunus.* However, the plum shows greater diversity in its range of distribution and in its physical characteristics. It might be a low-growing shrub, a small tree, or one that can attain twenty to thirty feet in height. The fruit ranges from olive-size to three inches in diameter, and can be blue purple, yellow, green, and various shades of red, from pale to nearly black.

Most of our table fruit is of the Japanese type, with nearly 90 percent of our domestic supply grown in California. Other important plum-producing states are Oregon, Washington, Michigan, and New York, where much of the crop is devoted to canning. In Europe plums are grown from Italy in the south to Norway and Sweden in the north. Yugoslavia has extensive acreage in plums, and produces a plum brandy called Slivovica. Some of the earliest European plums were the sloes, *P. spinosa*, a small, bitter fruit best known for its singular use in making sloe gin.

All prunes are plums, but not all plums can become prunes. Only those that can be dried without first removing the pit are suitable; other types ferment at the pit before drying. A high sugar content and firm flesh are other desirable qualities. Even the fresh fruit is often referred to as "prunes." Before harvesting, the fruit must ripen fully on the tree to develop the proper amount of sugar. Formerly, the ripened fruit was allowed to fall to the ground for gathering, but now mechanical tree shakers are used, with a fabric catching frame spread under the tree to retrieve the harvest. Once dried in the sun, nearly all plums are now dried in dehydrators. The production of prune fruit is largely confined to California, Washington, and Oregon.

❧ HOME CULTIVATION ❧

Plums include so many varieties, owing to cross-breeding, that in order to produce fruit the gardener needs to know the exact cultural requirements of the type selected. Some trees are self-pollinating while others require very specific pollinators. It is best to consult a reliable local nursery or extension service before making your purchase. The ornamental plums are just that—very beautiful landscape trees, but nonfruiting. The beach plum, in addition to its useful fruit, has a pretty spring bloom, and is frequently used in seaside plantings where a natural landscape is desired.

❧ NUTRITION ❧

Plums contain vitamins A, B, and C, have the minerals potassium and iron, and are one of the very best sources of fiber. Calories vary somewhat with the variety, but in general one three-ounce plum, two inches in diameter, has 30 calories. Five dried prunes have 110 calories.

❧ SELECTION ❧

When plums are ripe, most types will yield with gentle pressure. Some of the green-yellow varieties are quite firm and color is the determinant, but rock-hard fruit will not have the fullest flavor. Avoid fruit if the stem end shows a moist, brown discoloration.

Prunes are packaged either pitted or with pits, and usually with a size designation of small, medium, and large, or the number per pound. The lower the number, the larger the prune.

Varieties

Santa Rosa—Red-skinned with yellow flesh, tart flavor, and very juicy. The early sort appear about mid-July, the late ones in mid-August. Any plum with "Rosa" in its name will be of similar characteristics.

El Dorado—Large, heart-shaped, almost black skin and light amber flesh that turns red when cooked. This is a midseason type, July to August.

Laroda—Large, with reddish-yellow skin and sweet, firm yellow flesh.

Kelsey—Dark green turning to yellow when ripe. It has firm yellow flesh with a mild, sweet flavor.

President—Blue-skinned European type with firm, yellow flesh. This is not one of the best flavored varieties.

Italian or Prune—European blue variety, usually freestone, with a firm green to golden flesh. They are a good choice for stewing and baking.

Damson—Small, blue, very tart. It is used primarily for preserves, which are of excellent flavor.

Equivalents	
1 pound plums	= 6 medium size (2-inch diameter)
	= 2½ cups sliced
	= 2 cups diced
	= 1¾ cups pureed
20 whole prunes	= 1 cup
1 pound whole prunes	= 2⅔ cups
One 12-ounce box pitted prunes	= 40 prunes

STORAGE ❧ AND PREPARATION ❧

Plums may be kept at room temperature to ripen. Once ripe, store them in the refrigerator. Prunes keep best when refrigerated in glass containers.

Plums require little preparation beyond removal of the pit, which usually comes away easily from the halved flesh. The thin skin of the plum does not require its removal for most uses.

To plump prunes, pour boiling water over them and let stand about 5 minutes.

❧ ❧

Fresh plums are found in more varieties than almost any other fruit, with an incredible range of flavor from sweet to tart depending on the type. Some such as the Santa Rosa are tart near the skin, with a sweet very juicy flesh, while others, although with less juice and a firmer flesh, are totally sweet. The firmer blue Italian plums hold up best when poached or baked and are an excellent choice for open tarts and kuchen. Use more than one variety to get the full range of flavor in sauces and compotes, and for a further accent use cinnamon and lemon juice.

In this country prunes have in the past been relegated to a stewed breakfast food, while in France they have found a well-deserved place in haute cuisine, appearing in such varied dishes as sauces and stuffings for pork roasts and poultry as well as dessert soufflés and tarts. They are combined in compotes with both fresh fruits such as apples and pears and other dried fruits. Orange or lemon slices, with a stick of cinnamon, can add variety to the flavor. Prunes soaked in Port wine can be pureed to add to sauces for roast meats and fowl, or served by themselves with a cream or custard sauce for dessert.

Cabbage and Prune Salad

Serves 6–8

It's important to use a good mayonnaise, not a mayonnaise-type salad dressing which tends to be somewhat sweet. This salad is great for a buffet; it is easy to serve and combines well with other foods, such as baked ham or barbecued meats and poultry.

- ½ cup mayonnaise
- ¼ cup sour cream
- 4 teaspoons lemon juice
- ¾ teaspoon salt
- ⅛ teaspoon freshly ground pepper
- 8 cups chopped or coarsely shredded green cabbage
- 6 ounces pitted prunes, cut into quarters (about 20 prunes)

Mix the mayonnaise, sour cream, lemon juice, salt, and pepper to make the dressing. Place cabbage and prunes in a large serving bowl, add dressing, and mix well. Chill until serving time.

Prune and Chestnut Turkey Stuffing

Yields sufficient stuffing for 20-pound turkey

Rolce's childhood memories of Thanksgiving will always be associated with the flavor of prunes and chestnuts in the holiday turkey. This was her mother's recipe, probably a variation of one from her grandmother. Since her brothers have also carried on this family tradition, it's interesting to know at Thanksgiving that they are "sharing" the same meal although thousands of miles apart.

- 1½ pounds pitted prunes
- 1½ pounds chestnuts (canned may be used)
- 1 pound bulk sausage
- 12 cups bread cubes (not a dense type) (see Note)
- 2 large eggs, lightly beaten
- ¼ cup chopped fresh parsley
- 1 teaspoon salt
- ¼ teaspoon freshly ground pepper
- 1 scant tablespoon poultry seasoning
- 2 cups chopped onions
- 2 garlic cloves, minced
- 2 cups trimmed and chopped celery
- 1 cup (2 sticks) lightly salted butter

Cook and chop the prunes; set aside. Boil or roast chestnuts, remove shells and skins, and crumble into coarse pieces. Cook and drain the sausage. Combine sausage with prunes, chestnuts, bread cubes, eggs, parsley, and seasonings in a large bowl or pan.

In a medium skillet, cook the onions, garlic, and celery in 2 tablespoons of the butter until transparent, then add to mixture in the bowl and mix well. Melt the remaining butter in a skillet large enough to hold the entire mixture. Add the stuffing and stir to lightly brown. Stuff the body and neck openings of turkey, filling lightly as stuffing swells in cooking.

NOTE: Bread cubes should be prepared ahead and allowed to dry out a bit. Even though fresh chestnuts have an extra special flavor, don't hesitate to use canned for convenience sake.

⌁   ⌁

Flaumen Tzimmes
(Prune Tzimmes)

Serves 8–10

Traditionally this Jewish dish is served on Rosh Hashanah or as the main course for the seder dinner on Passover. It is rich and sweet, and a complete meal in itself. When served with crunchy bread and a green salad there is nothing better for a cold, blustery winter's night. A few more or less prunes, carrots, or potatoes really don't make any difference to the outcome of the dish. What's important is the long cooking period at a low temperature. Tzimmes makes wonderful leftovers, either reheated or for sandwiches with the meat.

This dish can also be frozen very successfully for up to three months.

> 3 *pounds boneless single beef brisket*
> 1 *tablespoon canola or other vegetable oil*
> 12 *ounces pitted prunes*
> 1½ *(20-ounce) packages frozen small whole carrots*
> 2 *tablespoons golden syrup or honey*
> 3 *tablespoons dark brown sugar*
> 2 *tablespoons lemon juice*
>   *Salt and freshly ground pepper to taste*
> 6 *medium potatoes, peeled and quartered*

Trim most of the fat from the brisket. In a large heavy ovenproof pot, heat the oil, add the meat, and brown on both sides over medium-high heat. Add water just to cover, then add all the ingredients except the seasonings and potatoes. Bring to a boil, cover, and simmer for 1½ hours, stirring occasionally.

Preheat the oven to 325° F.

Turn the meat, season with salt and pepper, add the potatoes, and transfer to oven to bake for a further 1½ hours, or until the meat is tender and brown and the sauce thick and syrupy. The slow long baking time improves the texture and flavor of the tzimmes, but care must be taken to prevent burning. If necessary, add a little water to the pot during the cooking period and stir occasionally.

Remove from oven and lift out the meat. Wrap and refrigerate overnight. The meat should be sliced across the grain, which is far easier to do when cold. Chill the vegetable and fruit mixture.

Before serving, slice the brisket thinly, return to the mixture, and place over low heat on top of the stove. Adjust seasonings, check the sauce for consistency, add a little water if it appears to be too thick, reheat thoroughly, and serve.

Karla's Curry

Serves 6

We've made this a spicy hot curry but the cook can adjust the flavor to his or her own taste by using less of the hot curry powder. It should be served along with condiments such as chutney, shredded coconut, diced green pepper, tomatoes, and boiled white rice.

2   pounds lean boneless beef, cut into 2-inch cubes
¼   cup flour seasoned with pepper to taste
6   tablespoons canola or other vegetable oil
1   large onion, finely chopped
2   garlic cloves, chopped
½   cup dried apples, cut in half
½   cup coarsely chopped dried apricots
1   cup coarsely chopped dried pitted prunes
½   cup slivered almonds
2½ cups beef stock
2   tablespoons white wine vinegar
1   tablespoon lemon juice
2   tablespoons hot curry powder
     Pinch of cayenne pepper
     Freshly ground pepper to taste

Dredge the meat in the seasoned flour and shake off the excess. In a heavy saucepan over medium-high heat, lightly brown the meat in the oil, then remove it to a plate and set aside. In the same saucepan, scraping the bottom and sides, add the onion and garlic and cook until softened but not brown. Add the apples, apricots, prunes, and almonds, stirring until well mixed. Return the meat to the saucepan, add the remaining ingredients, and bring to a boil. Lower the heat, cover, and simmer for about 1½ hours. The dish should be a rich brown color with aromas that are tantalizing.

Pork Chops with Prunes

Serves 4

12   pitted prunes
¾   cup orange juice
2   tablespoons red wine vinegar
4   center-cut lean pork chops (about 4–5 ounces each)
2   tablespoons flour
1   tablespoon canola or other vegetable oil
1   small onion, chopped
½   cup beef stock
     Salt and freshly ground pepper to taste

Put the prunes in a medium saucepan, add the orange juice and vinegar, and bring to a boil. Lower the heat to medium-low and cook uncovered for about 15 minutes. Remove and set aside.

Dredge the chops with flour and shake off any excess. In a heavy skillet, heat the oil, add the chops, and cook over medium-high heat for 4 to 5 minutes on each side or until golden brown and done. Transfer to a serving dish and cover lightly to keep warm.

Pour off any remaining fat from the skillet, lower the heat to medium, add the onion and cook for 3 minutes or until softened but not brown. Increase the heat and deglaze the pan with the beef stock, scraping the bottom and sides to free any particles. Add the prune mixture and cook for about 4 minutes over medium-high heat or until the sauce has been reduced and thickened. Return the chops to the skillet, stir them around in the sauce just to heat, season with salt and pepper, and serve.

Plum Kuchen

Yields one 9-inch cake

The first time Dorrit saw this cake in Rolce's kitchen she exclaimed, "That's my mother's recipe—she made it all the time with different fruits!" And no wonder, it's easy and, above all, absolutely delicious.

1/2 cup (*1 stick*) *lightly salted butter*
1 *cup plus 1 tablespoon sugar*
2 *large eggs*
1 *cup all-purpose flour*
1 *teaspoon baking powder*
1 1/4 *pounds Italian or prune plums,
   quartered*
1 *tablespoon lemon or lime juice*
1/8 *teaspoon ground cinnamon*

Preheat the oven to 350° F. Butter a 9-inch springform pan.

Cream together the butter and 1 cup sugar until well blended, then beat in eggs, followed by the flour and baking powder. Beat to mix well and turn into the prepared pan. Place plum quarters on top of the batter, close together in circles starting at the outside, in a flower petal pattern. Sprinkle with lemon juice. Mix cinnamon with remaining sugar and sprinkle over the top. Bake on center rack of the oven for 1 hour or until a cake tester inserted in the center comes out clean and top is golden brown. Serve warm or cool, with unsweetened whipped cream, if desired.

Gingered Prune Cake

Yields one 9-inch round cake

This recipe makes a single 1½-inch layer, rich enough to serve in small slices, pretty enough for any occasion.

CAKE

1 *cup coarsely chopped prunes*
2 *tablespoons diced preserved ginger*
1 *cup all-purpose flour*
1/2 *teaspoon baking powder*
1/2 *teaspoon baking soda*
1/2 *teaspoon ground ginger*
1/2 *teaspoon ground cinnamon*
1/4 *teaspoon ground nutmeg*
1/4 *teaspoon ground cloves*
1/8 *teaspoon salt*
3/4 *cup sugar*
1 *large egg*
1/2 *cup canola or other vegetable oil*
1/2 *cup buttermilk*
1/2 *teaspoon vanilla extract*

TOPPING

3 *ounces bittersweet chocolate* (*1 Swiss
   chocolate bar*)
1 *tablespoon lightly salted butter*
2 *tablespoons whipping cream*
15 *pecan halves*
1/4 *cup coarsely chopped pecans*

Preheat the oven to 300° F. Grease and flour a 9-inch cake pan.

Place prunes in a saucepan with water to cover, bring to a boil, and cook for 5 minutes, drain, and reserve. Dust ginger with 1 tablespoon of the flour to separate pieces, and set

(continued on next page)

aside. Blend the flour, baking powder, baking soda, ginger, cinnamon, nutmeg, cloves, and salt in a small bowl, and set aside. In a mixer bowl, beat together the sugar and egg, add oil, and beat to blend well. Mix in the dry ingredients alternately with the buttermilk and vanilla, beating on medium speed after each addition. Stir in chopped prunes and ginger, and distribute throughout the batter.

Turn batter into prepared pan and bake on center rack for about 50 minutes, or until tester comes out clean. Place pan on cake rack to cool for 10 minutes, then turn out upside down on a rack. Allow to cool briefly, then turn right side up onto another rack. Place on serving plate only after cake has cooled completely.

Break chocolate into pieces and melt with butter and cream in the top of a double boiler or over very low heat, stirring until smooth and liquid. Pour onto center of cooled cake and spread smoothly with a broad spatula just to the edges (do not spread on sides). Encircle cake with pecan halves, evenly spaced, about ½ inch from the edge. Press gently into the soft chocolate. Distribute chopped nuts evenly in center of cake.

Cake may be stored in a tightly closed tin for several days, or up to a week in the refrigerator. The flavor improves if made the day before it is to be served.

Plum Tart

Yields one 9-inch tart

Any of the large, red California plums may be used for this French-style tart.

PASTRY (FOR 2 TART SHELLS)

1¾	cups all-purpose flour
¼	teaspoon salt
1	teaspoon sugar
½	cup (1 stick) *lightly salted butter, cut in bits*
1	large egg yolk
4	tablespoons cold water, as needed

FILLING

9	large plums cut in half
⅓	cup plus 2 teaspoons sugar
1	tablespoon lemon juice
1	large egg

Mix the flour, salt, and sugar in a medium bowl. Add the butter and blend with fingertips until the mixture resembles coarse meal. Make a well in the center, drop in the yolk and half the water, and mix with fingers just until dough comes together. If dough is slightly crumbly, add just enough water to make dough form a ball. Form into 2 flattened disks, wrap in plastic (reserve one for future use), and place in refrigerator for 30 minutes.

To roll out, flour board well, sprinkle flour on top of the disk, and flour the rolling pin. Roll dough in a 10-inch circle ⅜ inch thick and fit into a 9-inch tart pan. Press into bottom and up sides, cutting off any excess to make a clean edge.

Preheat the oven to 350° F.

Arrange plums cut side down in pastry-lined pan with removable bottom. In a medium mixing bowl combine the ⅓ cup sugar with the lemon juice and egg, using a hand beater or whisk. Pour over the fruit and sprinkle with the 2 teaspoons of sugar. Place in oven and bake until filling is set, about 1 hour.

⊷ ⊷

Wine~Soaked Prunes

Yields 2 cups

This recipe was given to us by our friend Norma. Keep a jar of it in the refrigerator and there will always be a sauce to serve with ice cream, or to use with pork, chicken, or roast duck and of course to puree for prune soufflé. These prunes may be used immediately, but their flavor will improve with time.

12 *ounces medium pitted prunes*
 1 *cup Port wine*
 1 *cup dry red wine*
½ *cup light brown sugar*
 1 *cinnamon stick*

Put all the ingredients in a saucepan, bring to a boil, and simmer for 15 minutes. Remove from heat and cool. Place in mason jars and refrigerate.

VARIATION: For Prune Puree, place 1½ to 1¾ cups soaked prunes and ⅓ cup of the syrup in a food processor or blender and puree until smooth. Use as desired.

Cold Prune Soufflé

Serves 6

A soufflé is customarily served directly from the oven when piping hot, requiring perfect timing, so the cook is usually concerned that it is "either ready too soon, or, sorry, not quite ready yet." With some experimenting, we found that the traditional soufflé ingredients result in an excellent cold soufflé, freeing the hostess from all anxiety. Try it for a change.

 5 *large egg whites*
½ *teaspoon lemon juice*
 1 *cup Wine-Soaked Prune Puree (recipe at left, Variation)*

Preheat the oven to 275° F. Grease a 2-quart baking or soufflé dish.

In the bowl of an electric mixer, beat the egg whites until foamy, add the lemon juice, and beat on high until very stiff but not dry. Carefully fold one quarter of the egg whites into the prune puree and blend really well. Fold this mixture of prunes and egg whites back into the remaining whites and gently continue folding until completely blended. Pour into the prepared dish and bake for 30 minutes, or until the top is firm but not cracked.

Turn the oven off, open the door slightly, and leave soufflé inside the oven for an additional 40 minutes. (This gradual cooling will minimize the shrinkage.) Transfer to a rack and allow to cool completely for 30 minutes, then cover with plastic wrap and refrigerate. Chill for at least 2 hours before serving. This soufflé is best served on the day of preparation.

Armagnac Prune Ice Cream

Yields 1½ pints

Very thin and crisp ginger cookies are an excellent accompaniment for this ice cream.

⅓ cup pitted prunes, coarsely chopped
3 tablespoons water
5 tablespoons Armagnac or other good-quality brandy
2 large egg yolks
⅓ cup sugar
1 cup whipping cream
1 cup milk
½ teaspoon vanilla extract

Combine the prunes, water, and Armagnac in a small saucepan, bring to a boil, then lower heat and simmer until almost dry. Let stand for 4 hours or overnight.

Beat egg yolks lightly and set aside. Combine sugar with cream and milk, and scald. Gradually beat about ½ cup hot liquid into the yolks, then slowly return egg and cream mixture to pot. Return to heat, bring to a boil, reduce heat, and cook, stirring constantly, until mixture thickens and coats the spoon, about 5 to 7 minutes.

Place the pot in a pan of ice and water and beat until cool. Stir in vanilla and chopped prunes. Place in an ice cream maker and follow manufacturer's directions. Or place in a wide, shallow metal pan in freezer compartment. When edges are frozen and the center is nearly so, spoon into a bowl and beat with a rotary beater or an electric mixer until light and smooth. Pack into a freezer carton and replace in freezer.

Plum Sorbet

Yields 1 pint

This sorbet is both attractive and delicious when served in combination with a scoop each of Champagne Pear Sorbet (page 206) and Peach Wine Sorbet (page 193).

1¼ pounds purple or red plums, quartered
2 tablespoons water
6 tablespoons sugar
   Pinch of salt
2 tablespoons cognac
½ teaspoon balsamic vinegar

Combine the plums and water in a nonreactive saucepan, place over medium heat, and bring to a simmer. Cook until tender. Puree with the sugar and salt in a blender or food processor. Chill, then stir in cognac and vinegar. Freeze in an ice cream maker following manufacturer's instructions and pack in a freezer carton. Or pour into a flat pan (the wider the pan the faster mixture will freeze) and place in freezer. When the mixture is frozen, spoon into a chilled bowl and beat with an electric or hand rotary beater until light and smooth. Pack lightly in a freezer carton and return to freezer.

NOTE: When fresh fruit is to be stewed for a recipe, it is possible to substitute an equal amount of canned fruit. If it is sweetened (and it usually is), reduce the sugar in the recipe.

Matzo Fruit Pudding

Serves 10

Usually served during the Passover holidays, this pudding goes well with meat or fish and can stand on its own when served as a dessert.

   5   *squares plain matzos (7 ounces)*
   4   *eggs, separated*
  1/2 *cup sugar*
   1   *cup pitted prunes, chopped*
  1/2 *cup raisins*
   1   *cup walnuts, chopped*
   1   *(20-ounce) can pineapple chunks in natural juices, drained and diced into 1/2-inch cubes*
   1   *(20-ounce) can peach halves in syrup, drained and diced into 1/2-inch cubes*
   2   *ripe bananas, sliced into 1/4-inch rounds*
   2   *large tart apples, peeled, cored, and diced into 1/2-inch cubes*
  1/2 *cup fruit juice from the canned fruits*
   4   *tablespoons margarine, melted*

Preheat the oven to 375°F. Grease a 13 × 9 × 2-inch ovenproof dish.

Break each matzo square into quarters, place in a bowl, and cover with boiling water. Soak for 5 minutes, then drain and set aside. In the bowl of an electric mixer beat the egg whites until stiff and set aside. In another bowl beat the yolks and sugar until thick and creamy. Mix in the remaining ingredients except for the matzos and beaten egg whites. Then fold in the matzos and the egg whites. Pour into the baking dish and bake for 1 hour or until the top is set and golden in color. Remove, cover with foil, and leave for 30 minutes before serving. This pudding may be refrigerated for 3 days, or frozen for up to 6 weeks.

Prune, Apple, and Nut Dessert

Yields one 8-inch square

Making this dessert ahead of time improves the flavor. Serve plain or with lightly whipped cream.

   1   *cup prunes, chopped*
   1   *cup tart apples (8 ounces), peeled and chopped into 1/2-inch pieces*
  1/4 *cup dry sherry*
   6   *tablespoons lightly salted butter*
  3/4 *cup light brown sugar*
   1   *egg, lightly beaten*
   1   *teaspoon vanilla*
  3/4 *cup all-purpose flour*
  1/2 *teaspoon baking powder*
  1/4 *teaspoon salt*
   1   *teaspoon cinnamon*
  1/4 *teaspoon allspice*
  1/4 *teaspoon cloves*
  1/4 *teaspoon nutmeg*
  1/2 *cup chopped pecans*

Preheat the oven to 350°F. Grease an 8-inch square pan with butter.

Combine the prunes, apples, and sherry and allow to macerate for two hours. In a large bowl, cream together the butter and sugar, then beat in the egg and vanilla. In a separate bowl, mix together the flour, baking powder, salt, cinnamon, allspice, cloves, and nutmeg. Add dry ingredients to the creamed mixture, blending well. Stir in the fruit mixture and nuts until just combined. Spoon into the prepared pan and bake for 35 minutes, or until lightly browned. When cool, dust with confectioners' sugar and cut into 2- or 3-inch squares.

R·H·U·B·A·R·B

Basic Stewed Rhubarb

Cod in Rhubarb Sauce

Rhubarb Chutney Sauce

Rhubarb Betty

Strawberry Rhubarb Pie

Rhubarb and Pineapple Sorbet

Rhubarb and Fig Marmalade

Pecan-Topped Rhubarb Muffins

As early as 2700 B.C. mention of rhubarb appeared in a Chinese herbal *Penking,* describing its medicinal properties. It was so highly valued for its astringent and purgative qualities that it was carried with spices and luxuries of the Far East along the trade routes to the West. It was, however, many centuries later, about 1800 in England and somewhat earlier on the continent, that it came to be used as a food. One nineteenth-century American cookbook has a recipe for rhubarb pie, and in another publication are found directions for various tinctures, syrups, and extracts. Well into the twentieth century par-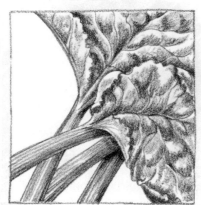ents regularly dosed young Americans with "spring tonics" that contained rhubarb as a principal in-gredient.

Although botani-cally a vegetable, rhubarb is used more like a fruit to make preserves and espe-cially pies. In fact, an old name still used in some parts of the country is "pie plant." This conversion from vegetable to fruit may have come about because rhubarb's extreme acidity re-quires large amounts of sugar to make it palatable, resulting in a tart-sweet flavor desirable in desserts.

Rhubarb grows readily in temperate and cold climates. As a perennial plant, it dies back to the ground in the fall, and is one of the earliest plants to reappear in the spring. It's an attractive plant, with broad, somewhat ruffled, dark green leaves on the ends of edible red stalks that grow to as much as two feet in length. To harvest, the stalks are pulled from the ground, not cut, and the leaves are discarded, since they contain a high degree of oxalic acid. They are said to be so toxic that some who have unknowingly eaten them have died.

❧ HOME CULTIVATION ❧

When planting rhubarb, you should select an area where it can grow permanently, since once established it does not like being moved. Many gardeners take advantage of its attractive foliage to make a border at the edge of the vegetable garden.

❧ NUTRITION ❧

Rhubarb contains vitamins A, B, and C. One-half cup of fresh rhubarb cooked with sugar has 190 calories, ½ cup frozen has 192 calories.

❧ SELECTION ❧

Rhubarb is usually sold in whole stalks with leaves removed. Look for stalks that are crisp, and if leaves are attached, they should not be badly wilted. There are two kinds of rhubarb: field grown and hot-house raised. Field grown is marketed in the late spring and early summer, with the season extended by hothouse plantings.

EQUIVALENTS
1 pound fresh = 4 cups chopped
12 ounces frozen = 1½ cups sliced

STORAGE ❧ AND PREPARATION ❧

To store for a few days, put rhubarb in a plastic bag or wrap (do not seal tightly) and place it in the refrigerator. Rhubarb can be frozen fresh, cut into pieces, or as a cooked sauce.

To prepare for immediate use, wash stalks, remove any coarse outer fiber (it is not necessary to peel rhubarb) with a paring knife, and cut into desired size.

❧ ❧

A typical American pairing is the popular rhubarb with strawberries, usually baked in pies. Not as well known is the rhubarb-pineapple combination, a lovely balance of their tart and sweet flavors. Try this pair to make a delicious sorbet, sauces, and pies. Cinnamon and lemon are good seasoning companions for rhubarb, and ginger is wonderful; use crystallized pieces in jam, add powdered ginger in pies, and grate in some of the fresh root when stewing. Rhubarb can be made into wine but we cannot vouch for the drinkability.

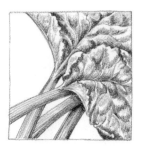

Basic Stewed Rhubarb

Yields 2 cups

If you are planning to use stewed rhubarb as a side dish or in meat or poultry sauces, it can be cooked without sugar by adding a little fruit juice as the cooking liquid.

> 4   *cups diced rhubarb*
> 1–1½ *cups sugar, depending on sweetness desired; 1 cup of sugar will yield a tart sauce*
> *Lemon zest, nutmeg, cinnamon, or ginger (optional)*

Mix the fruit and sugar in a ceramic or glass bowl, cover, and allow to stand, covered, for at least 1 hour or even overnight, stirring occasionally. This will allow the juice to accumulate and no water will be necessary for cooking. To cook, pour into a nonreactive saucepan and bring to a boil, lower heat, and cook, uncovered, for 5 minutes. If you wish a very smooth sauce, puree in a blender or food processor. Before cooking you may add a bit of lemon zest, a few gratings of nutmeg, cinnamon, or grated fresh ginger.

Cod in Rhubarb Sauce

Serves 4

The rhubarb is not too assertive in this pleasingly tart sauce. It is important to use one of the sweet variety of onions and cook everything briefly.

> 1½ *cups chopped rhubarb*
> 2¼ *cups water*
> 2   *quarter-size pieces fresh ginger, peeled and cut into fine julienne strips*
> ⅓   *cup cider vinegar*
> ¾   *cup sweet onion, such as Vidalia, peeled and sliced ¼ inch thick, slices cut in half*
> ⅓   *cup red bell pepper, cut into strips 1 inch long, ¼ inch wide*
> ¼   *teaspoon salt*
> 4   *cod fillets, about 6 ounces each, broiled or grilled*

Place the rhubarb, ¼ cup water, and ginger in a small nonreactive saucepan, cover, and simmer for about 5 minutes; set aside. Add cider vinegar to remaining 2 cups water and bring to a rapid boil. Add the onion and pepper strips to blanch for 2 minutes, drain, and add to rhubarb. Season with the salt. When fish is ready, heat the sauce briefly, arrange around fish on a heated platter, and serve.

Rhubarb Chutney Sauce

Yields 2½ cups

This unusual sauce, quite simple to make, has multiple uses. Try it as a condiment with roasted or grilled lamb, poultry, and pork, or with a rich grilled fish such as tuna or sword-fish. It is also surprisingly good as a spread with cream cheese on raisin bread. If fresh rhubarb is unavailable, frozen may be substituted.

    4 cups rhubarb, cut into 1-inch pieces
    2 tablespoons finely minced garlic
    1 tablespoon ground ginger
    1 tablespoon fresh ginger, minced
    3 mild, canned chiles, chopped
  ½ cup cider vinegar
  ¾ cup dark brown sugar
  ¾ cup golden raisins
    2 tablespoons fresh lime juice

Combine all the ingredients in a heavy saucepan, bring to a boil, cover, and cook over medium-low heat for 15 minutes, stirring occasionally to prevent the mixture from sticking to the bottom of the pan and burning. Uncover and continue cooking for another 10 minutes, stirring several times. Remove from heat, cool, and immediately store in airtight jars.

Rhubarb Betty

Serves 4–6

This is one of those desserts, like cobblers, that are old-fashioned, good, and easy to make.

    2 pounds rhubarb, washed, cut into 1-inch pieces
1⅓ cups sugar
  ⅓ cup raisins
    2 tablespoons solid vegetable shortening, or butter
    1 large egg
    1 cup all-purpose flour
1½ teaspoons baking powder
  ¼ teaspoon salt
  ⅓ cup milk
  ½ teaspoon vanilla extract

Preheat the oven to 350° F. Butter a 1½-quart baking dish.

Mix the rhubarb with 1 cup of the sugar. Place in prepared baking dish, mixed with the raisins. Cream the shortening with the remaining ⅓ cup sugar; add egg and beat well. Sift together the flour, baking powder, and salt; add alternately with the milk to the creamed mixture, then stir in vanilla. Spread batter over the fruit and bake 40 to 45 minutes, or until the top is golden-brown and the fruit bubbling.

Strawberry Rhubarb Pie

Yields one 9-inch pie

How fortunate that these two fruits arrive together in the spring. The flavors blend so well that it has been a favorite combination for desserts for generations. However, for an out-of-season treat, substitute frozen fruit for either or both.

PASTRY

2 cups all-purpose flour
1 teaspoon salt
2/3 cup plus 1 tablespoon solid vegetable shortening
4 tablespoons cold water
1 teaspoon vinegar

FILLING

6 tablespoons all-purpose flour
1 cup sugar
1 pint strawberries, halved
4 cups chopped rhubarb, in 1-inch pieces
2 tablespoons (¼ stick) lightly salted butter

Preheat the oven to 450° F.

Measure the flour into a mixing bowl with the salt. With a pastry blender cut in the shortening until the mixture resembles coarse meal. Sprinkle with the water and vinegar, a tablespoon at a time, mixing with a fork until all the flour is moistened. Press into a ball and divide in half. Roll out on a lightly floured board into a 10-inch circle.

Line a 9-inch pie pan with pastry, allowing a slight overhang.

Mix the flour and sugar, blending well. Place strawberries and rhubarb in a large bowl and stir in the sugar mixture to coat fruit, then turn into pastry-lined pan and dot with butter.

Roll out remaining pastry for lattice strips, about 7 by 12 inches, and cut 14 strips with knife or pastry wheel. Place 7 strips evenly spaced across fruit, then place remaining strips diagonally across the first ones. Press ends into edge of crust, trim evenly, fold overhang over strip ends and press together, making a high fluted edge. The high edge should prevent the juice from spilling over, but a baking sheet can be placed under the pan as further protection for the oven. Bake on the middle rack for 10 minutes, then lower to 350° F. and bake for 30 minutes more, or until the crust is golden brown and the fruit is tender and bubbling. Remove to a rack to cool for at least 30 minutes before cutting.

Rhubarb and Pineapple Sorbet

Yields 1 pint

This sorbet is the loveliest shade of pink imaginable. Try garnishing with fresh blueberries or a few shreds of candied lemon zest.

1   *cup sweetened Basic Stewed Rhubarb (page 233)*
1   *cup unsweetened pineapple juice*
½   *cup water*

Stir rhubarb, pineapple juice, and water together in a ceramic or glass bowl, then freeze in an ice cream maker according to manufacturer's directions, and pack in a freezer carton. Or pour into a flat pan (the wider the pan the faster the mixture will freeze) and when an inch of mixture is frozen, place in a chilled bowl and beat with an electric or hand rotary beater until light and smooth. Return to tray and refreeze. For an even smoother sorbet, repeat procedure once more.

Rhubarb and Fig Marmalade

Yields 2 pints

The seeds and peel added to the rich rhubarb color give this marmalade a most intriguing appearance. Allow the flavors to mellow for a few days for best flavor.

4   *cups diced rhubarb (about 1 pound), in ¼-inch pieces*
10 *dried Calmyrna figs, finely sliced*
2   *cups sugar*
1   *small lemon, sliced with rind, then finely julienned*
    1½-inch piece fresh ginger, peeled and cut into very fine julienne

Combine the rhubarb, figs, sugar, lemon, and ginger in a ceramic or glass bowl. Allow to stand, covered, for 24 hours. Place in a nonreactive pot, bring to a rapid boil, and cook rapidly until it reaches jelly stage, 220° F. If you have no thermometer, do a spoon test: Take up a spoonful of juice, cool a moment, then pour from side of spoon; the drops of jelly will come together or "sheet" off the spoon. Pour into sterilized pint or half-pint preserving jars, seal, and store in refrigerator.

Pecan~Topped Rhubarb Muffins

Yields 12 muffins

Serve these fruity muffins hot from the oven with butter at breakfast or lunch. Have leftovers with late morning coffee or your afternoon cup of tea.

- ¼   *cup (½ stick) unsalted butter, softened*
- *1   cup sugar*
- *1   large egg*
- *2   cups all-purpose flour*
- *4   teaspoons baking powder*
- ½   *teaspoon ground cinnamon*
- ½   *teaspoon salt*
- *1   cup milk*
- *3   cups diced rhubarb, in ½-inch pieces*
- ¼   *cup chopped pecans*

Preheat the oven to 400° F. Grease 12 muffin cups or line with paper cups.

Beat the butter with the sugar by hand or with an electric mixer until smooth and blended. Add the egg and blend. In another bowl, mix the flour, baking powder, cinnamon, and salt, then add with milk to the butter mixture. Stir just to completely moisten dry ingredients; the batter will be lumpy. Fold in the rhubarb quickly and thoroughly. Spoon batter into muffin cups, distributing evenly. Sprinkle tops with chopped nuts. Place on the middle rack and bake for 30 minutes or until a cake tester inserted in the middle comes out clean and tops are lightly browned.

S·T·R·A·W·B·E·R·R·I·E·S

Chilled Strawberry Wine Soup

Strawberry and Spinach Salad

Artichokes with Strawberry Sauce

Stir-Fried Scallops with Strawberries and Snow Peas

Strawberry Shortcake

Fresh Strawberry Sauce

Hot Strawberry Sauce

Strawberry Wine Gelatin

Fresh Strawberries in Meringue Shells

Strawberry and Blueberry Compote

Strawberries with Caramel Sauce

Strawberry Sorbet

The strawberry was enjoyed in its natural wild state centuries before it came under cultivation and eventual hybridization. It appears in early Greek and Roman writings, and is seen in fourteenth-century religious paintings and illuminated manuscripts in the fifteenth century. It may have originally been transplanted from the wild simply as an ornamental, but in the fourteenth century the royal gardens in France saw the planting of as many as 1,200 strawberries at one time. These were the small wild, or wood, type berries. They were used in various medicinal potions before they were appreciated as a  food. They have also en- joyed a certain popularity as a skin beautifier; in Na- poleonic times a well- known courtesan was said to bathe in strawberry juice to maintain a soft and silken skin, and many of the special herbal masks sold at the cosmetic counters today tout the wonders of strawberries for the complexion. Mean- while, discoveries of the strawberry were being made in the Americas. In South America it was first found in Chile and named *Fragaria chiloensis* (it was later discov- ered that this variety grows along the entire Pacific coast all the way to Alaska), and along the Atlantic coast of North America we find the variety *F. virginiana*. These varieties, both of which were larger than the European berries, are considered the parents of all cultivated strawberries grown today.

A perennial herb, the strawberry might be called an inside-out fruit. One definition of a fruit is a seed surrounded by a pulpy flesh; in the strawberry, we have the flesh surrounded by seeds. These seeds, known botanically as achenes, are actu- ally the true fruits, each with a seed within its thin wall. The name may have derived from an Anglo-Saxon description of the way runners "strew" or stray away from the mother plant to set new plants. An old method of stringing the berries together on straws for marketing suggests yet another explanation. In any case, judging from the frequency with which he is quoted, many agree with Samuel Butler in saying, "Doubtless God could have made a better berry, but doubtless God never did."

Strawberries were first grown in home gardens, or in farm gardens where they could be delivered to nearby markets, because of the problems with spoilage, which made them a special seasonal luxury for most city dwellers. With the advent of rail transportation in the late nineteenth century, strawberries could be supplied to fancy produce markets and restaurants in distant cities, and with the introduction of refrigeration for shipping, and the development of hardier, albeit less flavorful types, fresh berries soon became available to nearly everyone. California grows more strawberries than any other place in the world, and produces 75 percent of U.S. consumption. Fresh berries are now available, to some extent, all year. They are also marketed as frozen, in preserves, and, to a small degree, canned.

⊷ HOME CULTIVATION ⊷

Strawberries can be grown in nearly all states, including parts of Alaska and Canada. There are so many hybrids available that you can find one to specifically suit your climate and soil. They are not difficult to grow, but do require a location that provides full sun. They should be allowed to ripen on the plant for sweetest flavor. Because they throw out runners, they are usually allotted a "patch" of land rather than rows, but they can be kept

in rows with careful cultivation. The alpine strawberry, known as the *fraise des bois*, does not throw runners and can, therefore, be used as a border plant. This is an especially nice way to edge an herb garden. The berries are small, but the flavor is wonderfully intense, and the plants are everbearing.

⊷ NUTRITION ⊷

One cup of strawberries has just 55 calories and is an excellent source of vitamin C. The quantity of vitamin C in the ripe fruit increases with the amount of sun it receives prior to picking. It retains the vitamin for two to three days if the berries are not cut or injured.

⊷ SELECTION ⊷

Strawberries should have good red color, no brown or soft spots, and have their pointed green hulls in place. As with other fruits shipped long distances, they are kept at controlled temperatures, which may make them relatively scentless, but if they are fragrant, with a characteristic strawberry scent, you can be assured of good flavor. Check the bottom of the basket for staining—the evidence of crushed or spoiled berries. Huge berries often have hollow centers and may be dry; for best flavor and juice select medium fruit. Those oversize berries with stems attached and sold at a premium price have only their novel appearance going for them.

EQUIVALENTS
1 pint basket = 2 cups sliced berries

STORAGE AND
֍ PREPARATION ֍

Strawberries may be kept for one or two days in the refrigerator, but are best used the same day (see nutrition note). Wash and hull only when ready to use them; after washing, pat dry with paper towels. Remove hulls only after washing, with fingers or using the point of a paring knife. When serving strawberries, you'll find the flavor will be better if they are allowed to come to room temperature. They can be frozen, sliced or whole, and will retain a good flavor; however, they will be soft once thawed.

֍   ֍

Strawberries and cream is almost a cliché but the flavor is unbeatable, rich yet light. The presence of strawberries lends an elegance to any dish it graces and, by association, any meal. Start with a bright chilled soup, take advantage of the color contrast with a spinach salad, or end with a glorious strawberry-filled shortcake. For great color and flavor, mix strawberries with bananas and pineapple in fruit salad, or add them to a summer pudding with blueberries and raspberries. That same flavor can be used to good advantage when made into vinegar for salad dressings, or as a hot or cold fresh fruit sauce over ice cream. Dry and sweet wines, liqueurs, and lemon juice can all be used to good advantage in strawberry desserts, sauces, and drinks. The flavorsome combination of strawberries and rhubarb in pies, compotes, and jams has continued in popularity from generation to generation, and strawberry ice cream ranks in the top three flavors year after year. (The other two are vanilla and chocolate.) Shakes made with strawberries and ice cream are among the most popular of soft drinks, but for the ultimate in romantic food serve strawberries and champagne.

Chilled Strawberry Wine Soup

Serves 4

This recipe makes a fruit soup that is not too sweet for a first course, is easy to prepare, and is an economical dish for early spring when using only fresh berries would be expensive. If using unsweetened frozen fruit, add ¼ cup sugar.

    1 (16-ounce) package frozen strawberries, thawed
    1 cup dry white wine, chilled
    2 tablespoons lemon juice
    ¼ teaspoon grated lemon rind
    1 cup plain soda water, chilled
    ½ cup sliced fresh strawberries
       Mint leaves, for garnish

Place frozen strawberries in a blender or food processor, puree briefly, then add wine, lemon juice, and lemon rind and blend just to combine. Just before serving add soda water and stir in sliced berries. Garnish each bowl with fresh mint leaf.

Strawberry and Spinach Salad

Serves 6

The colors make quite a dramatic presentation and the salad can be tossed or arranged on plates with strawberries placed on top of the greens.

    1   pound fresh spinach
    1½ tablespoons lemon juice
    3   tablespoons light olive oil or other light vegetable oil
    ¼   teaspoon salt
        Freshly ground pepper to taste
    4   very thin slices sweet onion, such as Vidalia (see Note)
    ½   cup sliced strawberries

Wash the spinach, pick out any coarse stems, and tear leaves into bite-size pieces; set aside to drain well or spin dry. Mix the lemon juice, oil, salt, and pepper and blend well until slightly thickened. To assemble the salad, place the spinach in a bowl, add onion and strawberry slices, and when ready to serve, pour dressing over and toss gently.

NOTE: If sweet onion is not available, soak yellow onion slices in a bowl of cold water for 10 minutes, drain, and rinse once more.

Artichokes with Strawberry Sauce

Serves 4

First sampled with fresh strawberries picked in an English country garden, this unusual combination of ingredients provides a fragrantly delicate flavor and a striking contrast of colors.

> 4 *artichokes*
> *Salt*
> 4 *tablespoons plus 1 teaspoon canola or other vegetable oil*
> 2 *tablespoons lemon juice*
> 12 *large strawberries*
> 2 *tablespoons raspberry vinegar*
> ¼ *teaspoon Dijon mustard*
> 1 *teaspoon sugar*
> *Freshly ground pepper to taste*

Pull off a few of the lower outer tough leaves from each artichoke. With a sharp knife or scissors, trim the tips off the outer leaves. In a large nonreactive saucepan stand artichokes upright, cover with water, and add a pinch of salt, 1 teaspoon of the oil, and the lemon juice. Bring to a boil and cook for 45 minutes or until the outer leaves pull off easily. Remove from saucepan, rinse under cold water, and drain. Set aside.

Clean and hull the strawberries, then place in a food processor or blender. Puree the fruit, then add the remaining ingredients leaving the oil until last. Season to taste.

Slice each artichoke in half vertically and remove the choke with a spoon. Serve, facing upward on individual plates, and put the sauce along one side.

Stir-Fried Scallops with Strawberries and Snow Peas

Serves 4

This quick low-fat recipe demonstrates the marvelous results that can be achieved by blending foods of different colors and textures.

> 1¼ *pounds scallops*
> ¼ *teaspoon salt*
> ¼ *teaspoon sugar*
> 1 *tablespoon rice vinegar*
> 1 *teaspoon sesame oil*
> 1 *teaspoon cornstarch*
> 1 *egg white*
> 10–12 *large strawberries*
> 4 *ounces snow peas*
> 1 *tablespoon canola or other vegetable oil*
> ¼ *cup chopped scallions, including 2 inches of green*
> *Juice of 1 lime*
> ¼ *teaspoon finely julienned pickled or fresh ginger*
> *Salt and freshly ground pepper to taste*

Wash and pat the scallops dry with paper towels. If they are very large, cut them in half. In a shallow pie plate or flat serving plate, combine the salt, sugar, rice vinegar, sesame oil, cornstarch, and egg white. Mix thoroughly. Place the scallops in the marinade, coat well, cover, and refrigerate for 1 hour. Drain and pat dry with paper towels.

Clean and hull the strawberries; halve, then slice each half into 3 pieces. Cut the stems and string the snow peas, place in small

(continued on next page)

saucepan of water, bring to a boil, blanch for 10 seconds, and immediately drain under cold water. Put on paper towels to dry.

In a wok or large skillet, heat the oil, add the scallops, and cook over medium-high heat for 3 to 5 minutes, stirring just until opaque. Add the remaining ingredients and cook for a minute more to heat through, stirring constantly. Serve immediately with plain white rice or a fried rice mixture.

Strawberry Shortcake

Serves 6–8

This is a real American classic—shortcake made with a rich biscuit base, lots of fresh strawberries, and a reasonably lavish hand with the whipped cream.

SHORTCAKE

- 1¾   cups all-purpose flour
- 2   teaspoons baking powder
    Pinch of salt
- 4   tablespoons (½ stick) lightly salted butter, cut into pieces
- ⅔   cup whipping cream

TOPPING

- 1   quart fresh strawberries, washed, dried, hulled, and halved
- 2   tablespoons sugar plus 2 teaspoons
- 1½   cups whipping cream

Preheat the oven to 425° F. Butter an 8-inch round cake pan.

Mix the flour, baking powder, and salt in a bowl. Cut the butter into the flour mixture with a pastry blender, 2 knives, or your fin-

gers until mixture resembles coarse meal. Add the cream and stir until mixture just comes together. Shape into a flat disk and press lightly into the prepared pan, patting evenly to the edges. Bake on the center rack for about 20 minutes; the top should be lightly colored and feel firm to the touch. Turn out of pan and right side up on a cake rack to cool.

When shortcake is completely cool, slice in half horizontally with a long thin knife. Slice strawberries in half and sprinkle with 2 tablespoons of the sugar; set aside for about 30 minutes. When ready to assemble whip the cream with the remaining 2 teaspoons of sugar. Spread two-thirds of the strawberries with their juice over the cut surface of the bottom half, cover with whipped cream, place the top half over the filling, press lightly, then spoon berries on center of top only and top with more whipped cream.

Fresh Strawberry Sauce

Yields 2 cups

What could be more tempting than luscious, ripe, flavorsome bright red strawberries, pureed to create a sauce that will embellish any ice cream or fresh fruit salad. Also delicious spooned over a poached pear or blended together with oranges in Grand Marnier.

- 1   pint fresh strawberries
- 2   tablespoons superfine sugar
- 3   tablespoons fresh lemon juice
- 1   tablespoon Cointreau
- 1   tablespoon cognac

Wash and hull the strawberries, and cut them in half. Combine with the sugar and lemon juice in a blender or food processor and puree until well blended. Add the Cointreau and cognac, and process for a few more seconds. Chill before serving. Covered tightly, this sauce will keep in the refrigerator for up to 2 weeks.

Hot Strawberry Sauce

Yields 1½ cups

On a hiking tour in the Italian Dolomites we first discovered hot fruit sauces served with ice cream (usually vanilla) in Brixen-Bressanone, near the Austrian border, and then found this delightful practice was common throughout the region.

   1 *cup water*
  ⅓ *cup sugar*
  ½ *cup crushed strawberries*
   1 *teaspoon lemon juice*
   1 *teaspoon orange-flavored liqueur*
   1 *cup fresh halved strawberries*

Mix water and sugar in a saucepan and bring to a boil. Simmer for 3 minutes, then add the crushed berries, lemon juice, and liqueur. Cook gently for another 3 minutes and add the halved berries. Heat through but do not boil. Serve while hot.

Strawberry Wine Gelatin

Serves 6–8

Other fruits may be substituted for the strawberries, such as very ripe chopped peaches, whole raspberries, or chopped mango. Gelatin can be topped with whipped cream, with garnish added.

   2 *tablespoons unflavored gelatin*
  ½ *cup cold water*
   1 *cup boiling water*
  ¾ *cup sugar*
   2 *cups wine (Madeira, medium-dry sherry, or Port)*
   2 *tablespoons brandy*
   2 *tablespoons lemon juice*
   1 *pint strawberries*
      Mint leaves, for garnish

Add the gelatin to the cold water and let stand 5 minutes to soften. Add boiling water and stir until gelatin is dissolved; stir in the sugar. When cool, blend in the wine, brandy, and lemon juice. Pour into 6 to 8 wine glasses, about ½ cup per glass. Wash, dry, hull, and slice berries. Divide sliced berries among glasses, reserving a few slices for garnish after gelatin has set. Top with a mint leaf for added color.

Fresh Strawberries in Meringue Shells

Serves 4

These shells can be filled with other fresh berries, a fruit mixture, or a fruit sorbet. Don't make meringues in very humid weather because they will remain sticky.

 2 *large egg whites, at room temperature*
½ *cup sugar*
½ *teaspoon vanilla extract*
 1 *pint fresh strawberries, sliced*
½ *cup whipping cream, whipped*

Preheat the oven to 250° F. Cover a baking sheet with brown, parchment, or wax paper.

In an electric mixer beat the whites until they're very stiff and dry, then beat in the sugar, a tablespoon at a time, until the mixture holds its shape. Add the vanilla and beat until mixture is no longer gritty when rubbed between thumb and fingers.

Use either a pastry bag with star tip or a spoon to shape 4 meringue shells on the baking sheet. The rims should be about 1 inch high and ¾ inch wide. Bake 50 minutes or until meringues feel dry and firm to the touch. They should be nearly colorless or very lightly browned.

Slide meringues off paper onto rack using a broad thin spatula and allow to cool. Shells may be used at once or stored for 2 days in a tightly closed container. Fill with sliced berries and top with whipped cream. If berries are tart, sprinkle with sugar to taste before placing in shells.

NOTE: The shells can be filled with ice cream and then topped with the strawberries.

✧ ✧

Strawberry and Blueberry Compote

Serves 6–8

When fresh strawberries and blueberries are in season, a compote, cooked for only a brief period and served warm, makes a festive presentation. The juices of the two fruits blend together and the color has a jewellike appearance.

½ *cup orange juice*
     Juice of 1 lime
¼ *cup sugar*
 1 *quart fresh strawberries, cleaned, hulled, and halved*
 1 *pint fresh blueberries, rinsed and picked over*
     Crème Anglaise (recipe follows)

In a large shallow saucepan, combine the orange and lime juices and the sugar. Bring to a boil and cook over medium heat until the sugar has dissolved, about 3 minutes altogether. Add the berries, bring the liquid back to a boil, lower the heat to medium, and cook, stirring, for about 2 minutes. Remove from heat and cool to serve at room temperature. May be prepared several hours ahead, or almost at the last moment. Serve with the Crème Anglaise.

Crème Anglaise

Yields 1½ cups

- 1¼ cups milk
- 4 large egg yolks
- ⅓ cup sugar
- 1 teaspoon cornstarch
- 1 teaspoon vanilla extract
- 1 tablespoon liqueur of choice (*optional*)

Place the milk in a saucepan and heat, but do not boil. Set aside and keep hot. Place the egg yolks in a heavy saucepan, beat for about 3 minutes, then gradually add the sugar. Continue beating until the mixture is pale yellow and creamy. Mix in the cornstarch. Place over medium-low heat and while stirring constantly with a wire whisk, add the milk, a little at a time. Continue stirring until the sauce is sufficiently thick to coat the back of a spoon, about 20 minutes. (An instant-read thermometer should register 170° F.) Take great care not to allow the sauce to boil, since the eggs will curdle. Remove from the heat, stir in the vanilla, and flavor with a liqueur, if you wish. Cover with plastic wrap and chill. The crème may be prepared one day in advance.

NOTE: This sauce may be prepared in a double boiler. Make certain that the egg mixture never comes to a boil, or that the water in the bottom of the double boiler never boils. This method will take about 10 minutes longer.

Strawberries with Caramel Sauce

Serves 4

This is an adaptation of a popular dessert enjoyed at Skipjack's restaurant in Boston. The blending of the strawberries with the caramel is a treat.

- 2 large Heath Bars
- ¼ cup sugar
- ¼ cup whipping cream
- 2 tablespoons light corn syrup
- 1 tablespoon unsalted butter
- 1 pint fresh strawberries
- Whipped cream (*optional*)

At least a day before, freeze the Heath Bars. Then place the frozen bars in a plastic bag and break into small pieces, but do not crush. If not using immediately, keep refrigerated.

In a saucepan, combine the sugar, cream, corn syrup, and butter and bring to a boil. Cook over medium-high heat, stirring, for about 3 minutes. Remove from heat and add the pieces of Heath Bar to the mixture. Set aside to cool slightly.

Wash and hull the strawberries and divide among 4 individual serving dishes. Top with the sauce, garnish with a dollop of whipped cream if desired, and serve immediately. The sauce may be refrigerated and reheated, thinning with cream if necessary.

Strawberry Sorbet

Yields 1 pint

For a tricolor Fourth of July dessert, try serving with blueberry and pear sorbets. The colors are fun to do and the flavors are great together.

- ½ cup sugar
- 1¼ cups water
- 1½ cups crushed fresh strawberries
- 1 tablespoon lemon juice
- 2 tablespoons dry white wine (*optional*)

Boil together the sugar and water for 5 minutes. Set aside to cool to room temperature, then stir in the strawberries, lemon juice, and wine. Puree in a blender or food processor. Freeze in an ice cream maker according to manufacturer's directions, and pack in a freezer carton. Or pour into a flat pan (the wider the pan the faster mixture will freeze) and place in freezer. When the mixture is frozen, spoon into a chilled bowl and beat with an electric or hand rotary beater until light and smooth. Pack lightly in a freezer carton and return to freezer.

·E X O T I C·
A N D   L E S S
A V A I L A B L E
F R U I T S

Early in this century grapefruit would have been listed here, and perhaps fifteen years ago the avocado would have headed the list. Within the past year or two we have seen mangos and papayas move into the mainstream. Most of the fruits described in this section have made their appearance very recently, but some, such as currants and gooseberries, are still restricted to specialty produce markets. As demand increases, encouraging growers to produce more, the cost will come down so that we, too, can make a recipe calling for a cup of passion fruit.

Carambola

This is also known as star fruit because of the star-shaped slices when cut crosswise, forming a five-pointed star. Asian in origin, it is now grown in Hawaii, the Caribbean, and mainland states of Florida and California. It is about three to five inches in length, oval in shape, and has a thin, waxy, yellow skin with deep ribs that have sharply defined edges. Those with wider ribs tend to be the sweeter ones; narrow ribbed, or

less ripe fruit can be quite tart to sour. If it has a green color, keep at room temperature until it becomes a deep, golden yellow, with rib edges turning brown. The texture will remain crisp even when fully ripe. Remove the few seeds, but peeling is not necessary. It is often eaten out of hand as a fresh fruit. As a Chinese dessert, it is cut up and placed around a bowl of sea salt used for dipping. The unique star-shaped slices and the tangy taste lend an exotic note to salads, fruit bowls, and as a garnish for meat and seafood. It is a good source of vitamin C, and also provides vitamin A and potassium.

Cherimoya

The cherimoya is also known as the "custard apple," with its flesh of a creamy, soft consistency. It is variously described as tasting like a pineapple, a strawberry, a baked apple, or combinations of several tropical fruits. In appearance it somewhat resembles a plump, green pine cone or, perhaps, an artichoke. It is about the size of a medium avocado. The skin is thick, a medium, dull green, and easily bruised; the flesh is creamy white with a central core, and many hard, black seeds throughout. Originating in South and Central America, it is now being grown in California and Florida, as well as Spain and New Zealand. The cherimoya is at its best when tree ripened, and it must be packed and handled with care. Select those that have started to soften, then allow them to become slightly soft overall, at room temperature before using. Cherimoyas should be chilled for best flavor, but not until fully ripe. Lemon or lime juice may be used to perk up the rather bland taste. They may be made into a sauce, added to fruit salads, or more often, cut in half and eaten with a spoon. The atemoya, a cherimoya hybrid developed in Florida, has a sweet flavor and a bumpy, pale green skin. Other related fruits are the soursop, known as *guanabana* in Spanish-speaking countries, the sharifa, and the llama. All are the *Annona cherimola* species. They contribute some vitamin C and niacin to the diet.

Currants and Gooseberries

Currants and gooseberries are both of the Ribes family, and are produced on low-growing shrubs of similar appearance. Currants are a beautiful clear red; the clusters look like tiny blown glass ornaments on the shrub. There is a black variety, and a less-known white type. The most popular gooseberry is a pale green to yellow, is larger than the currant, and is without its translucence. A red variety is more of a blush on green than a real red. Both are tart in taste, but when fully ripened the gooseberry is sweeter than the currant. All of these berries have vertical veining, slightly more pronounced on the gooseberry. These fruits are much more common in Great Britain and Europe than in the United States, which may be partly a matter of taste. Another reason is, undoubtedly, the fact that the plants are host to a serious disease affecting white pine trees, called blister rust. Once infected, the trees die. This is so serious a problem that the plants are banned in many states or parts of them north of Florida where there are white pine forests. They are easy to grow and are often used in English and European fruit gardens as hedges, but cannot be grown where the climate is very hot or dry.

All varieties of both berries are popular for making jams and jellies. In France the black currant is made into the liqueur, crème de Cassis. Red currants and gooseberries are especially popular for making tarts, sauces, and syrups. Select intact fruit and wash only when ready to use. All provide some vitamin C, especially the black currant. After a long absence from the produce shelves, red currants are once again making an appearance in specialty fruit stores, and occasionally, even in the produce sections of the general markets.

Feijoas

The feijoa also has a second name, "pineapple guava"; although related to the guava, it is of another species. Originally from South America it is grown in Europe, Africa, Asia, New Zealand, and the United States. Feijoas are about the size of large plums, oval in shape, with a dark, dull green skin. The flesh is pale yellow with small edible seeds. Some describe the flavor as similar to pineapple, or minty. Use sparingly in fruit salads since it will dominate those fruits of more delicate flavor. Select those that are beginning to soften; they can be kept at room temperature for further ripening. They are a fairly good source of vitamin C.

Guava

The guava, a native of South America, is grown in nearly all tropical and subtropical parts of the world. It is commercially grown in such widely divergent areas as Southeast Asia, Australia, South Africa, and the Caribbean, as well as countries of its native South America. It propagates readily, and can easily become a pest. Because it's a host to the fruit fly, guavas cannot be imported into the United States. Those found in our markets are grown in Florida and California. It is a medium tree, growing to about thirty feet, with fruits about the size and shape of a plum. When fully ripe guavas are yellow and slightly soft to the touch, but if purchased somewhat green, they can be left to ripen at room temperature. The flesh can range in color from white to dark pink, with numerous small seeds in its center. Remove the seeds and eat out of hand or puree as a base for custard or cream desserts. A preserve known as guava paste, often sold in blocks, is a popular dessert in the Caribbean, and is often served with crackers and cream cheese in the United States. Guava is also sold as juice, either alone or in combination with other tropical fruit juices. It has an unusually high vitamin C content.

Kiwano (Horned Melon)

The horned melon comes from New Zealand, where it is known as the kiwano. This has to be one of the stranger-looking fruits you will ever come across—oval in shape, about six inches long, a vivid orange color, and covered with sharp spikes. This unusual covering encloses a brilliant green pulp filled with edible white seeds, similar to those of the cucumber, but with very tough connecting membranes. The flavor is mild, slightly tart, and somewhat like a cucumber. The shells make interesting serving containers, but the pulp has few uses. The kiwano can be stored at room temperature up to six months! At present this is a very expensive fruit.

Kiwi

The kiwi, formerly called the Chinese gooseberry, has become a very well-known exotic owing to an incredible advertising campaign waged by the growers. Originally from China, it has had phenomenal success as a commercial crop in New Zealand, where it received

its new name. The fruits are usually about three inches long, with rounded ends, and a fuzzy, thin, green-brown skin. Inside is a bright green flesh with a central white core surrounded by tiny black seeds. When ripe the entire fruit should feel slightly softened. Unripe fruit can be irritating to the mouth, but fully ripe, it is an appealing, sweet yet tangy fruit to eat out of hand. Using a peeler remove the skin, then slice crosswise to reveal the unusual pattern that makes this fruit so useful as a garnish for a variety of salad and fruit dishes. It contains an enzyme that tenderizes meat, and has an extremely high vitamin C content. It is available nearly year round. When the California crop is in, the price becomes very reasonable.

Lychee

The lychee (or litchi) originated in China, where it has been cultivated for more than 2,000 years. It has long been grown in Thailand and the Philippines, and is now grown in India, South Africa, New Zealand, and Australia. The medium-sized trees bear bunches of fruit the size of small plums. Within the reddish-brown, rough skin is a pearly-white flesh centered by a hard, shiny brown seed. The flavor is a wonderful combination of acid and sweet, and quite aromatic. The canned fruit is comparable to canned Queen Anne cherries, both in flavor and texture, although the lychee is slightly larger and the flavor is more exotic. Select fresh ones with the pinkest color and intact stems. They may be stored briefly in the refrigerator or frozen whole. Generally, oriental markets are the best source for fresh or canned fruit. When dried they are called lychee nuts. To make a lovely refreshing drink, place ten canned lychees in an eight-ounce glass, add half a cup of crushed ice, fill with the lychee juice, and stir. Nutritionally, lychees contain both vitamin C and potassium.

Passion Fruit (Granadilla)

A native of Brazil, the passion fruit's name refers to the Passion of Christ. Jesuit missionaries saw in its beautiful and unusual blossoms a symbol of the crucifixion: the three nails, crown of thorns, twelve apostles, and the cross. The fruit is about the size and shape of a large egg, and either purple or yellow with reddish overtones. The pulp and juice are yellow-green with many edible seeds embedded in the flesh. The taste is unique and defies comparison with other fruit flavors; it is pleasingly tart and sweet, with a delightful fragrance. When selecting, look for fruit that is partly smooth but beginning to wrinkle. A smooth fruit will take several days at room temperature to become fully ripe, at which point it will become totally wrinkled. It may then be stored in the refrigerator for several days. To use, cut into the thin, hard skin, holding over a dish to catch any juice. South African dishes requiring passion fruit by the cup would be far too costly to reproduce here, where the fruit is still incredibly expensive. However, just a few seeds sprinkled over a fruit cup will contribute a wonderful exotic flavor. It is popular as a fruit juice, either alone or in combination with other tropical fruits, and adds a special flavor and unusual appearance when the seeds are added to the icing on a cake.

Pepino

The pepino may also be known as mellowfruit, treemelon, or melon pear. In shape it resembles neither a pear nor a melon, since it is rounded at the stem and quite pointed at the opposite end. The skin is satin smooth, slightly glossy, with a pale yellow color that develops purple striations as it ripens. The pulp is pale yellow with the consistency of a melon, centered by an edible seed section. Those found in our markets are about four inches long and two inches across at the top. When ripe it should be just slightly softened. It may be peeled and eaten plain, cut up with other fruits in salads, used as a main course garnish, or served with sugar and lime. Although it has the sweetness and delicate melon flavor that would make it an excellent addition to the breakfast menu, the cost prevents popular usage. It is a good, low-calorie source of vitamin C.

Persimmon

The persimmon has its origins in China, but has been under cultivation for centuries, both there, and in Japan, where it is known as "kaki." It is grown in all the subtropics, and in Israel a new cultivar has been developed. This fruit appears to be very much like the Chinese fruit, but is marketed under a new name, Sharon. California produces most of the oriental varieties sold in this country. These are the Hachiya and the Fuyu. They have an acorn shape, and are about the size of a large peach with a glossy vivid orange-red skin. Our native variety is found growing wild from Pennsylvania south to the gulf states and west to Illinois. This is a small fruit, about the size of a blue Italian plum, with several large, flat seeds. The Virginia settlers learned about the fruit from the Indians, and used it dried, for puddings, sauces, and as preserves. It ripens in the fall and is usually allowed to stay on the trees until after first frost. It will then be a pale, dusky purple, soft, wrinkled, and quite sweet. This native persimmon is not raised commercially; those you find in the produce markets are all of the oriental type. A ripe persimmon should be very soft. If it isn't, keep it at room temperature for a day or two. It may be peeled and sliced, or simply cut in half and scooped from the skin with a spoon. The oriental persimmon is a very rich source of vitamin A.

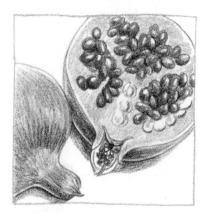

Pomegranate

A unique and ancient fruit, the pomegranate has been the subject of art and poetry for centuries. Mentioned in the Bible in describing a priest's robe as having a pattern of pomegranates in its border, in 1 Samuel 14:2, Saul is said to have tarried under a pomegranate tree, and the Israelites in the wilderness longed for the refreshment of the pomegran-

ate. It is a small tree (ten to fifteen feet), or more often, grown as a bush, with narrow green leaves, brilliant red blossoms, and red fruits about the size of a large orange. Indigenous to Persia, today it is cultivated in Morocco, Egypt, and the Middle East in general, and in Afghanistan, India, and Spain. In this country, commercial production is centered in California, although the plant has a fairly wide growth range in temperate climates. It does not produce fruit in the colder regions. Because of its brilliant, hibiscuslike flowers, the pomegranate is valued not only as a landscape plant but also planted in pots or tubs indoors. The blossoms make it an outstanding subject for bonsai. The fruit has a slightly hexagonal shape with a "coronet" formed by the calyx and stamens at one end. The thin, leathery, red skin covers a pulp of many seeds, each embedded in pink to red flesh. These seeds are separated into compartments by a pale yellow, inedible membrane.

In Mediterranean countries the rather tart juice has for centuries been a popular thirst-quencher and is a principal ingredient of grenadine syrup, made in France. To open the fruit, score the rind with a sharp knife from top to bottom, and gently remove the seeds from the membrane. The fruit may be rolled to break down the pulp, then a hole cut in one end from which to pour the juice. As children, we would drink the juice directly from the fruit in this manner. It is quite messy, and stains fingers, face, and clothes. The bright red seeds look like jewels strewn over a bowl of cut fresh fruit. Or use them to garnish a salad; the juice can be used in sauces for meat and poultry. Pomegranates contain some vitamin C and are unusually rich in potassium.

❧ BIBLIOGRAPHY ❧

GENERAL

Bianchini, F., and Corbetta, F. 1973. *The complete book of fruits and vegetables*. New York: Crown Publishers.

Cavendish, Richard, ed. 1983. *Man, myth and magic*. New York: Marshall Cavendish.

Condit, Ira J. 1947. *The fig*. Waltham, MA: Chronica Botanica Co.

Darrow, George M. 1966. *The strawberry*. New York: Holt, Rinehart and Winston.

Duval, Marguerite. 1982. *The king's garden*. Charlottesville: University Press of Virginia.

Encyclopedia Britannica. 1991, 15th ed.

Herbst, Sharon Tyler. 1990. *Food lover's companion*. New York: Barron's.

Little, R. John, and Jones, C. Eugene. 1980. *A dictionary of botany*. Van Nostrand Reinhold.

Luchine, Alexis. 1987. *The new encyclopedia of wines and spirits*. 5th ed., rev. New York: Knopf.

Magnes, J. R. 1951. *How fruit came to America*. Washington, DC: National Geographic.

Masefield, G. B. 1969. *The Oxford book of plants*. London: Oxford University Press.

Root, Waverley. 1980. *Food*. New York: Simon and Schuster.

Schneider, Elizabeth. 1986. *Uncommon fruits and vegetables*. New York: Harper and Row.

SELECTION OF PRODUCE

Carcione, Joe, and Lucas, Bob. 1972. *The greengrocer*. San Francisco: Chronicle Books.

Murdich, Jack. 1986. *Buying produce*. New York: Hearst Books.

GROWING INFORMATION

Bilderback, Diane E., and Patent, Dorothy H. 1984. *Backyard fruits and berries*. Emmaus, PA: Rodale Press.

Loewer, H. Peter. 1972. *Growing unusual fruit*. New York: Walker and Co.

Perper, Hazel. 1965. *The avocado pit grower's indoor how-to-handbook*. New York: Walker & Co.

Rodale, J. I., ed. 1977. *The encyclopedia of organic gardening*. Emmaus, PA: Rodale Books.

Swenson, Allan A. 1977. *Landscape you can eat*. New York: David McKay.

Taylor, Norman, ed. 1961. *Encyclopedia of gardening*. 4th ed. Boston: Houghton Mifflin.